Isaac Levi's new book is concerned with how one can justify changing one's beliefs. The discussion is deeply informed by the belief–doubt model advocated by C. S. Peirce and John Dewey, of which the book provides a substantial analysis. Professor Levi then addresses the conceptual framework of potential changes available to an inquirer. A structural approach to propositional attitudes is proposed that rejects the conventional view that a propositional attitude involves a relation between an agent and either a linguistic entity or some other intentional object such as a proposition or set of possible worlds. The last two chapters offer an account of change in states of full belief understood as changes in commitments rather than changes in performance; one chapter deals with adding new information to a belief state, the other with giving up information.

THE FIXATION OF BELIEF AND ITS UNDOING

THE FIXATION OF BELIEF
AND ITS UNDOING

Changing beliefs through inquiry

ISAAC LEVI

Columbia University

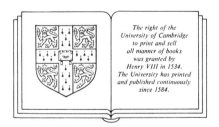

CAMBRIDGE UNIVERSITY PRESS

Cambridge

New York   Port Chester   Melbourne   Sydney

Published by the Press Syndicate of the University of Cambridge
The Pitt Building, Trumpington Street, Cambridge CB2 1RP
40 West 20th Street, New York, NY 10011, USA
10 Stamford Road, Oakleigh, Melbourne 3166, Australia

First published 1991

Printed in the United States of America

Library of Congress Cataloging-in-Publication Data
Levi, Isaac, 1930–
The fixation of belief and its undoing : changing beliefs through
inquiry / Isaac Levi.
p.   cm.
Includes bibliographical references and index.
ISBN 0-521-41266-8
1. Belief and doubt.   2. Probabilities.   3. Epistemics.
4. Knowledge, Theory of.   I. Title.
BD215.L45   1991
121'.6 – dc20   91-14207
                                                         CIP

British Library Cataloguing in Publication Data
Levi, Isaac *1930–*
The fixation of belief and its undoing : changing beliefs
through inquiry.
1. Beliefs
I. Title
121.6

ISBN 0-521-41266-8 hardback

FOR
REBECCA, GABRIEL, AND AMELIA

Contents

Preface

This book elaborates, modifies, and extends some of the themes of the first three chapters of *Enterprise of Knowledge*. I was prompted to return to these matters by reading the excellent paper of Carlos Alchourròn, Peter Gärdenfors, and David Makinson, "On the Logic of Theory Change: Partial Meet Functions for Contraction and Revision," and the substantial literature anticipating and emerging from this important paper. In addition, Gärdenfors presented me with an excellent target of criticism. Thanks to his book *Knowledge in Flux*, we have available a superb introduction to the contemporary discussion of belief change from the best-known student of the subject. To a very considerable degree, my book focuses on the points of disagreement between Gärdenfors and myself. I want to emphasize at the outset, therefore, my profound admiration for the quality of his work and the work of his colleagues Alchourròn and Makinson, and my gratitude to Gärdenfors for his collegial friendship and his generous assistance to me in writing this book. He has written extensive notes on all of the chapters, and I have relied on them heavily in preparing the final version.

As time goes by, I become more indebted to my former student, current colleague, and good friend, Teddy Seidenfeld. He sent me detailed comments on the first draft that have helped me clarify many obscurities and improve the final version.

While writing Chapter 2, I found enlightenment and stimulation in speaking with Akeel Bilgrami, Arnold Koslow, and Shaughan Lavine. I also benefited from the need to think through the relations between my view of conceptual schemes and Koslow's use of implicational structures.

I began preliminary work on this project in tandem with research on sequential choice in the summer of 1987, when I spent two and a half months at the Research School of Social Sciences of the Australian National University. I am especially grateful to Philip Pettit and Frank Jackson for their kind and intellectually stimulating hospitality and to the lively group of research students in Canberra – especially Andre Fuhrmann, Peter Lavers, and Michaelis Michael.

In January 1988, I took up a visiting fellowship at All Souls College. I owe the Fellows of All Souls College a profound debt of gratitude for making it possible for me to pursue my work while staying in Oxford in such a congenial and beautiful setting.

Thanks are also due to the History and Philosophy of Science Division of the National Science Foundation for providing me with a grant that enabled me to extend my sabbatical to one year.

I am fortunate to have a family whose warmth and love have always nourished me. I have a wonderful wife, Judith; two sons, Jonathan and David, whose achievements and moral character are a source of pride to me; and a lovely daughter-in-law, Stephanie, who is mother to my three grand-children, to whom this book dedicated. My thanks and love go out to all of them.

Isaac Levi
New York

1

Introduction

As inquiring agents modify their evolving doctrines, they come to believe where they were initially doubtful. Conjectures or hypotheses are thereby converted into settled assumptions free from serious doubt and, therefore, counted as certainly true. Such erstwhile conjectures are shifted to the status of evidence or knowledge and are deployed as premises in subsequent inquiries (pending future reconsideration).

Inquiries that terminate with the settling of an issue are provoked by the presence of doubt. To be sure, the presence of doubt does not automatically induce the doubter to engage in inquiry. We attach greater urgency to the solution of some problems than to the solution of others, and often disagree, and disagree intensely, as to the priority to be attached to various unsettled issues. Even so, when agents seek to justify the termination of inquiry by adding to the body of settled assumptions some proposed solution to the problem under investigation, their effort at justification is predicated on a distinction between those propositions taken for granted as settled and beyond reasonable doubt, and others that are not regarded as certainly true but as conjectural, more or less probable or improbable and, hence, as both possibly true and possibly false. And, given that distinction, the effort to justify the conversion of a conjecture into a certainty is an effort to justify a *change* in the set of assumptions accepted as evidence and as certainly true and, with this alteration, to institute a change in the way in which truth value–bearing claims are separated into those whose truth is seriously possible and those whose truth is not seriously possible.

Some philosophers seem to deny this truistic point. They wish to insist that we do or should take nothing for granted except, perhaps, the truths of logic and some fragments of set theory and mathematics. All logical and mathematical possibilities should be serious possibilities. No rational agent should ever change this standard for serious possibility but should hold on to it permanently. There is no good reason for becoming certain of the truth of a proposition concerning which one was initially in doubt (unless the becoming certain is nothing more than recognizing the implications of those fragments of logic and mathematics one does take for granted).

For such authors, inquiry cannot be understood as motivated by reasons that include a concern to remove doubt. Doubt is never justifiably eliminable. One may, to be sure, be more or less certain of the truth of conjectures. One may judge them to be more or less probable. But no matter how close the probability one assigns to a hypothesis is to 1, it remains a hypothesis or a conjecture because there remains a serious possibility that it is false as far as the agent is concerned.

I suggest that advocates of this view are guilty of confusing two theses:

1. We can never completely remove doubts on all issues, although we may hope to come closer to doing so by removing more and more doubts.

2. We can never remove doubts about any (extralogical) issue, although we may hope to come closer to doing so by becoming more and more certain of answers to at least some questions.

Thesis 1 amounts to little more than an acknowledgment that attaining a complete view of the world is a messianic pipe dream. No matter how successful we have been in finding answers to urgent questions, there will always be some aspect of issues under investigation that remains unsettled. We may manage to establish that the average wage of women doing work comparable to that of men was less than that of men in 1989 while failing to establish whether or not this wage differential prevailed among tenured faculty in universities. And even if we manage to fix on an answer to this question, there will be others that remain unsettled. Inquiry into a particular issue will terminate when enough doubts concerning the questions raised are completely removed, rendering the remaining doubts less urgent in comparison to the doubts provoked by other problems that seem more pressing.

Thesis 1 acknowledges that we may hope to make progress toward settling more and more questions. Thesis 2 denies that we can make any such progress whatsoever. We cannot remove doubts concerning any extralogical question. The only "progress" we can make is to become more and more confident of the truth of a given answer to a given question. We can never settle the matter.

If inquiry cannot be motivated by a concern to remove doubt, what is its rationale? If we cannot incorporate the solution we come close to establishing into the evidence and background information for future investigations, why should we care that we come close? The truth of the well-established conjecture remains an open question and a legitimate issue for future investigation. Inquiry never settles anything and, hence, inquiry – even inquiry into a specific problem – never legitimately terminates because the matter is settled but only, so it seems, because the investigators are tired or bored or have run out of funds. No matter how minute a question might be, if inquiry into that question is free of costs, it should go on forever.

Thesis 2 is not to be confused with the entirely plausible view that an inquiry initially designed to answer one question might provoke an inquiry into other questions in a manner that, if fruitful, could become endless. We are now considering the position that one should never be certain of anything except, perhaps, logic and mathematics. On this view, no matter how close to certain we become concerning a definite answer to a specific question, as long as there are no costs to future inquiry, it pays to continue focusing on that particular question. Advocates of this view are saved from blatant absurdity by the fact that preoccupation with the same question indefinitely incurs excessive costs and, in any case, is not feasible. Observe, however, that the only thing that prevents reopening of a question that has been studied for a long time is cost. Hence, a long neglected question may be reopened for the sole reason that the cost of doing so has decreased. There is no need to seek an inducement to open a question. Because questions never get settled but only more nearly settled, there is always some benefit to pursuing them further.

Many well-known philosophers and scientists have endorsed some variant of this view, even if they tend to avoid formulating their attitudes as bluntly as I have done. And there are reasons that may be offered for insisting that, insofar as the costs of inquiry can be ignored, every issue is always unsettled and open to further inquiry. According to the opposing view, when a claim is settled and taken for granted, there is no point in testing it or otherwise subjecting it to criticism, even if such further testing is free of costs. Consequently, so the argument runs, if we were to regard some issue as settled, it would be permanently ruled out as a legitimate issue for inquiry in the future. To render a claim immune to critical scrutiny is the hallmark of dogmatic and authoritarian thinking.

This anxiety derives from a failure to distinguish between certainty and incorrigibility. To regard some proposition as certainly true and as settled is to rule out its falsity as a serious possibility for the time being. As long as it is taken to be settled that it is true, there is, indeed, no point in testing it or subjecting it to criticism, even if cost-free opportunities for such testing and criticism abound. As long as the proposition is taken for granted, any such test presupposes the truth of the proposition.

But from this, it does not follow that good reasons will not become available in the future for a change of mind and for calling into question what is currently considered to be true and, as a consequence, for undertaking investigations to check on its truth. Just as we are sometimes justified in ceasing to doubt some erstwhile conjecture and thereby converting it into a certainty, so too we may sometimes be justified in coming to doubt some erstwhile certainty and in converting it into a conjecture. To be certain that middle-sized bodies moving at moderate speeds almost always obey the laws of Newtonian mechanics to a high degree of approximation does not entail certainty that one will never change one's mind or, indeed, that one will never have good reason to change one's mind. Certainty does not imply incorrigibility.

Currently settled theories may have only a limited capacity to explain and predict phenomena in some domain. For example, classical thermodynamics could not explain brownian motion. Efforts to construct theories – even theories incompatible with settled assumptions – may be justified by the concern to seek comprehensive systematizations of the phenomena.

Once such theories are constructed, their availability may, under suitable circumstances, provide good reason for coming to doubt the erstwhile settled assumptions, so that a non-question-begging inquiry can be undertaken to decide between the new proposal and the old theory.

In such cases, efforts are undertaken to construct theories for one purpose – namely, the comprehensive systemization of some domain. If such efforts are successful, they have as a by-product the unsettling of erstwhile settled assumptions. Such results are not, it should be emphasized, benefits of the enterprise but rather costs – at least from the vantage point of the inquiring agent who initially takes the settled assumptions for granted. To be justified in ceasing to believe what is initially settled, the inquirer must regard the benefits of giving the new proposal a non-question-begging hearing to be great enough to outweigh the costs.

The idea just sketched needs further elaboration. But, as it stands, it ought to indicate that those who deny that we should completely remove doubt because doing so requires a rigid dogmatism have themselves been guilty of a dogmatic conflation of certainty with incorrigibility.

The thought that certainty does not imply incorrigibility rejects a shared shibboleth of many philosophical traditions. So-called foundationalists insist that one does not have a right to be certain of the truth of a proposition unless one can justify its truth on the basis of self-justified "first" premises and principles. But it is difficult to offer a characterization of self-certified premises that provides for the correction of such premises. Consequently, it appears that if there are claims the understanding of which justifies certainty that they are true, the justification must provide a guarantee against deception. Foundationalists, therefore, tend to equate certainty with incorrigibility. If, starting from such a foundationalist perspective, one is skeptical about providing self-certifying first principles and premises sufficient to justify a body of claims as certainly true rich enough for the purposes of science and ordinary life, one may well conclude that, with the exception of whatever weak assumptions (such as logical truths) one is prepared to take as secure against the melan genie, our substantial beliefs ought to be less than certain and, at the same time, subject to critical scrutiny and revision. Such skeptics agree with the foundationalists that certainty and incorrigibility amount to the same.

Following the tradition of Peirce and Dewey, I reject the requirement of self-certified first premises and principles for justifications of belief. This is not to say that questions of justification do not arise concerning beliefs. When seeking to answer some question that is as yet unsettled, we seek either to justify coming to full belief in a potential answer to the given question or to settle the matter by responding to the testimony either of the senses or of witnesses according to some "rule" or "program" for eliciting information from a source whose reliability we already take for granted. The significance of the distinction between the two modes of legitimate coming to believe will be discussed later. In either case, however, the revision of a set of full beliefs by adding new ones is a legitimate object of criticism.

But if a system of full beliefs may be changed by "expansion" – that is, by coming to believe new ones, why should we be prevented from altering such a system of full beliefs by coming to doubt or ceasing to believe erstwhile settled assumptions? Why is there an obstacle to revising a system of full beliefs by "contraction" once we have turned our backs on anxieties concerning malevolent demons? Why should we insist that certainty implies incorrigibility? I do not think that there are any good reasons for doing so, although there are plenty of bad reasons. Some of the bad reasons will be addressed in the subsequent discussion. But deep-seated prejudices tend to be resistant to the refutation of the bad reasons that are deployed to rationalize them. It is desirable to combine such refutations with a positive account of rational belief change that gives a sensible characterization of the conditions under which ceasing to be certain is legitimate. Although I have proposed such a positive account elsewhere (Levi, 1980a, ch. 3), I have focused primarily on the topic of expansion – that is, the justification of coming to be certain. I have left the discussion of contraction (the justification of ceasing to be certain) in outline form. The details of this outline need to be made more explicit. In this volume, I try to flesh out the sketch.

As a preliminary to offering this positive account, I review in summary but, I hope, elementary form some of the general themes about belief revision that I have defended elsewhere and that characterize the core of the approach to belief revision I favor. This review furnishes the background relative to which the discussion of ceasing to believe will be elaborated.

2

Full belief

2.1 Commitment and performance

My subject is changing states of full belief. Preliminary to that discussion, it is desirable to make some general remarks about the respects in which changes of states of full belief are under study.

I begin with the assumption that a useful distinction may be made between two kinds of change in full belief:

1. Changes in doxastic commitment.
2. Changes in doxastic performance.

At time t_1, X fully believes that Albany is north of New York and that being north of is a transitive relation.

At time t_2, X comes to believe fully, in addition to what he believes fully at t_1, that Montreal is north of Albany.

At time t_3, X comes to believe fully that Montreal is north of New York.

I consider the transition from t_1 to t_2 to be a change in doxastic commitment, whereas the change from t_2 to t_3 is a change in doxastic performance without a change in doxastic commitment. At t_2, X is already committed to full conviction that Montreal is north of New York. But prior to t_3, X does not recognize that his beliefs that Albany is north of New York, that Montreal is north of Albany, and that being north of is transitive commit him to believe that Montreal is north of New York. At t_3, he recognizes his commitment and fulfills the obligation it entails.

In this volume as elsewhere, my attention is focused on changes in doxastic commitment (Levi, 1980a, ch. 1, sect. 5). I have emphasized this in previous publications. However, in this chapter, I try to elaborate on some facets of the approach I am taking that may have some relevance to contemporary preoccupations with meaning and the relations between propositional attitudes and the world. I hasten to add that I am not much concerned with these matters and have a somewhat dimmer view of their philosophical importance than others do. In the hope, however, that the theses to which I do attach importance may be better appreciated, I try to situate my position as best I can within contemporary discussions.

When a contract is written and signed by two parties, it is a fact that each of the parties acted in various ways that are describable as natural processes representable in physical or biological terms. Both X and Y put pen to paper.

However, if the action of X is described as signing a contract, we mean to convey more than that X put pen to paper. By that act, X undertook certain obligations. X acquired commitments.

X's commitment may have been to pay Y $200,000 in exchange for a house by the end of the week. X may or may not live up to the commitment. A description of X's performance on the contract specifies how well he succeeds in fulfilling his commitments.

Suppose that at the end of the week, X gives Y state bonds assessed as worth $200,000. Y wants cash instead of bonds. A dispute arises as to whether X fulfilled his commitment under the contract. There is no question that X offered Y the state bonds. The issue is whether X paid $200,000 as required by the contract. This dispute concerns the behavioral conditions under which X has paid $200,000 as required by the contract. A resolution of this dispute determines more specifically than was hitherto recognized just what X's commitment was when X undertook to pay $200,000.

I contend that when an agent X is in a state of full belief, X has undertaken something. Unlike the case of contracting, X may not have committed himself to someone else. But there are forms of undertaking or commitment that involve no obligation to anyone else. For example, X may vow to be the batting champion of the American League.

Such undertakings need not involve a public ceremony like signing a contract. Still, I want to say that X, in a state of full belief, does something or is in some state that "generates" the commitment X has undertaken. When X shifts from his state at t_1 to his state at t_2, X has a commitment to be certain that Montreal is north of New York. But, as described, X may not be living up to his commitment at t_2. He does better at t_3.

Of course, X does better at t_3 only if his doxastic performance at t_3 fulfills the commitment he undertook at t_2. Suppose that, at t_3, X uttered the words "Montreal is north of New York." Was X fulfilling the doxastic commitment he undertook at t_2?

The mere utterance of the words would not be enough. The utterance would have to express X's conscious full belief that Montreal is north of New York or, as I shall say, X's full recognition that Montreal is north of New York.

Not only is the mere utterance of these or other words insufficient, such linguistic performances are not necessary. Other forms of action may express full recognition that Montreal is north of New York.

As in the case of fulfilling the contract, neither X nor we may be in a position in advance to anticipate all questions that might arise as to the extent to which X is fulfilling his doxastic commitment.

Furthermore, there may be several different behavioral, neurophysiological, or other physical occurrences that might be expressions of X's recognition that Montreal is north of New York. At t_3, X might express such recognition and also express recognition that Montreal is not north of New York. If this should happen, we may well wonder whether both "expressions" are fulfillments of X's doxastic commitment – in which case the commitment is inconsistent – or whether one of these performances is a fulfillment of X's commitment and the other is a violation of it – in which case the doxastic performances are inconsistent but the commitment is consistent.

None of these issues can be settled by considering the acts and processes as described in behavioral, neurophysiological, or physical terms. To describe them as doxastic performances presupposes that they are fulfilling or violating a doxastic commitment, and to decide whether they are fulfilling or violating such a commitment presupposes a judgment as to what the commitment is – that is, what doxastic obligations the agent has.

In this case, at any rate, the gap between the intensional and the physical reduces to the gap between "ought" and "is." I am inclined to think that this is generally so for all the so-called propositional attitudes.[1]

If this is correct, to say that X fully believes that h threatens to be ambiguous. It can be construed as partially describing X's doxastic commitment at a given time or as characterizing X as fulfilling a doxastic commitment.

To avoid confusion, I reserve "X fully believes that h" as a partial description of X's doxastic commitment. I use "X fully recognizes that h" for the description of the doxastic performance as fulfilling the commitment. Sometimes X may attempt to fulfill a commitment but fail, either through some linguistic or other behavior. In such cases there is no full recognition, even though there is an abortive attempt at it. Yet, the behavior is a manifestation of a performance, one that fails to live up to X's commitment.

With this understood, we may say that when X fully believes that h at t, he may not fully recognize that h at that time, even though he is committed at t to doing so. On the other hand, if X does fully recognize that h at t, he fully believes that h at t. Yet, X can attempt to recognize fully that h at t and yet fail to believe fully that h at t. Attempting to recognize fully that h at t is a doxastic performance. It can fulfill a doxastic commitment (in which case it is a full recognition that h) or fail to do so (in which case it is an abortive attempt at such recognition).

There is one important respect in which doxastic commitment differs from contracting. If X signs a contract without having the ability to meet its terms and fully recognizes this to be so, his contract may be regarded as fraudulent. Incapacity is no excuse for failing to live up to a nonfraudulent contract. Contracts are, in this sense, indefeasible.

Doxastic commitments may appear to be fraudulent in just this sense. None of us is logically omniscient. Yet, X is doxastically committed to recognize fully the truth of the deductive consequences of what he fully believes.

To avoid the charge of fraudulence, one can deny that X has a doxastic commitment to recognize the truth of the deductive consequences of what he fully believes. That appears to be the view of authors like Harman (1986). Any prescriptions regulating our commitments as to what we should recognize should be tailored to meet our capacities.

To suppose that they are always fraudulent is unacceptable. But so is trimming the standards of doxastic commitment. Doxastic commitment must, therefore, be commitments different from contracts. They must be defeasible.

Perhaps another analogy will help. Consider the case of an individual who seeks to be a righteous person. The agent may know in advance that she can never fully succeed. But she has undertaken to realize this condition to the maximum extent to which she is capable. Doxastic commitments are of this kind. X is committed to recognize fully the truth of the deductive consequences of what he fully believes. But the obligation he has incurred is not a categorical one. Rather, it is one that he may fail to satisfy with a good excuse.

I cannot pretend to furnish a complete and precise list of good excuses. I can say this much: Severe emotional distress, failures of memory, lack of mathematical and logical training, and unavailability of appropriate computing technology, encyclopedias, and other records helpful to the memory can all provide good excuses unless the opportunity to remedy these deficits is available and the process is not excessively costly.

There is, to be sure, something more that needs to be said. Defeasible undertakings or commitments of the sort under consideration would, indeed, be fraudulent if the agent did not judge it desirable to devise cheap and effective remedies for his disabilities so as to extend his capacity to live up to his commitments.

There is a fairly broad consensus that it is good to enhance computational capacity. Many resist the study of logic and mathematics, regarding it as too costly, but few resist using devices that aid computation when they are available. Consider the modern cash register, which relieves the cashier of the burden of doing any computations at all. I suggest that those who acknowledge such desirability are in favor of encouraging therapies and technologies that will enhance our capacity to live up to our doxastic commitments. Authors who trim the standards of rationality to match our capacity can make no sense out of the positive view we take of such therapies and technologies.

The distinction between doxastic commitment and doxastic performance is crucial to the approach to belief change I am exploring. My concern is with revisions of doxastic commitment and not of doxastic performance. The remaining sections of Chapter 2 explore various aspects of this distinction.

2.2 Conceptual frameworks

How should an inquiring agent choose between the modifications of his current state of full belief that are available to him? Some conception of the range of available changes is presupposed by the question. An account of this conception is needed, therefore, in order to answer it.

Any potential revision of the agent's current state of full belief is a transition from the agent's current state to a potential state of full belief. Since failing to change the current state is a degenerate revision, the agent's current state is a potential state, and we may characterize the range of potential revisions of states of full belief available to the agent by the set K of potential states of full belief available to him. These constitute the agent's conceptual framework.

The agent's conceptual framework at a given time characterizes certain abilities or entitlements (more will be said about whether they are abilities or entitlements subsequently) of the inquirer at that time. I am supposing that the agent is in a given state $\mathbf{K}$ at time t and is able or entitled to make certain kinds of changes in his doxastic condition from t to t'. Such changes are being represented as shifts from $\mathbf{K}$ to some potential state $\mathbf{K}^*$. But $\mathbf{K}^*$ represents a kind of doxastic condition. To call it "potential" is to say no more than that the agent is able or entitled to satisfy that condition.[2]

The set of potential revisions of X's current state $\mathbf{K}$ of full belief changes, of course, with his current state of full belief. It is determined by the set K of potential states of full belief (i.e., the agent's conceptual framework) and the agent's current state $\mathbf{K}$ of full belief. However, the set K of potential states of full belief itself need not change. Change in belief does not entail change in conceptual framework. The question as to whether conceptual frameworks can be revised will be discussed briefly later on.

Changes in states of full belief come in one of four varieties. Some changes are "ampliative" in the sense that the new state is "stronger" than the initial one, so that an agent in the new state believes more than an agent in the initial one. Some changes weaken the state of full belief in the sense that the inquirer believes less than before. Some changes cannot be compared with respect to whether the inquirer believes more or less than before. Among these changes, some lead to states in conflict with the initial state and others do not.

$\mathbf{K}^*$ is stronger than $\mathbf{K}$ according to a conceptual framework K if and only if a person in state $\mathbf{K}^*$ believes more than a person in state $\mathbf{K}$ according to the framework. The comparison with respect to strength will be assumed to generate a partial ordering of the potential states of full belief in a conceptual framework.[3] The partial ordering is from stronger to weaker potential states of full belief. If $\mathbf{K}^*$ is stronger than $\mathbf{K}$, the latter is a "consequence" or "implication" of the former. The consequence relation is between potential states of full belief and not between sentences in a language or propositions or sets of possible worlds. Syntactic or semantic consequence relations are of secondary interest here, being useful primarily when representing potential states of full belief linguistically.

The focus on the consequence relation as a relation between states of full belief rather than as sentences or propositions seems warranted given the preoccupation of this volume with changes in belief. In evaluating rival changes in belief state, the inquirer needs to take into account how well the alternatives promote the goals of his inquiry. One of the aims of inquiry is the acquisition of valuable new information. Although the way such information is represented linguistically may or may not facilitate such acquisition, in seeking valuable new information, the inquiring agent is seeking to shift to belief states satisfying his curiosity. Linguistic representations of such belief states ought not to be confused with the states themselves. The partial ordering of potential states of full belief with respect to strength imposes an important constraint on how changes in belief states are to be evaluated with respect to informational value. If K^* is stronger than K, it carries at least as much informational value as K.

The second desideratum of inquiry is the avoidance of error. That is to say, the inquiring agent is concerned to restrict movements in his state of full belief to error-free states of full belief. Truth, or freedom from error and falsity or erroneousness, is a property of states of full belief in the first instance and only derivatively of sentences or propositions.

In seeking to avoid error, the inquirer is committed to judging elements of a subset of the potential states in the conceptual framework error-free and to judging elements of another subset erroneous. It is conceivable that the two sets exhaust the domain of potential states of full belief; but, in general, there is a residual set of potential states for which no verdict with respect to truth and error is rendered. Even so, the inquirer takes for granted that the potential states that remain in suspense are either error-free or erroneous (but not both). Consequently, the inquirer recognizes a distinction between what is error-free (erroneous) and his judgment as to what is error-free (erroneous). To be sure, from the inquirer's point of view, what he judges error-free (erroneous) is error-free (erroneous). The distinction is based on the inquirer's recognition that he is in doubt with respect to the error or absence of error in some potential states and, hence, that some states are error-free (erroneous), though he does not judge them so. But when seeking to avoid error, the inquirer grounds his evaluations of potential changes of belief on his current judgments as to what is error-free (erroneous). Moving to a state judged error-free incurs no risk of error. Moving to one judged erroneous incurs error for sure. Moving to one where no judgment is made incurs a risk of error and a prospect of avoiding error.

There are three constraints on the way inquirers should judge truth and error in potential states of full belief:

I. A potential state of full belief K is judged error-free by an inquirer if and only if it is a consequence of the inquirer's current state of full belief.

II. A potential state of full belief K is judged erroneous if and only if all states having both the current state and K as consequences are judged erroneous.

III. At least one potential state is judged error-free, and at least one potential state is judged erroneous. (This does not preclude judging the same state both error-free and erroneous.)

When an inquirer seeks to avoid error, he does so on the presupposition that his current state of full belief is error-free. Other inquirers may disagree, since they judge truth and error from their own states of full belief. But in keeping with the Peircean belief–doubt model, the inquirer is free of doubt as to the truth of his current state. This claim is one of the implications of condition I.

Another implication of condition I is that all potential states of full belief that are consequences of a state of full belief the inquirer judges error-free should be judged error-free.

Condition I, in effect, ensures not only that all potential states that are consequences of the current state are judged error-free, but also that only these states are so judged.

Condition II implies that all states stronger than a state judged erroneous are judged erroneous.

Condition III is introduced to prevent judgments of truth and error from becoming vacuous. It does not specify any specific potential state as being one that must be judged error-free (erroneous) no matter what the current state of full belief. It could be satisfied in different ways relative to different states.

I take these three conditions to be a characterization of the sense in which judgment of truth and error is to be understood when it is claimed that the inquirer is concerned to avoid error as judged from his point of view. I am claiming that inquirers should be concerned to avoid error. I do not know how to demonstrate to the skeptical that, in inquiry, avoidance of error in this sense is a desideratum, any more than I can demonstrate that the acquisition of valuable new information is a desideratum. For better of worse, however, I take for granted that these are two cognitive goals of inquiry and, in particular, that the concern to avoid error is a concern to avoid error as judged by the inquirer in a sense meeting conditions I–III.

Condition I implies that all consequences of the inquirer's current state of full belief are to be judged error-free. From the inquirer's perspective, shifting to such a state from his current state incurs no risk of error. On the other hand, given the constraint on assessments of informational value, informational value tends to be lost by making such shifts.

To obtain more informational value, the inquirer should shift to a state of full belief stronger than his current state. Because the new state is stronger than the current state, condition I prohibits the inquirer from judging it error-free prior to the shift. Either the potential states stronger than the current state are judged erroneous or the inquirer is in suspense concerning their status as erroneous or error-free. No matter how this judgment is made, the inquirer incurs a risk of error in shifting to such a state. The moral of the story is that those shifts that increase informational value incur risk of error.

This conclusion can be obtained from the assumption of a partial ordering of the potential states defining a consequence relation together with the constraints on assessments of informational value and judgments of truth and falsity I have described that are built on the consequence relation. Conceptual frameworks, however, should exhibit more structure than that given by saying that they are partial orderings. We now consider some further structural conditions that may be imposed on conceptual frameworks.

Given any pair of potential states of full belief K_1 and K_2, there should be a potential state that is the least upper bound of the potential states that are consequences of each of the two states in the pair – that is, the strongest such common consequence. This potential state is the *join* $K_1 \vee K_2$ of the states in the given pair.

Observe that although this requirement is formally a strengthening of the conditions we have imposed on the partial ordering of potential states of full belief, it prohibits restricting the inquirer's conceptual repertoire in certain ways and should be endorsed in order to minimize dogmatism. To appreciate the force of this point, consider two inquirers, X and Y, sharing a common framework. X is in state K_x and Y is in state K_y. On some occasions, it may be desirable for both X and Y to modify their views by adopting a belief state representing the shared agreements or common ground between them. To do this entails that they both give up informational value and, hence, incur a cost that they seek to minimize. In particular, they do not want to give up any more information than will be needed to bring them into agreement. The assumption of the existence of the join of K_x and K_y allows for the conceptual availability of such a move to both X and Y. It does not claim that exercising the option is always or even sometimes justifiable. However, we should not preclude such moves at the outset by denying that belief states representing such shared agreements are conceptually available. To do that violates the Peircean injunction against placing roadblocks in the path of inquiry. The assumption that joins exist is one expression of the conceptual liberality I mean to defend.

In a similar spirit, we may argue that given any pair of potential states K_1 and K_2, there should be a weakest potential state that is as strong as each of the states in the pair. This potential state is the *meet* $K_1 \wedge K_2$ of the pair of states.

The rationale for this assumption is analogous to the case of the join. Sometimes X may seek to strengthen his current view by adding Y's view (or, more realistically, some consequence of Y's view) to it. This strengthening, as we have seen, incurs a risk of error. Given the risk to be incurred, X will not want to increase it gratuitously by shifting to a stronger state than is necessary. He should shift to the weakest state that will incorporate the new information. To deny the existence of such a "greatest lower bound" or meet is to place roadblocks in the path of inquiry by disallowing states from the agent's conceptual repertoire that, if available, are surely worthy of consideration. Perhaps there are good reasons in some cases for considering a shift to the meet illegitimate; but the reasons should be displayed by showing what is wrong with the shift to the meet, and not by forbidding the inquirer to consider the shift at all.

A partially ordered set in which each pair of elements has a meet (greatest lower bound) and a join (least upper bound) is called a *lattice*. I have argued that a conceptual framework ought to be a lattice because (1) we are concerned to obtain informational value in a sense that depends on a partial ordering of potential states with respect to strength; (2) because we are concerned to avoid error, as judged by the inquirer, where such judgments are constrained in a manner depending on the same partial ordering; and (3) because we should not place conceptual roadblocks in the path of inquiry by creating unnecessary constraints on the inquirer's freedom of conceptual movement.

In the same spirit of conceptual generosity, the inquirer should have available to him a potential state that is the uniquely weakest of the potential states in his conceptual repertoire. It is a consequence of all other potential states and shall be labeled 1. State 1 is the state of maximum ignorance allowed in the conceptual framework. Clearly, 1 should be judged error-free no matter what the inquirer's state of full belief is.

There should also be a strongest potential state 0 that has every other state as a consequence. We cannot allow this potential state to be judged error-free without allowing every potential state to be judged error-free according to condition I on judgments of truth and error. According to condition II, 0 should be judged erroneous if any potential state is judged erroneous. Condition III requires that at least one potential state be judged erroneous relative to any given state of full belief. Hence, 0 should be judged erroneous relative to every state of full belief, including 0 itself. Of course, relative to 0, it is also judged error-free. I take for granted that when an inquirer is concerned to avoid error, he does so on the assumption that there is error to avoid and, hence, that at least one potential state is erroneous. Hence, 0 should be judged erroneous no matter what the inquirer's current state of full belief happens to be. If the inquirer happens to be in 0, he judges it both erroneous and error-free. State 0 is, of course, the inconsistent state of full belief. As I shall argue in Chapters 3 and 4, it is useful to recognize circumstances in which inquirers may legitimately move to 0 and, hence, to countenance it as a potential state of full belief.

Even though we have assumed the existence of both a meet and a join for every pair of potential states of full belief, we have not removed all conceptual obstacles that might be imposed concerning such meets and joins. For example, although the join of two potential states is the strongest common consequence of both of them, it could be that there is no potential state in the conceptual framework whose consequences are *just* the common consequences of that pair. If there were such a potential state, it would be the join; but in the situation envisaged, this state might not be available. If it did not exist, the join of K_1 and K_2 could still exist, but it would not represent the state we have in mind presystematically when speaking of what the two belief states share in common. On the other hand, positing the existence of the state whose consequences consist of all and only the common consequences of K_1 and K_2 does not rule out any other potential states (although the potential state that qualifies as the join has been altered). Conceptual liberality argues for making the existential assumption.

In the same spirit, we should assume that there is a potential state whose consequences are all and only the consequences of K_1 or K_2 and the meets of these consequences. If such a state exists, it is the meet of K_1 and K_2.

The two assumptions just added ensure that the conceptual framework is not only a lattice but a *distributive* lattice satisfying the following conditions: For every x, y, and z in the conceptual framework,

$$\text{(i)} \quad (x \vee y) \wedge z = (x \wedge z) \vee (y \wedge z)$$
$$\text{(ii)} \quad (x \wedge y) \vee z = (x \vee z) \wedge (y \vee z)$$

Although I have supposed that the inquirer judges some potential states erroneous and, in particular, that 0 is so judged, judgments of error have not been shown to be determined by the inquirer's current state of full belief in the same manner as judgments of freedom from error. To do this, I shall not add a further principle to conditions I–III constraining judgments of truth and error, but rather shall make some further assumptions about the availability of potential states in the conceptual framework that can be justified by the Peircean injunction against conceptual roadblocks.

Given a potential state of full belief K in the framework, there should another potential state K^* in the framework such that $K \wedge K^*$ has 0 as a consequence (and, hence, is identical to 0). If any such potential state is a consequence of the current state of full belief, then the meet of K and the current state has 0 as a consequence and, hence, is judged erroneous. This meet has both K and the current state as consequences; hence, by condition II, K should be judged erroneous.

In the spirit of conceptual generosity motivating Peirce's injunction against roadblocks in the path of inquiry on which I am repeatedly relying, I assume that there is a weakest K^* having the given relation to K and label that $\rightarrow K$.

A partial ordering that is a lattice with a least element and with a *pseudocomplement* $\rightarrow K$ is called a *pseudoboolean algebra* (Rasiowa and Sikorsky, 1963, pp. 58–9) and provides the "algebraic semantics" for intuitionistic propositional logic (Gärdenfors, 1988, p. 139). I have motivated the requirement that a conceptual framework of potential states of full belief should satisfy the requirements for a pseudoboolean algebra by appealing (1) to the theme I shall be alluding to in various places that the desiderata of inquiry should be acquisition of new informational value and avoidance of error and (2) to the need for conceptual generosity contained in the Peircean injunction against placing roadblocks in the path of inquiry. Similar considerations support the additional requirements needed to ensure that the conceptual framework is a boolean algebra that provides the algebraic semantics for classical propositional logic.

Even in the intuitionist framework, we are in a position to say that potential state K' is judged erroneous relative to current state K if and only if the meet of K and K' has $\rightarrow K$ as a consequence.

Consider now the join $K \vee \rightarrow K$ of K and $\rightarrow K$. If this join is different from and, hence, stronger than 1 (as intuitionists might maintain), there should be at least one potential state K^* different from 0 relative to which $K \vee \rightarrow K$ is judged false. If K^* did not exist, not only would the inquirer be deprived of judging $K \vee \rightarrow K$ false, except relative to 0, but the inquirer could not suspend judgment as to the truth value of $K \vee \rightarrow K$. That is to say, there could be no consequence of $K \vee \rightarrow K$ distinct from itself and from 1. The inquirer would be constrained to judge $K \vee \rightarrow K$ true relative to every state other than the state of maximal ignorance 1 even though it is stronger than 1. A conceptual roadblock would have been placed in the path of inquiry.

The roadblock cannot, however, be removed by positing a potential state K^* distinct from 0 relative to which both K and $\rightarrow K$ are both judged false. If K^* existed, $K^* \vee \rightarrow K$ would be weaker than $\rightarrow K$ even though its meet with K is identical to 0. This result would contradict the assumption that $\rightarrow K$ is the pseudocomplement of K. K^* cannot, therefore, exist.

The only way to remove the roadblock, therefore, is to abandon the intuitionist approach and to assume that $K \vee \rightarrow K$ is identical to 1. The pseudocomplement $\rightarrow K$ becomes the *complement* $\sim K$ of K.

Thus, I contend that the conceptual framework should be a distributed and complemented lattice. That is to say, the potential states of full belief in a conceptual framework *IK* are partially ordered in a manner satisfying the requirements of a boolean algebra.[4]

Three considerations have motivated the adoption of this structural requirement:

1. Assessments of informational value are weakly monotonic in strength, as partially ordered by the consequence relation.
2. Judgments of truth and error satisfy conditions I–III.
3. One should not place conceptual roadblocks in the path of inquiry.

Considerations 1 and 2 refer to the aims of efforts to revise states of full belief. Neither consideration suffices to support the requirement that the conceptual framework should be a boolean algebra. But they provide crucial preliminary support for the idea. We need, in addition, to make assumptions about the options available to the inquirer seeking to change the state of full belief. Consideration 3 is just such an assumption.

To be sure, consideration 3 itself would not suffice. There would be no point to the conceptual generosity involved in shifting from a pseudoboolean algebra to a boolean algebra were we not concerned to avoid error in a sense in which truth and error are judged as required by conditions I–III. We might argue from the interest in informational value invoked in consideration 1 together with consideration 3 on behalf of the requirement that the conceptual framework be a pseudoboolean algebra. But without the appeal to a concern to avoid error, it becomes unclear why we should be concerned to make judgments of truth and error at all and, hence, why we should worry about the availability of a potential state that is judged true when **K** is judged false.

One may wish to exploit consideration 3 still more and enlarge the number of options (e.g., by requiring the boolean algebra to be complete by ensuring the availability of potential states that are error-free if and only if at least one element of a set of potential states of arbitrary cardinality is error-free). I am perfectly happy to indulge such liberality. In this discussion, however, I rest content with the minimal liberalism involved in requiring a conceptual framework to be a boolean algebra.

We can envisage conceptual frameworks that are atomic boolean algebras. The atoms of a boolean algebra correspond to potential states of full belief that remove doubt maximally or carry maximal information short of inconsistency. State **0** carries stronger information but is judged erroneous relative to every potential state of full belief. To be sure, in state **0**, every potential state is also judged error-free. State **0** is, of course, the inconsistent state.

Although a conceptual framework representable as an atomic boolean algebra does not itself specify the class of error-free potential states of full belief, an inquiring agent who endorses a given conceptual framework is committed to the view that exactly one atom is error-free. Potential states of full belief are elements of a conceptual framework. Each of these potential states generates a principal filter (i.e., a filter with a strongest element). This principal filter is the set of consequences of the given state judged error-free in that state. No set of potential states can represent the set judged error-free by an inquirer unless that set is a principal filter. From the inquirer's point of view, the set of error-free potential states must contain the set of states the inquirer judges to be error-free. The inquirer cannot reach a state relative to which he judges all and only the error-free potential states to be error-free unless there is a strongest element of that set. That is to say, unless the set is a proper principal ultrafilter, the inquirer cannot, even in principle, judge all and only elements of the ultrafilter to be error-free. Hence, insofar as avoidance of error is a desideratum of concern to the inquiring agent, the set of error-free potential states will be supposed to be a largest set of potential states that could be judged error-free. When the framework is atomic, this set is a proper principal ultrafilter generated by an atom. Hence, from the inquiring agent's point of view, exactly one atom is error-free.[5]

In general, we should not suppose that conceptual frameworks are representable by atomic boolean algebras. There need not be any maximally consistent states of full belief in the framework, and in reasonably sophisticated framework, such states do not exist. Hence, in such frameworks, the inquiring agent cannot, even in principle, be in a state of judging all error-free states to be so. Even so, there are atomic subalgebras of the algebra representing the conceptual framework. For every such subalgebra, the agent is committed to the existence of exactly one error-free atom of the subalgebra and to the set of error-free elements of the subalgebra belonging to the proper principal subalgebra generated by that atom, by the reasoning of previous paragraph. Since 0 and 1 of any such atomic subalgebra are identical to the 0 and 1 of the full algebra, respectively, the 1 element of the full atomless algebra must be error-free and the 0 element erroneous for all agents who share the same conceptual framework – that is, who share the same ability to realize states of full belief.

To sum up, I require that the set of potential states of full belief constituting a conceptual framework meet two requirements: (1) The conceptual framework should have the structure of a boolean algebra. (2) In every atomic subalgebra of the framework, the set of error-free potential states should belong to exactly one proper principal ultrafilter.

Every appeal to presystematic judgment runs the risk of being little more than an expression of the prejudices of the author. My endorsement of conditions (1) and (2) is a reflection of the goals and values characterizing efforts to change states of full belief that I am advocating and the liberal conception of the resources available for promoting these goals I have defended. Those who reject my argument should consider which element of my conception of the aims of efforts at changing belief states and the resources available they judge questionable and offer a rival view.

2.3 Abilities and entitlements

Describing a conceptual framework as a boolean algebra allows us to bracket certain controversies concerning the character of full belief and other so-called propositional attitudes in examining questions of revision of full belief and other attitudes. Nothing in the characterization of potential states of full belief just mentioned requires us to assume that when agent X is in a state of full belief, X has a belief relation to a sentence in some language accessible to X in some sense or to a proposition eligible to be the "meaning" of a sentence and explicated, perhaps, as a set of possible worlds or maybe in some other way.

To be sure, beliefs and other propositional attitudes are manifested linguistically, and such manifestations bring X into relation to sentential tokens and types and other linguistic expressions. In particular, we partially describe intensional states by means of sentences that can take the form "X *A*'s that *h*," where "*A*'s" is intended to be replaced by a specification of an attitude such as "is certain," "judges it seriously possible," "judges it probable," "desires," "hopes," and so on, and *h* is replaced by a sentence. It should be explained why this form of representing aspects of states of full belief is useful even if propositional attitudes are not relations between individuals and propositions or sentences.

Nonetheless, characterizing potential states of full belief as elements in a boolean algebra identifies the set of potential states of full belief with a minimum of commitment to controversial aspects of the issues just raised.

The set of potential states of full belief constituting the conceptual framework for an agent X at *t* time consists of those states that agent X at *t* is conceptually capable of adopting at that time. But what is meant by conceptual capacity here? X is alleged to have some sort of ability to change her state of full belief in certain ways. But did physicists before 1900 have the ability to shift to states of full belief embracing the modern quantum theory developed in the 1920s? Or did those physicists who survived the transition to quantum theory suffer a change in their frameworks? To take another example, prior to Einstein's introduction of special relativity theory, the concept of light moving in the ether seemed to be embedded in the conceptual repertoire of many physicists. Afterward, this claim was alleged to have become meaningless, according to many physicists and philosophers. According to others, the concept remained intelligible but inapplicable. This dispute seems to boil down to a controversy as to whether Einstein's special theory of relativity argues for a conceptual shift involving a reduction of the conceptual framework by removing certain potential states of full belief from that status. Before Einstein, scientists were conceptually capable of believing that the ether exists, but afterward they were not capable of believing it or of believing that it does not exist. This seems odd because surely a historian of science ought to be able to understand (at least in principle) the views of physicists before Einstein. Ether theories ought to be in the historian's conceptual repertoire.

The problem here has to do with the notion of conceptual capacity. On the one hand, we may take conceptual capacity to refer to the intellectual abilities of inquiring agents, in which case we should acknowledge that such agents have diverse capabilities. Some individuals cannot understand quantum mechanics, and others can. Moreover, the same individual may be able to understand quantum mechanics under one set of conditions but not under another. On the other hand, we wish to identify a notion of conceptual accessibility such that whatever is conceptually accessible to one intelligent agent is accessible (at least in principle) to any such agent.

If we take conceptual capacity in the first subjective sense, then few individuals have conceptual frameworks characterizable by boolean algebras of potential states of full belief, whether these are atomless or not. If we take conceptual capacity in the second sense, there should be exactly one conceptual framework common to all intelligent agents, and no revision of conceptual frameworks. The shared framework, though perhaps a boolean algebra of potential states of full belief should be atomless.[6]

I suggest that we consider a third sense of conceptual capacity. In revising states of full belief, the inquiring agent ought, so I contend, to be concerned to increase the informational value of his belief state and to avoid error. The evaluation of *informational value* is constrained by the partial ordering of potential states of full belief with respect to *information* that determines the boolean algebra. The evaluation of potential states as error-free or not is constrained by the requirement that the set of error-free states in any atomic subalgebra form a proper, principal ultrafilter in that subalgebra and by the inquirer's assumption that the inquirer's current state is error-free.

Now suppose that the inquiring agent has the intelligence to understand Lorentz's theory of the electron in the ether, so that he is conceptually able, in both senses initially mentioned, to be in a state of full belief embracing Lorentz's theory. The agent might not only recognize such a potential state of full belief, he might be able to embed it in a partial ordering of potential states constituting a boolean algebra. But suppose that the inquiring agent interested in relieving doubt and in avoiding error sets bounds on his interest in doing so. He does not care whether belief states embracing Lorentz's theory are free of error or not. Although one can, if one likes, say that such belief states are *truth valued* in the sense that they are either free of error or not, the inquiring agent is not seeking to avoid error in any sense in which such belief states are so truth valued. But if the agent does not consider such belief states as truth valued in any sense of concern to him, he will not contemplate shifts to such belief states as removing doubts or yielding information in any sense of concern to him.

The notion of conceptual capacity in the third sense is a notion that is relativized to the aims of the inquiring agent. It characterizes those potential states of full belief that the agent considers truth valued (error-free or not error-free) in the sense in which the agent is concerned to avoid error and that remove doubt in a sense of concern to him.

Other agents may differ from agent X with regard to the interest in error-free information. Yet, in principle, nothing prevents them from endorsing states of full belief in X's conceptual repertoire, and vice versa. And for all we know, they may have the intelligence to do so. They will still resist X's view that belief states involving affirmation or rejection of Lorentz's theory bear truth values in any sense of interest to their concern with error-free information.

Thus, it seems to me that there is a sense in which different agents may embrace different conceptual frameworks and the same agent may endorse different frameworks at different times. But disagreements over and revisions of conceptual frameworks are *au fond* disagreements over and revisions of cognitive values. To say this does not imply that such differences correspond to differences in the several agents' capacities to understand one another conceptually in either of the first two senses. To the contrary, if such agents are to confront their differences or if an agent is to contemplate changing his conceptual framework, an understanding of the ramifications of embracing alternative frameworks must be available.

A conceptual framework as a set of potential states of full belief meeting the specifications of a boolean algebra is a conceptual framework in this third sense. Thus, a potential state of full belief is not just a state of full belief to which an inquirer is able to shift in one of the first two senses, but is one to which he is entitled to move insofar as he is restricting moves to states that are either error-free or erroneous in a respect that is of concern to him in inquiry. The characterization of an inquirer's conceptual framework is as much a characterization of the inquirer's cognitive value commitments as it is of his conceptual capacities.

I shall not attempt to offer an account of criteria for evaluating revisions of conceptual frameworks. However, I shall indicate from time to time limitations I currently favor on conceptual frameworks. But if I take the position, for example, that belief states concerning the existence or nonexistence of possible worlds neither carry error nor are error-free, I do so acknowledging that circumstances might arise when there would be good reason for me to revise my conceptual framework. The kind of good reason that needs to be supplied would call for good reasons for me to modify concern with error-free information in certain ways.

Given a conceptual framework, any change of a state of full belief within the framework can be taken to be of one of four types:[7]

1. *Expansions* are changes in which one shifts from a state of full belief to one that is at least as strong.

2. *Contractions* are changes in which one shifts from a state of full belief to one that is at least as weak.

3. *Replacements* are changes in which the meet of the initial state and the subsequent state is the inconsistent state.

4. *Residual shifts* are changes in which the initial state and the subsequent state are not comparable according to the partial order, as they are in (1) and (2), and their meet is not the inconsistent state, as in (3).

This classification exhausts the possibilities. Degenerate cases in which no changes take place can be viewed both as expansions and as contractions.

2.4 Propositions

When an agent X shifts from a state of full belief to a stronger one (i.e., expands his state of full belief), it is tempting to say, as we did indeed say in the previous section, that X has come to full belief that some claim or proposition is true. This way of speaking suggests that X has come to bear a relation to some item called a *proposition* that he did not previously bear.

This view suggests another conception of conceptual framework distinct from the one we have just introduced. We might introduce a boolean algebra of propositions. If p precedes q in the partial ordering of propositions in the algebra, p entails q. The minimum proposition is the contradictory one. The maximum one is the necessary truth. Each proposition corresponds to a potential state of full belief. An inquiring agent fully believes that the proposition corresponding to his state of full belief is true and does the same for all of its entailments.

According to this vision of things, two boolean algebras are involved here: the boolean algebra of potential states of full belief and the boolean algebra of propositions. One might well ask why it is necessary to have a boolean algebra of propositions in addition to the boolean algebra of potential states of full belief. I myself do not think it is necessary to do so, but others clearly do.

To assume that two algebras are required because full belief at time t simply is a relation between an inquiring agent at time t and a proposition is to beg the question. A marginally more promising response would be to suggest that the conceptual abilities of the agent are explained by the boolean algebra of propositions and the assumption that the agent is conceptually able to be in a state of full belief in which he fully believes all propositions in a filter in the boolean algebra of propositions. If full belief is a relation between inquiring agents and propositions, X's state of full belief at time t is reducible to the set of propositions X fully believes at t. The boolean algebra of potential states of belief can be reconstructed as a boolean algebra of the sets of propositions defined by principal filters generated by the propositions in the boolean algebra of propositions.

If the conceptual capacity involved is the value-driven one I suggested as the focus of attention, then the explanation of conceptual ability should show why the inquiring agent is concerned to avoid error among potential states of full belief belonging to a particular boolean algebra. Presumably an account involving propositions will assume that the propositions in the given boolean algebra of propositions are themselves truth valued. But this appeal is scarcely illuminating. Even if propositions are postulated to be truth valued, all that can be shown is that sets of propositions closed under a consequence relation can be characterized as error-free if and only if no proposition in the set is false. It cannot be explained why the inquiring agent is prepared to regard that set of propositions as representing a potential state of full belief whose freedom from error is a matter of concern to the agent in efforts to obtain error-free information. Of course, one might specify a set of propositions the truth values of which are of concern to the agent. I fail to see why this affords an advantage over simply specifying the boolean algebra of potential states of full belief concerning whose truth values the agent is interested.

One might defend the introduction of propositions on the grounds that certainty or full belief is just one of several propositional attitudes. One can be in doubt that h, judge that h as seriously possible, judge that h as probable or probable to some degree, hope that h, want that h, prefer that h over that g, and so on. In spite of the differences in these attitudes, they all share a common feature: They are all directed toward the same proposition that h. We need to introduce propositions because there are different propositional attitudes that can share the same content in order to identify what it is that they share in common.

In spite of its surface plausibility, this claim too is false.

When we use statements like "X believes that h," we are not compelled to take this to claim that X bears a belief relation to a proposition that h distinct from a potential state of full belief. I suggest that the expression "that h" represents a potential state of full belief. I have no objection to describing that potential state of full belief as the proposition that h. Indeed, I shall mimic this terminological practice by calling potential states of belief *doxastic propositions.* My current concern is to emphasize that such that-clauses do represent potential states of full belief and not sets of possible worlds or some other type of nondoxastic propositions distinct from potential states of full belief.

On this view, "X believes that h" does not assert that X stands in a belief relation to the nondoxastic proposition that h. Rather, it asserts that X is in a state of full belief that is at least as strong, according to the partial ordering, as the state of full belief identical to the doxastic proposition that h. "X believes that h" partially describes X's state of full belief by partially locating his state of full belief in the boolean algebra of potential belief states according to the partial ordering of potential beliefs states.

The situation is quite analogous to representing points in three-dimensional Euclidean space by triples of real numbers. A full specification of a point might be obtained by specifying a particular triple of real numbers. A partial specification might be given by saying that the point is one represented by one of a given class of triples. To say that the point in question is represented by $(1,1,1)$ is not to imply that the point is related to $(1,1,1)$ in some way other than that the triple represents the point. To say that the point is represented by a triple all of whose components are greater than 1 is not to relate the point to $(1,1,1)$ in some other way than to say that $(1,1,1)$ represents a point that is itself related to the point under study in a special way.

In our case, we could envisage representing the potential belief states that are atoms of the boolean algebra by n-tuples of numbers (assuming, for the sake of the argument, that the conceptual framework is an atomic boolean algebra) and potential belief states by sets of such n-tuples. From this it does not follow that when an agent is in a belief state represented by such a set, X stands in a belief relation to the set of n-tuples. And if we say that X is in a state of full belief stronger than the belief state represented by a given set of such n-tuples, we are not saying that X stands in a belief relation to the set of n-tuples.

We frequently use that-clauses to describe states of full belief rather than elaborate sets of n-tuples of numbers. The point I am belaboring is the same. To say "X believes that h" is not to assert a relation between X and a nondoxastic proposition represented by "that h," but rather a relation between X's belief state and a belief state or doxastic proposition represented by "that h" – a relation defined by the partial order of the potential states of full belief. If one likes, one can say that "X believes that h" partially describes one doxastic proposition by stating that it is X's state of full belief and relating it to the potential state of full belief or doxastic proposition that h.

We are also now in a position to examine some of the other propositional attitudes.

Consider, first, judgments of serious possibility. X judges it seriously possible that h if and only if the doxastic proposition that h is in a principal ultrafilter to which her current state of full belief belongs. But this is tantamount to saying that the doxastic proposition that $\sim h$ (which is the complement of the doxastic proposition that h) is not in the filter generated by X's current state of full belief. The judgment that h is seriously possible and that $\sim h$ is also seriously possible implies that X is in doubt as to the truth of the doxastic proposition that h. It implies that the doxastic proposition that h is a conjecture or hypothesis rather than a certainty. That is to say that, from X's point of view, shifting from her current belief state to the belief state represented by that doxastic proposition risks error.

On the account just given, the claim that "it is seriously possible that h according to X at t" is, like "X is certain at t that h," a partial description of X's state of full belief at t.

If the doxastic proposition is that h is seriously possible according to X at t, it is *equivalent given X's current belief state* **K** with the doxastic proposition that g that is associated with the meet of **K** and the state of full belief associated with that h. From X's point of view at t, expanding her belief state by coming to be certain that h is tantamount to coming to be certain that g. The equivalence class of all doxastic propositions under **K** equivalence is, in effect, the **K** proposition that, again, is the state of full belief associated with g. In effect, the agent's judgments of serious possibility indicate the range of potential expansions of her current state of full belief. As such, to declare that h is seriously possible according to X at t is to provide a partial description of her state of full belief, just as the ascription of a judgment of certainty is.

Notice that, relative to **K**, a quasi-ordering of the doxastic propositions or potential states of full belief is induced that corresponds to a partial ordering of the **K** propositions.

On this account, therefore, the state of full belief serves as the agent's standard for serious possibility. Hypotheses that are judged possibly true are determined relative to the agent's settled convictions.

On this view, we may also identify hypotheses that are logically possible as those that are seriously possible relative to the weakest potential state of full belief 1 in the partial ordering characterizing the boolean algebra of potential belief states constituting the conceptual framework.

Agent X may discriminate between seriously possible hypotheses with respect to credal probability. On the view being developed, such judgments of credal probability are evaluations of potential expansions of the current state of full belief with respect to how likely they are to be free of error. Alternatively put, they are evaluations of these potential expansions with respect to the risk of error that would be incurred by implementing these expansions. Once more, to ascribe a judgment of credal probability that h to agent X at t is to partially describe his state of full belief. A judgment of serious possibility that h is ascribed to him that, as we have seen, supplies partial information about his state of full belief.

However, ascription of a judgment of credal probability does more than this. It also partially describes X's credal state relative to his state of full belief K. Given X's state of full belief K, any two propositions that are equivalent given K should be counted as equally probable, so that each K proposition has a univocal credal probability assessment. Moreover, if K proposition h is stronger than K proposition g according to the partial ordering induced by K, h is not more probable than g. However, we do not require that h be less probable than g.

Thus, X's state of credal probability or credal state relative to K amounts to a consistent extension of the partial ordering characterizing the boolean algebra of K propositions, with the qualification that if h is stronger than g, h need not be less probable than g but only equally probable. If the state of credal probability is represented completely by a real valued probability function from K propositions to real numbers between 0 and 1, the extension will amount to a weak ordering. But the ordering need not be complete and may yield nothing better than a partial or quasi-ordering of the K propositions.[8]

The point I wish to emphasize here is that a credal state relative to K supplements the state of full belief K by adding further structure to the partial ordering of K propositions induced by K itself.

Consequently, the claim that X judges that h with credal probability r is not only a partial description of X's state of full belief, as we have already stated, but of his credal state as well. It locates the potential expansion of K represented by the K proposition that h in the structure induced by the credal state that completes the structure induced by K itself.

In so locating this potential expansion of K, it characterizes the risk of error that X assigns to expanding K by shifting to the meet of K and the doxastic proposition that h.

Thus, we have a way of stating how X can judge it seriously possible that h and judge it probable to degree r that h without stating that the two attitudes reveal different relations between X and a nondoxastic proposition that h. The judgment of serious possibility relates X's state of full belief to the state or doxastic proposition that h by reference to the partial ordering characterizing the boolean algebra for X's conceptual scheme. The judgment of credal probability relates X's state of full belief to the doxastic proposition that *h* by reference to the set of probability functions that supplement the boolean structure over the potential states of full belief.

Agent X may also discriminate among seriously possible hypotheses with respect to how morally, economically, politically, cognitively, aesthetically, or personally desirable they are – that is, with respect to how desirable it is that the associated potential expansions are free of error. Again, ascribing such evaluations to X at *t* is a partial description of X's state of full belief. But it is also a partial description of X's goals, values, and desires at *t*.

Once more, the structure imposed on **K** propositions or potential expansions of **K** by the agent's values at *t* is related to the partial ordering of **K** propositions induced by **K** and the boolean algebra of potential states of full belief or doxastic propositions. An examination of how it is related entails an even more complicated discussion than a discussion of how the structure imposed by X's credal state is related. We shall not undertake it here. But the idea I wish to emphasize is the same one presented earlier: If X values that *h* be true more than that *g* be true, the **K** propositions *h* and *g* have been partially located in the structure that X's values relative to **K** induce on potential expansions of **K**.

I do not wish to discuss the diverse and subtle differences between propositional attitudes here. What I am suggesting, however, is that the intentional element in propositional attitudes like probability judgment and value judgment has two components:

1. A partial description of X's state of full belief or standard for serious possibility **K** that locates the potential expansion of **K** associated with the doxastic proposition that *h* under consideration in the partial ordering characterizing the boolean algebra of potential expansions of **K**.

2. A partial specification of the location of the same potential expansion of X's state of full belief associated with the doxastic proposition that *h* in a different structure of potential expansions representing the attitudinal state (e.g., of credal probability or value judgment) under consideration.

The differences between propositional attitudes are, therefore, representable as differences in the structures they induce on potential expansions of X's state of full belief. Thus, all other attitudes presuppose states of full belief or standards for serious possibility. They do not presuppose a boolean algebra of propositions distinct from potential states of full belief.

I do not mean to suggest that states of full belief are more fundamental than other attitudinal states. I am suggesting, to be sure, that when attributing other propositional attitudes such as judgments of credal probability or value to an agent, one is implicitly attributing to the agent judgments of serious possibility and full beliefs. It is also true that on the view I am suggesting, only states of full belief are error-free or erroneous. Neither states of probability judgment, states of modal judgment, nor states of utility judgment are truth valued in this way except insofar as they presuppose states of full belief.

However, when it comes to evaluating revisions of states of full belief, judgments of probability and value often play an indispensable role. In that sense, no claim that one type of attitude is more fundamental than the others is being advanced.

Perhaps an analogy, superficial no doubt, may help make the point I am belaboring. One can envisage a physical field theory that makes a distinction between the geometrical structure of space–time and the various force fields defined on space–time. But it may also be possible to identify the geometrical field with one of the force fields – say, the gravitational field – without any loss of systematizing power.

In our case, we can envisage a structure of propositions and a family of other structures defined on the propositions each of which is characteristic of a propositional attitude. But it may turn out that the structure associated with one type of attitude – states of full belief – can, without any loss of systematizing power, be identified with the propositions. As far as I can tell, this is precisely the situation before us. Under the circumstances, there seems to be no advantage to beginning with a view of a conceptual framework as a boolean algebra of propositions. We shall still need to consider potential states of full belief anyhow. To insist on two isomorphic structures where one will do for the purpose of giving an account of the revision of states of full belief seems gratuitous in the way *verdoppelte Metaphysik* typically is.

Gratuitous metaphysics has, in recent years, been raised to the second power by those who characterize propositions as sets of possible worlds. This view is not only doubly gratuitous but presupposes that the boolean algebra of propositions is atomic. It thereby restricts conceptual frameworks to atomic boolean algebras of potential states of full belief – a restriction that is as questionable as it is needless.

It should be emphasized that the proposal to characterize conceptual frameworks as potential states of full belief is not undertaken in order to dispense with abstract entities. A conceptual framework and the states of full belief that are its elements are abstract enough. But for the purpose of giving a systematic account of inquiries where states of full belief, credal states, and value judgments are revised, we do not need the bells and whistles that introducing propositions and possible worlds provides.

Recently we have begun to witness a trend among philosophers away from the bells and whistles. Two notable examples may be worth mentioning here. Arnold Koslow (in press) offers an account of the logical and modal operators, beginning with the idea of an implication structure. An *implication structure* is a domain of entities and a relation on the domain of arbitrary finite degree (the implication relation) satisfying Gentzen-style axioms. One might consider applying Koslow's approach to belief change by taking the domain to be the space of potential states of full belief and, instead of using the binary relation of consequence I have employed, using his implication relation. One can then construct operators corresponding to conjunction, disjunction, and classical negation, and assuming that these operators always have values, ensure that there are enough elements in the domain of belief states to generate the binary consequence relation yielding a boolean algebra. The consequence relation will simply be the implication relation in the binary case. This approach will not, however, allow for the existence of potential states of full belief that are least upper bounds and greatest lower bounds of sets or belief states of arbitrary cardinality, and this may seem to be an excessive limitation on conceptual capacity. Moreover, it has seemed to me preferable to avoid endowing potential states of full belief with too much syntactical structure, leaving syntax to our linguistic means for representing such states.

Koslow does not focus on the topic of change of belief, and the intended applications uppermost in his mind are such that implication structures have the right shape for handling them. I do not mean to fault Koslow for not sharing my preoccupations. What is instructive for present purposes is that Koslow seeks to characterize the logical and modal operators using a structural account. I have sought to do something similar for conceptual frameworks focusing exclusively on the structure needed for representing the kinds of changes that seem necessary for approaching change of belief state in a systematic manner. Obviously an abstract structural approach does not do justice to an account of the intended application. Some motivation for endorsing the structural constraints I have proposed has already been offered, and more needs to be said concerning how belief states are connected with inquirers' actions and linguistic performances. But exhibiting the structure does show why certain kinds of apparatus (such as possible worlds semantics) are not needed. Koslow's approach, like the one I favor, contributes effectively to this endeavor.

Peter Gärdenfors is interested, as I am, in change of belief. And just as I have posited a domain of potential states of full belief, Gärdenfors (1988, ch. 6) has introduced a domain of epistemic states. However, Gärdenfors does not impose a structure on this domain, except for positing the existence of an epistemic state $\mathbf{K}_\perp$ called the *absurd epistemic state* corresponding to $\mathbf{0}$. Rather, he introduces a set *Prop* of functions from epistemic states to epistemic states called *propositions*. (He calls a pair $<K, Prop>$ a *belief model*.) These functions correspond intuitively to types of expansion. For example, $\mathbf{A}$ is a function that, when applied to an epistemic state $\mathbf{K}$, is the epistemic state that is the expansion of $\mathbf{K}$ by adding $\mathbf{A}$. By laying down axioms or conditions on these functions, he is able to introduce a relation of logical consequence between propositions and to introduce the logical connectives. $\mathbf{B}$ is a logical consequence of $\mathbf{A}$ if and only if for every epistemic state $\mathbf{K}$, $\mathbf{B}(\mathbf{A}(\mathbf{K})) = \mathbf{A}(\mathbf{K})$. His axioms suffice to allow for a representation of the propositions as a pseudoboolean algebra and for the identification of an additional axiom yielding a boolean algebra.

Gärdenfors does, therefore, have two kinds of artifacts in his scheme: the epistemic states and propositions that are expansion functions. But the propositions are not a gratuitous extra here; for, according to his approach, the structure is introduced by constraints on expansion functions. Otherwise, there is no structure on the epistemic states.

Observe that once one has the expansion functions, one can introduce a consequence relation on the epistemic states. If **A** implies **B**, then, for any epistemic state **K**, the expansion of **K** by adding **B** is a consequence of the expansion of **K** by adding **A**. So the existence of a partial ordering of epistemic states with respect to consequence is assured. However, there is no guarantee that the set of epistemic states has a maximum 1 corresponding to a state of maximum ignorance or the structure of even a lattice. For example, one might have a pair of epistemic states K_1 and K_2 and generate separate lattices for each, where each of the pair of states is the weakest in the associated lattice and the strongest is the absurd epistemic state. Otherwise, however, the two structures remain completely unrelated, having neither meets nor joins (nor being complements of one another). Inquirers beginning in such incommensurable states could not move to shared agreements to engage in a joint inquiry or contemplate endorsing both of their positions. For reasons offered in Section 2.2, conceptual frameworks recognizing such incommensurabilities nip inquiry in the bud and ought not to be countenanced.

However, as Gärdenfors, in effect, shows (1988, pp. 139–140), if the conceptual framework is a pseudoboolean or boolean algebra, as the case may be, one can obtain a belief model consisting of the epistemic states and expansion functions meeting Gärdenfors's requirements. Whether one calls the epistemic states (potential states of full belief) *propositions* or applies this term to the expansion functions becomes a matter of terminological convenience. Once one has ensured that the space of potential states of full belief has the structure of a boolean algebra, Gärdenfors's approach and the one I follow come out equivalent. What I insist on, however, is that the conceptual framework should be a boolean algebra for reasons already explained. This is not ensured by starting with expansion functions.

Gärdenfors also appears to think that the requirements for expansion functions needed to secure a classical propositional logic are less compelling than those needed to ensure an intuitionistic logic alone. In part, this is due to his failure to appreciate the objectionable aspects of beginning with unstructured spaces of epistemic states just mentioned. In all fairness, however, I think there is another aspect of Gärdenfors's philosophical outlook that contributes to his caution about classical logic. Recall that my argument for the classical view depends not only on the Peircean injunction against conceptual roadblocks but also on my assumption that avoidance of error is an important desideratum in changing belief states. Gärdenfors, on the other hand, not only seeks to bypass modal metaphysics, as I do, but also seeks an account of change of belief that dispenses with avoidance of error as a desideratum in inquiry. He explicitly disavows taking truth into account in constructing a view of change of belief (Gärdenfors, 1988, pp. 19–20). To this extent, his view resembles what appears to have been John Dewey's attitude toward inquiry rather than that of Charles Peirce. Although I differ from Peirce's understanding of truth and avoidance of error as a desideratum in inquiry, dispensing with avoidance of error as a goal of inquiry seems to me excessive and I seek to provide for it. But if one adopts Gärdenfors's attitude, perhaps a case can be made for caution in endorsing the classical view.

2.5 Sentential representations

The topic is change of states of full belief. In Section 2.1, I said that these states are states of doxastic commitment. In Section 2.2, I sketched an abstract structure characterizing a "space" of potential revisions of such commitments. Given this characterization, it is possible to say something about what the doxastic commitment is a commitment to. An agent in a state of full belief **K** fully believes all those potential states in the filter of the conceptual framework K generated by **K** to be free of error. We may also say that the agent fully believes (is certain) that all of the doxastic propositions (i.e., potential states of full belief) that are consequences of K in the conceptual framework are true. To say this, however, is not to claim that the agent fully recognizes or is able to recognize fully the truth of all of the doxastic propositions that are consequences of K. The agent X is no ideally situated, rational angel. X's state of full belief is a commitment to recognize fully the consequences of the state.

X's doxastic performance may fail to live up to his doxastic commitment in one of two ways:

1. X may misidentify a doxastic proposition as a consequence of his state of full belief when it is not. In this case, we may say that he has attempted full recognition of the doxastic proposition in question but that the attempt failed.

2. X may not attempt full recognition of a consequence of his state of full belief at all.

Both kinds of failure are failures of doxastic performance. We may judge the first kind to have occurred when the agent displays what appears to be full recognition of a doxastic proposition inconsistent with his commitment or, more generally, not a consequence of his commitment but where we may interpret the apparent full recognition as a failure of full recognition. The second kind may be judged to occur when a given doxastic proposition is a consequence of the agent's state of full belief and the agent gives no indication of full recognition of that proposition at all.

Even if the distinction I have insisted upon between commitment and performance is conceded, one may still ask for an identification of conditions under which an agent fully recognizes a doxastic proposition to be true. If the inquirer is going to keep his own attitudes under critical control, he will need to fulfill his commitments to some significant extent. And others interested in predicting and explaining his behavior may very well be interested in ascertaining the extent to which his behavior may be taken to be a manifestation of the inquirer's living up to his doxastic undertakings.

Thus, to say that X fully recognizes that h is to claim that X has dispositions to certain kinds of behavior under certain conditions. What the dispositions are dispositions to and what the conditions are will depend on background assumptions we make about X. If, for example, we assume that X is a competent English speaker and that the English sentence "New York is larger than Albany" represents the potential state of full belief that h in English, we may take one of the dispositions to be the disposition to answer positively the question "Is New York larger than Albany?" in situations where we can also take for granted the sincerity of X – that is, his interest in revealing what he recognizes to be true. Or X may have the disposition to take bets in which he discounts completely the risk of losing in case Albany has more people than New York. The kinds of disposition that instantiate full recognition that h are diverse, and can differ from person to person and context to context. Any general formula for characterizing these dispositions that avoids inaccuracy is quite likely to be vacuous. To recognize fully that h is to be disposed to certain kinds of behavior (either linguistic or nonlinguistic or both) under certain conditions. We may be in a position to be more specific in characterizing the dispositions in specific contexts, depending upon what we take for granted about X. Doing so is part of the hermeneutical task of interpreting X's behavior. All I am saying here is that to attribute full belief that h to X is to attribute to him a commitment to having some battery of dispositions to linguistic or other behavior. To the extent that he has such dispositions, he fully recognizes that h, and when appropriately prompted, he manifests that recognition.

If X fully recognizes that h, X fully believes that h or, equivalently, is in a state of full belief that has the doxastic proposition that h as a consequence. The converse, of course, does not hold. X may fully believe that h and be committed to full recognition that h without living up to his undertakings.

Hence, if X's linguistic or nonlinguistic behavior is understood by an interpreter as a manifestation of X's full recognition that h, two judgments are being made by the interpreter: (1) the agent has certain dispositions and (2) these dispositions satisfy the agent's doxastic commitments.

The first judgment is a factual claim about the agent. There is nothing in principle that prevents the integration of the attribution of such dispositions within a biological and physical account of the agent's behavior.

The second claim is more problematic. On the one hand, to claim that the dispositions satisfy the commitments is to presuppose that the agent has undertaken certain doxastic commitments and that the dispositions the agent is alleged to have, according to judgment (1), meet conditions required for fulfilling these commitments. This is also a factual claim. On the other hand, when one attributes doxastic commitments to an agent, one does so on the presumption that the inquirer ought to fulfill his commitments (insofar as he is able and costs permit). And this prescriptive assumption supports the value judgment that the agent has done what he ought to have done. Thus, the attribution of full recognition has a prescriptive dimension that is not "naturalizable" if the fact–value dichotomy holds.

That the so-called propositional attitudes cannot be "naturalistically" reduced is not exactly news. The only gloss I would make on this observation has already been noted in section 2.1: that the lack of a naturalistic account of such attitudes may be seen as having the same provenance as the lack of a derivation of "ought" from "is."

Because values cannot be fully reduced to facts, demands for a naturalistic reduction of either full belief or full recognition cannot be gratified. Just as the specification of the conditions under which someone fulfills a promise to pay a sum of money carries an irreducibly normative component, so too does fulfillment of doxastic commitments.

Nonetheless, it is possible to say something systematic about the doxastic commitments of inquirers with the aid of linguistic representations of potential states of full belief, and it will be useful to do so as a prolegomenon to the subsequent discussion of belief change. Such linguistic representations are useful to the inquiring agent for describing and criticizing the doxastic commitments and performances of other agents and for policing his own commitments and performances.

These uses of language to represent states of full belief should be distinguished from the use of language to manifest states of full belief. Just as physicists interested in formulating general laws regulating changes of physical state use language (often highly regimented, technical language) to represent physical states, regimented linguistic representations of potential states of full belief may be used to characterize changes of belief state.

Language is also involved in manifestations of linguistic dispositions instantiating doxastic performances fulfilling or violating states of full belief. Highly regimented language is, for the most part, less well suited to such linguistic manifestations than to the representation of belief states, although I advocate no precise principle regarding this point. For the purposes of this discussion, where the concern is to represent states of full belief, the complexities of representation with the aid of natural languages tend to obscure rather than illuminate the systematic account of belief revision under consideration. For this reason, the scheme I use deploys some regimented language L to represent potential states of full belief. I shall require L to have a first-order predicate logic. I also include vocabulary and axioms interpretable as set theory and arithmetic, as well as extralogical vocabulary. Depending on the richness of $\underline{L}$, it is possible to distinguish between belief states in the conceptual framework by representing them by means of different sets of sentences in $\underline{L}$. There may be distinct potential states of full belief represented by the same set of sentences in $\underline{L}$. This means that $\underline{L}$ is not sufficiently refined to be able to represent completely potential states of full belief in the given conceptual framework. Indeed, if K is an atomless boolean algebra, $\underline{L}$ is incapable of doing so, since we may suppose that the strongest consistent belief states characterizable within $\underline{L}$ will be represented with the aid of maximally consistent sets of sentences.

Someone may insist that where no distinction is marked by sets of sentences in $\underline{L}$, there is no distinction between potential states of full belief. Such a view might be attractive to someone who thinks that an inquirer's conceptual space is bounded by his language. I am rather skeptical of such views (insofar as I understand them at all). But I do not wish to enter into debates about such matters. They are largely irrelevant to my concerns. I am, of course, planning to represent states of full belief by sets of sentences in a regimented language $\underline{L}$. But this language is not necessarily one that the agent uses or would use to communicate his convictions or other attitudes. Nor, for that matter, is it a language that I would or do use to communicate my convictions except in a very restricted way. Just as a physicist might use points in phase space in a representation of mechanical states of a physical system without in any way implying that his method of representation is used by the physical system, I shall use sets of sentences in $\underline{L}$ (along with sets of sentences in other related regimented languages) to represent an agent's state of full belief at a given time. The agent X no more uses sentences in $\underline{L}$ than the physical system speaks the language of points in phase space. To the extent that the expressive means of $\underline{L}$ are limited, we may say that our linguistic means for characterizing belief states are limited to representing such states only partially, so that two distinct belief states might have the same representation in $\underline{L}$. The limitation is on our ability to represent X's conceptual framework with the aid of $\underline{L}$, and not on X's linguistic or conceptual capacity.

Let Φ be a mapping from sentences in $\underline{L}$ into the potential states of full belief in K such that the condition of deducibility preservation holds.

Deducibility preservation: If "g" is deducible from "h" in $\underline{L}$, $\Phi($"g"$)$ is in the filter generated by $\Phi($"h"$)$.

An immediate implication of deducibility preservation is that if "h" and "g" are logically equivalent sentences in $\underline{L}$, $\Phi($"h"$) = \Phi($"g"$)$.

Let S be all the doxastic propositions assigned sentences according to Φ. Consider some potential state of full belief $\mathbf{K}$ and the filter in the conceptual framework K generated by $\mathbf{K}$. Let $\underline{K}$ be the set of sentences in $\underline{L}$ that represent doxastic propositions in the intersection of this filter and S according to the function Φ. I am saying that the potential corpus $\underline{K}$ in $\underline{L}$ represents the potential state of full belief K insofar as that potential state is representable in $\underline{L}$.

It is possible that two distinct potential states of full belief are representable by the same corpus relative to $\underline{L}$ and Φ. To discriminate between the two potential states may require a richer language. I take for granted that we are focusing on revisions of states of full belief insofar as they are representable as shifts of potential corpora expressible in $\underline{L}$ according to function Φ. To represent finer-grained changes in states of full belief, a richer regimented language would be required.

Insofar as we focus on the conceptual subframework representable by potential corpora expressible in $\underline{L}$, a potential state K_2 is a consequence of K_1 if and only if the potential corpus $\underline{K}_2$ contains the potential corpus $\underline{K}_1$. Thus, the structure of the partial ordering of potential corpora with respect to set inclusion represents the consequence relation between potential states of full belief.

Deducibility preservation guarantees that every potential corpus is closed under deduction. The improper ultrafilter generated by 0 consists of all potential states of full belief in the conceptual subframework. Every sentence in $\underline{L}$ represents a potential state of full belief according to Φ in this improper ultrafilter. Hence, the set of such sentences (i.e., $\underline{L}$ itself) is the potential corpus representing 0 in $\underline{L}$. This corpus is the inconsistent corpus.

The filter generated by 1 contains only one element – to wit, 1. Hence, the potential corpus representing 1 consists of those sentences in $\underline{L}$ that represent 1. In virtue of deducibility preservation, this urcorpus $\underline{1}$ must include all the logical truths of $\underline{L}$. We might decide to include any other sentences that we mean to hold fixed, such as some set theoretic and mathematical truths. The urcorpus is, in virtue of deducibility preservation, closed under deduction, as is every other potential corpus.

The set of all potential corpora in $\underline{L}$ closed under first-order deduction will form a boolean algebra. Since we have already assumed that the conceptual framework (or the framework representable in $\underline{L}$) is a boolean algebra, we have not, to this extent, made any extra assumption in requiring that the mapping obey deducibility preservation. However, assuming that the logic for $\underline{L}$ is a first-order logic together with the deducibility preservation requirement allows for the possibility that the subframework representable by $\underline{L}$ does satisfy additional structural conditions. For example, suppose that $\underline{L}$ contains denumerably many singular sentences of the type "thing i is red." Call this set $\underline{I}$. Assume that these sentences represent distinct potential states of full belief according to the mapping. Call the set of potential states of full belief represented by the sentences in this set I. There must be a potential state in the framework representable by the deductive closure of $\underline{I}$.[9] This potential state is the greatest lower bound of I. The sentence "Everything is red" represents a potential state that is a lower bound for I. So we are assuming the existence of the greatest lower bound of I. Moreover, "Everything is red" should not represent that greatest lower bound; for the corpus that is the deductive closure of $\underline{I}$ is a proper subset of the corpus that is the deductive closure of "Everything is red" and, hence, represents a weaker potential state of full belief bounding I from below.

I rest content here with saying that the conceptual subframework must not only be a boolean algebra but must also satisfy further conditions that ensure that the conceptual subframework is representable by a mapping conforming to deducibility preservation from a regimented first-order language.

Consider a pair of potential corpora $\underline{K}_1$ and $\underline{K}_2$ such that $\underline{K}_1 \subset \underline{K}_2$. The doxastic proposition $\mathbf{K}_1$ is a consequence of the doxastic proposition $\mathbf{K}_2$. $\mathbf{K}_2$ is an expansion of $\mathbf{K}_1$, according to our preceding definitions. We shall also say that $\underline{K}_2$ is an expansion of $\underline{K}_1$. In the same way, we may speak of contractions, replacements, and residual shifts of potential corpora representing potential states of full belief rather than of the potential states of full belief.

Given a regimented language $\underline{L}$ and a translation function Φ, "X fully believes that h" can be understood to assert that the doxastic proposition that h (where "h" is in $\underline{L}$ and $\Phi("h") =$ that h) is in the filter generated by X's state of full belief. And this can also be restated as saying that "h" is in X's corpus $\underline{K}$.

At the outset, I suggested that the state of full belief distinguishes between what is settled and what is not. The distinction is captured with the aid of the corpus. Given any sentence "h" in $\underline{L}$ or the doxastic proposition that h it expresses, opinions concerning the truth of that h are settled if and only if either "h" or "$\sim h$" is in $\underline{K}$. Otherwise, the issue is open or unsettled.

We may reach the same point by considering the distinction between what is seriously possible according to agent X at time t and what is not.

The doxastic proposition that h is seriously possible, according to X, at t if and only if there is at least one ultrafilter in the boolean algebra of potential states of full belief that (1) has X's current state of full belief as a member and (2) has the doxastic proposition that h as a member.

We may say that the sentence "h" in $\underline{L}$ is possibly true in the sense of serious possibility if and only if the doxastic proposition that h is seriously possible. We could represent X's state of full belief by the set of sentences in $\underline{L}$ judged seriously possible. It should be clear that "h" is possibly true according to X at t if and only if "$\sim h$" is not in X's corpus $\underline{K}$ at time t.

Instead of locating a potential state of full belief by specifying those potential states of full belief that are in the filter generated by it, as we do when we report that X believes that h, we could proceed by specifying those doxastic propositions that are seriously possible, according to X, at t.

If the conceptual framework were an atomic boolean algebra, this would, in effect, specify the set of atoms of the boolean algebra that generate principle ultrafilters to which X's state of full belief belongs and, in this way, identify the state of full belief itself. The atoms of the boolean algebra correspond roughly to what are often called *possible worlds*. But on the account I am proposing, they represent doxastic propositions or potential states of full belief. Possible worlds, like propositions, belong to the gratuitous metaphysics dismissed in Section 2.4.

A maximally consistent corpus in $\underline{L}$ might itself be thought to correspond to a possible world. Such a corpus might represent an atomic doxastic proposition or a maximally consistent state of full belief if the conceptual framework K is atomic. However, this need not be so if $\underline{L}$ lacks the expressive power. Moreover, K need not be atomic. In that event, there are no maximally consistent states of full belief and, hence, the maximally consistent corpora in $\underline{L}$ cannot represent them and a fortiori cannot represent possible worlds.

The account I have given implies that if X is in a state of full belief, X believes all doxastic propositions in the filter generated by that state of full belief and, hence, given the assumptions for representing states of full belief adopted previously, believes all doxastic propositions whose sentential representations are logical consequences of sentential representations of doxastic propositions he believes.

In section 2.1 and at the beginning of this section, I suggested a distinction between between doxastic commitment and doxastic performance. To be in a state of full belief is to have undertaken a doxastic commitment. But one can undertake a doxastic commitment without living up to it.

To what is X committed by being in a state of full belief? I proposed distinguishing between "X fully believes that h," which partially describes X's current state of full belief and, hence, his doxastic commitment, and "X fully recognizes that h," which describes X as engaging in a doxastic performance.

To say the X is engaging in a doxastic performance is to claim that the activity or condition conforms to a doxastic commitment X has undertaken. Which commitment is obeyed if the doxastic performance obeys a doxastic commitment rather than violating one? Any doxastic commitment correctly described as involving full belief that h. Hence, when X fully believes that h, X is committed thereby to recognizing fully that h. (The converse, of course, does not hold.)

Of course, this characterization of X's doxastic commitment does not explain clearly how recognition that h is manifested in linguistic and other forms of behavior or is processed biologically. I do not know how to furnish comprehensive yet nonvacuous recipes for answering this question.

Even so, something more needs to be said about the structure of full recognition and doxastic commitment.

If X makes a promise to whistle "The Wabash Cannonball" and subsequently does so at the appointed time without having intended the musical performance as a fulfillment of the promise, has X nonetheless fulfilled her promise? In one sense, of course, the answer is "yes." X promised to whistle

"The Wabash Cannonball" and did it inadvertently at the appointed time. But if X did not recognize that she whistled the tune, and that in so doing she fulfilled the promise she made, she will not recognize that she has fulfilled the promise. She may think she should seek to do so and, hence, whistle the tune a second time.

In the case envisaged, X did not fully believe that she fulfilled the promise any more than she fully recognized it. But we can envisage an alternative scenario. X might have deliberately whistled "The Wabash Cannonball" so that she had at one time fully recognized that she had done so and, hence, fully believed that she fulfilled her promise and then subsequently forgotten that she had done so. In that case, X would remain committed to recognizing fully that she had whistled the tune, and that in so doing she had fulfilled her promise. She would have full belief that she kept her promise without recognition. In this case too, X might seek to keep her promise by whistling the tune again.

There is a difference, however, between the two cases. In the second case, we who have witnessed X's progress have a remedy for her malaise. We may seek to prod her memory so as to bring her full belief into full recognition. This remedy will not suffice in the first case. Even if we can bring X to recognize that she whistled "The Wabash Cannonball" inadvertently, both we and X may be undecided as to whether the act fulfilled her promise. I do not want to settle the matter. It is not obvious how it should be settled. But suppose that it is settled to X's satisfaction that she kept her promise. Then, among other things, X comes to recognize that she has kept her promise and terminates her efforts to do so.

The moral of the story is the same in both cases: If X fulfills her promise to whistle "The Wabash Cannonball," she not only whistles "The Wabash Cannonball" but also recognizes that she has done so. In making the promise, X undertook not only to whistle "The Wabash Cannonball" but also to recognize that she did so.

When X fully recognizes that h, she is fulfilling an undertaking character-ized as fully believing that h. But, from X's point of view, she will not have fulfilled the undertaking unless she fully recognizes that she fully recognizes that h, just as, from her point of view, she will not have fulfilled her promise to whistle "The Wabash Cannonball" unless she recognizes that she has done so. However, to describe X as fully recognizing that h is to describe X as fulfilling a doxastic commitment and, hence, as fully recognizing that she fully recognizes that h, fully recognizing that she fully recognizes that she fully recognizes that h, and so on. This is not the same as saying that when X has the dispositions that are instantiated when she has full recognition that h, she always has the dispositions instantiating full recognition that she has those dispositions. However, to the extent that she lacks these second-level dispositions, the fact that she has the first-order dispositions will not suffice for full recognition that h.

Moreover, to fully recognize that h is to judge with recognition that $\sim h$ is not a serious possibility. Hence, to judge with recognition that $\sim h$ is not a serious possibility is to recognize fully that one judges with recognition that $\sim h$ is not a serious possibility.

Consequently, we may say that when X fully believes at t that h, X fully believes at t that X fully believes at t that h and that X fully believes at t that $\sim h$ is not a serious possibility, according to X at t. X's full belief that h commits her to recognizing fully that h, recognizing fully that she fully recognizes that h, and so on.

These conclusions apply only to full beliefs and recognitions by a single agent at a given time. The inquirer is not undertaking to recognize what he fully recognizes at some other time or what others recognize. The difference does not reflect any first-person epistemic or doxastic privilege. It would be preferable to regard it as a first-person doxastic obligation imposed by the commitments or undertakings of the agent. The obligation is not only to have the dispositions instantiating full recognition but to be in a position to police and, hence, to recognize the full recognitions he has.

If we wish to represent this aspect of the inquirer's commitments in a regimented linguistic way, one way to do it is by introducing a hierarchy of regimented languages.

First, suppose that we have a hierarchy beginning with $\underline{L}$ and followed by $\underline{L}^1, \ldots$ of metalanguages, where each one in the hierarchy includes the previous one and has, in addition, resources for describing the syntax of the language immediately below it, to provide Tarskilike truth theories for the language immediately preceding and resources for identifying which potential corpus expressible in the language immediately preceding is the corpus of agent X or, for any other agent Y, for that agent.

In effect, we have suggested that agent X whose corpus is $\underline{K}$ is committed to having " 'h' is in $\underline{K}$ " in his metacorpus $\underline{K}^1$ if "h" is in $\underline{K}$, and conversely.

Suppose that h is a serious possibility, according to X at t. Does X's doxastic commitment generate an undertaking to judge with recognition that h is seriously possible, according to X, and so on? When X fully believes that h, an affirmative answer seems noncontroversially obvious. But suppose that X does not fully believe that h any more than he fully believes that $\sim h$? Should X be committed to judging with recognition that both h and $\sim h$ are seriously possible?

In Section 2.1, I suggested that X may undertake a doxastic commitment nonfraudulently even though X is certain that X will not fulfill all its conditions. The undertaking is to fulfill the commitments insofar as his computational abilities, memory, and emotional state permit and insofar as various technologies can be deployed at a reasonable cost.

However, if X's doxastic commitment involves an undertaking to recognize whether a doxastic proposition is seriously possible or not, X's doxastic commitment is representable as requiring that if and only if "h" is not in X's corpus $\underline{K}$, " 'h' is not in $\underline{K}$" is in $\underline{K}^1$. Hence, it would seem to follow that X is committed to being able to decide whether a given sentence in $\underline{L}$ is in $\underline{K}$ or not. This is so even though, in general, $\underline{K}$ will not be recursive and, hence, there will not be an effective decision procedure for deciding on membership in $\underline{K}$.

It may, perhaps, be argued that when this is so, insisting that X has a commitment to recognize what is not in his corpus as well as what is is fraudulent; for X could not achieve this even if X had the capabilities of a Turing machine.

I do not think this point is decisive. There are countervailing considerations.

When X makes judgments of credal probability and assigns positive credal probability to doxastic propositions, X presupposes that such doxastic propositions are serious possibilities.

I contend that X is committed to recognizing fully his judgments of credal probability and, hence, his judgments of serious possibility. When X fails to recognize what his credal probability judgments are, there is a failure of commitment, just as when he fails to recognize what his full beliefs are. Hence, X can be committed to assigning positive probability to the doxastic proposition that h less that 1 but fail to recognize this because he fails to recognize that both the doxastic proposition that h and that $\sim h$ are both serious possibilities. Even if there is no effective procedure for deciding whether "h" is in X's corpus $\underline{K}$, this could be so.

When X is in a state of full belief represented by $\underline{K}$ in $\underline{L}$, I have suggested that X is committed to judging his state of full belief to be error-free and all elements of the filter generated by that state to be error-free as well.

Notice that freedom from error, or truth, is taken here to be predicated of states of full belief (i.e., doxastic propositions) and not propositions or sentences (tokens or types). The inquiring agent ought to be concerned to avoid error in his state of full belief. Whether he ought to be concerned to avoid error in what he writes or says is entirely another matter.

If a sentence "h" in $\underline{L}$ represents a potential state of full belief **K** according to the mapping Φ, we may say that "h" is true in $\underline{L}$ if and only if **K** is error-free – that is, true (without relativity to $\underline{L}$ or the mapping). Relative to the mapping, therefore, to assert that X fully believes that h is to give a description of X's state of full belief equivalent to asserting that X fully believes that "h" is true in $\underline{L}$. The doxastic proposition that h is identical to the doxastic proposition that "h" is true in $\underline{L}$ according to the mapping.

Thus, the claim that X should be concerned to avoid error in his state of full belief **K** implies that X should be concerned to avoid error in the corpus $\underline{K}$ where truth and error are predicated of sentences in $\underline{L}$. $\underline{K}$ consists of all sentences representing consequences of **K**. These consequences are error-free if **K** is, and conversely.

Thus, the judgment that K is error-free is representable by specifying that corpus $\underline{K}^1$ contains a tarskilike truth theory for $\underline{L}$ according to which all sentences in $\underline{K}$ are true in $\underline{L}$.

We may summarize these claims for all $\underline{L}^i$ and $\underline{L}^{i+1}$ in the hierarchy as follows:

Full Recognizability Condition:

1. $\underline{K}^i \subseteq \underline{K}^{i+1}$
2. If "h" $\in \underline{L}^i$,"h" $\in \underline{K}^i$ if and only if " 'h" $\in \underline{K}^{i}$" $\underline{K}^{i+1}$.
3. If "h" $\in \underline{L}^i$,"h" $\notin \underline{K}^i$ if and only if " 'h" $\notin \underline{K}^{i}$" $\in \underline{K}^{i+1}$.

Truth Condition: $\underline{K}^{i+1}$ furnishes a characterization of "true in $\underline{L}^{i}$" meeting Tarskian requirements.

Notice that given $\underline{K}$ at time t, these four conditions uniquely determine a Tarskian truth theory for $\underline{L}$ according to $\underline{K}^1$ that secures the truth in $\underline{L}$ of every sentence in $\underline{K}$. $\underline{K}^1$ is not uniquely determined, however, by $\underline{K}$. That is because it may contain information about Y's corpus expressible in $\underline{L}$ at various times, as well as information about X's corpus at times other than time t. However, if we ignore this other information, X's corpus in $\underline{L}$ does, indeed, uniquely determine the hierarchy of metacorpora. Hence, in studying revisions of X's doxastic commitments expressible in $\underline{L}$, we do not have to worry about revisions in the hierarchy. They are automatically taken care of. Thus, in a systematic investigation of belief change, it will prove unnecessary, for the most part, to consider the entire hierarchy of metalanguagues and the matacorpora generated by the first-level corpus, and one will focus instead on changes in the first-level corpus alone. The only reason for introducing the more ramified representation is to provide an explicit characterization of commitments to full recognition relevant to the self-criticism ingredient in being in a given state of full belief.

It may be wondered why, in addition to the hierarchy of metalanguages and metacorpora, the associated Tarskilike truth theories are introduced. A partial answer is, of course, based on my claim that inquirers ought to be concerned to avoid error in changing belief states so that judgments of truth and error and of risk of error are to be made. But another consideration is also relevant. If one follows the practice I am following of representing potential states of full belief by sets of sentences in a regimented language, we may represent the judgment that a potential state K is error-free (erroneous) by the claim in $\underline{L}^1$ that no sentence (at least one) in $\underline{K}$ is false in $\underline{L}$. To do this, we need to have a truth predicate applicable to sentences of the regimented language. But all of this would be unnecessary if we could use a mapping from the sentences in $\underline{L}$ *onto* the potential states in K that preserved deducibility. In that case, the sentence itself could represent the judgment that the belief state it represents is error-free. If the conceptual framework is sufficiently rich, however, this condition will not hold. The condition demands that all corpora in $\underline{L}$ representing potential states of full belief are finitely axiomatizable and, hence, can be replaced by single sentences. I do not assume, however, that this will, in general, be so. Consequently, to obtain a sentential representation of the judgment of freedom from error or erroneousness, we need, in general, to appeal to quantified statements in $\underline{L}'$ over elements of deductively closed sets in $\underline{L}$ utilizing a truth predicate for sentences in $\underline{L}$. The truth predicate is not eliminable from such sentences, in general, as it would be in the case where all potential states are representable by finitely axiomatizable, deductively closed sets. The hierarchy of Tarskilike theories is needed to furnish coherence to linguistic representations of judgments of truth and error in the general case.[10]

A corpus $\underline{K}$ is intended to serve as a "standard" for serious possibility.

Standard for Serious Possibility Condition: "h" (in $\underline{L}^i$) is a serious possibility according to X at t if and only if "$\sim h$" is not in X's corpus $\underline{K}^i$ at t.

We may, therefore, abbreviate "$\sim h$ is not in X's corpus $\underline{K}$ at t" as " $\Diamond h$." "h is in X's corpus $\underline{K}$ at t" becomes "$\sim \Diamond h$" or "$\boxed{t}h$".

These sentences are elements of $\underline{L}^i$. We may use the same abbreviatory device for sentences in $\underline{L}^2$, and so on, up the hierarchy.

Hence, using the standard for serious possibility condition and the full recognizability condition, we may derive a set $\underline{K}^*$ of sentences in a language $\underline{L}^*$ containing $\underline{L}$ and all truth functional compounds of sentences containing finitely many modal connectives in a prefix. $\underline{K}^*$ is closed under the principles of sentential S5 modal logic and is uniquely determined by $\underline{K}$.[11]

Changes in standards for serious possibility are, therefore, equivalent to changes in states of full belief. I claim that the aims of belief change ought to be the acquisition of error-free informational value and have, therefore, presupposed that states of full belief are truth valued. Hence, standards for serious possibility are truth valued. This does not mean that judgments that specific doxastic propositions are seriously possible (or the sentences that represent such judgments by predicating the possible truth of sentences in $\underline{L}$) are truth valued. There is a fact of the matter as to whether inquirer X judges the doxastic proposition that h seriously possible or the sentence "h" possibly true; but there is no fact of the matter as to whether it is seriously possible that h. That is to say, when revising his state of full belief or standard for serious possibility, the inquirer is not concerned to avoid error in the judgments of serious possibility he makes, but only in the standard for serious possibility relative to which he makes them.

Suppose, for example, that X, who begins with corpus $\underline{K}$, expands his corpus by adding sentence $\underline{A}$ and forms the deductive closure. Initially he judged $\sim\underline{A}$ a serious possibility. Subsequently he judged it an impossibility.

If these judgments were truth valued in a sense relevant to the concern to avoid error, X would be deliberately courting error in changing his view. I conclude that X is not concerned to avoid error in any sense that involves a concern to avoid false judgments of serious possibility.

Such judgments could not be true or false anyhow. A judgment of serious possibility is not a potential state of full belief (standard for serious possibility) or a representation of one. But, according to the view I favor, only potential states of full belief or sentential representations of them are truth valued.

2.6 Comparative statics

What I am calling a *potential corpus* corresponds roughly to a *belief set* in the sense of Gärdenfors.[12] Gärdenfors understands such a belief set to be a *model* of the *epistemic state* of an agent. I take it that his epistemic state corresponds to my state of full belief.

Gärdenfors contrasts the actual psychological state of the agent to the ideal epistemic state represented by the belief set. Again, roughly speaking, his distinction corresponds to the one I mean to draw between commitment and performance.

Gärdenfors suggests that the epistemic state is to be understood as a sort of equilibrium state, and the kind of belief revision under consideration is to be analogized to the study of changes in equilibrium states in physics.

The idea of characterizing epistemic states as analogues of such equilibrium states has been suggested by Ellis (1979) and by me (Levi, 1970, 1980a, pp. 9–13). However, in my work, the study of changes in equilibrium states was explicitly intended to be normative or prescriptive and not explanatory. As I suggested in 1980, the principles of belief revision are principles of a normative analogue of comparative statics of the sort one might find in thermodynamics or economics. Ellis takes the analogy to thermodynamics more literally. He thinks of states of belief that are rational as equilibrium states of an ideally rational agent, just as one may think of the laws of thermodynamics as equilibrium conditions of ideal systems that real systems satisfy only to some degree of approxiamtion. When real systems fail to satisfy the ideal equilibrium conditions, they may still be useful, so Ellis contends, in explaining the behavior of the real systems.

This view would be more attractive than it actually is if we could show that it would be preferable to model behavior as approximating the requirements of rationality rather than shift to a different theory. If we were really concerned with explanation, I suspect that we would have long ago abandoned belief–desire models of rational behavior. In my judgment, we retain variants on such models of rationality for purposes of prescription rather than explanation. Our propositional attitudes are commitments in the sense I have explained. It may be helpful to point out that an agent has lived up to his commitment and this kind of information may enhance our understanding of his behavior. But it is not an explanation of his behavior in any "covering law" sense.[13]

The account of belief revision I am concerned to address is doubly normative. First, the contrast between equilibrium and disequilibrium corresponds to the distinction between doxastic commitment and doxastic performance. An agent would reach doxastic equilibrium if his doxastic performance completely fulfilled his doxastic commitment. To the extent that it does not, the agent is under an obligation to change his performance, so as to bring it into greater conformity – provided, of course, that such improvements are feasible for the agent and not too costly.[14]

Second, an agent may or may not have good reason to revise his doxastic commitment – that is, change the equilibrium state.

The two normative aspects of the account of belief revision should be carefully distinguished from one another, and both should be distinguished from the doxastic performances that fulfill and fail to fulfill doxastic commitments.

Gärdenfors, for example, suggests that inductive reasoning "belongs to the process of adjusting a state of belief to an equilibrium."[15] Gärdenfors seems to think of inductive reasoning as part of the therapeutic activity of modifying performance so as to fulfill doxastic commitment better. He suggests that recognizing inductive generalizations facilitates parsimonious representations of the "current information" and, hence, promotes realization of equilibrium. If I understand Gärdenfors's brief remarks correctly, inductive principles are techniques for enhancing our capacity to live up to our commitments, rather as the study of logic, psychotherapy, and the use of the computer are. I, for my part, understand induction as a form of belief change – that is, change in doxastic commitment or in equilibrium state. In particular, I regard it as a species of *expansion* (See Section 2.3.) In expansion, an agent shifts from one state of full belief to another in the lattice generated by the first. Such expansion is represented linguistically as a shift from a corpus $\underline{K}_1$ to a corpus $\underline{K}_2$ containing the $\underline{K}_1$. Sometimes the shift is justified by canvassing a range of available *expansion strategies* and concluding, given the initial corpus, one's credal probability judgments, and one's (cognitive) aims, that all things considered, the expansion strategy is the one to follow. Such deliberate or inferential expansion is a decision between alternative *cognitive options* and is to be evaluated in terms of how well it promotes one's cognitive aims.

Not all expansion is deliberate (= inferential = inductive). Sometimes one expands one's state of full belief in response to external stimuli – for example, the testimony of the senses or of other witnesses – in conformity with some habit, program, or routine. Although I am not inclined to do so, C. S. Peirce did think of induction as routine expansion.[16]

Although Gärdenfors does not seem to think of induction as a species of expansion but rather as a change in belief reflecting a move toward equilibrium, he does recognize changes in states of belief and, in particular, acknowledges the occurrence of expansions. However, he tends to think of changes in belief states as being driven by what he calls *epistemic inputs* (1988, pp. 13–15). Gärdenfors says too little for one to be sure of his intent, but he appears to think of all changes in belief as the result of "deliverance of experience," which he allows to be by linguistic or nonlinguistic means. He does not consider decision theoretic models of change of belief states where one of several alternative changes is chosen in order to promote some goal. Thus, Gärdenfors might allow for expansions having the properties of what Peirce called *inductions* even though Gärdenfors does not use this terminology.

The philosophically interesting issue is not what is meant by the term *induction*. What is important is the conception of the problem of belief change driving Gärdenfors's discussion. Whether he examines expansion, contraction, or other foms of change in belief state, Gärdenfors avoids considering the question of justifying one change rather than another. His neglect of criteria for evaluating inductive expansions is of a piece with his tendency to neglect an investigation of principles for justifying the making of one belief revision rather than another.

Thus, in discussing expansion, Gärdenfors lays down certain axioms that a change of the sort expansion is supposed to be should satisfy. He then shows that the only shifts from corpus to corpus that satisfy his axioms are those in which a sentence is added to the corpus, and all the "consequences" of that sentence and what is already in the corpus are added (Gärdenfors, 1988, p. 51, theorem 3.1).

In effect, then, the only conditions that Gärdenfors imposes on an expansion are those that distinguish expansions from other transformations of potential corpora to potential corpora. Nothing in Gärdenfors's discussion focuses on why inquiring agent X in a state of full belief representable by potential corpus $\underline{K}$ would be justified in expanding his corpus by adding "h" rather than "g" via inferential expansion, or would be justified in settling on which to add by following some program for relying on expert testimony or the testimony of the sentences.

I contend that there are important types of change in doxastic commitment through expansion that have been called *inductive* whether one wishes to continue the practice or not. Some of them are types of deliberate expansion and others of routine expansion. Gärdenfors has studied only those properties of expansion that are abstracted from the topics of routine and deliberate expansion. (In personal correspondence, Gärdenfors has acknowledged that, in this respect, his discussion of expansion is too coarse-grained.)

The import of these issues will emerge in subsequent discussion. For the present, I wish only to indicate that my concern with comparative statics is a prescriptive or normative one. It is consonant with my concern with specifying equilibrium conditions or, if one likes, general constraints on doxastic commitment.

Before turning, however, to the question of change of doxastic commitment or corpus in general and to the main topic – to wit, contraction – I shall close this chapter with some remarks about alternative views that ignore the distinction between commitment and performance in the context of revising and criticizing propositional attitudes.

2.7 Rationality unbound

My argument for the reducibility of the hierarchy of metacorpora and judgments of serious possibility to the corpus in $\underline{L}$ pivots on two assumptions mentioned in Section 2.5: the full recognizability condition and the standard for serious possibility condition.

Judgments of serious possibility are supposed to define the space of possibly true hypotheses over which judgments of credal probability and other judgments of uncertainty are made and over which assessments of value are determined. The view I have taken is that when at t X has full belief that h, it is not a serious possibility that h according to X at t, and conversely (Levi, 1980a, ch. 1).

Many philosophers will object to this claim on the grounds that full belief is not knowledge. X may have full belief that h and, hence, be certain that h is true and yet acknowledge that his belief might be wrong. Only if X knows that h is this precluded.

On my view, if X fully believes that h, he fully believes that h is true. (See the truth condition of Section 2.5.) That is to say, X is committed to recognizing fully that h is true. Hence, X fully believes that his full belief that h is free of error.

As I use the term *knowledge*, knowledge is error-free, full belief. Hence, if X fully believes that h, X fully believes that X knows that h, X fully believes that X knows that X knows that h, and so on.

Hence, if X were to acknowledge that his belief that h might be wrong, he would be acknowledging that his knowledge that h might be wrong, which, so the critics concede, would be incoherent.

Of course, those who press this line of criticism insist that knowledge is not merely error-free, full belief but rather error-free, justified, full belief. I am not concerned to enter into a tedious logomachy with those who define *knowledge* differently from the way I do. For the sake of the argument, let them use the term *knowledge* any way they wish. But then, as long as X's corpus represents his state of full belief and, hence, his standard for serious possibility, it follows that X is committed to recognizing every sentence in $\underline{L}$ and only such sentences that are inconsistent with his corpus as impossible. It is irrelevant whether the sentences in $\underline{K}$ represent knowledge in the sense that X has justifications for his full beliefs.[17]

The other point at which critics might complain about my reductions concerns the full recognizabilty condition of Section 2.5.

Part of the alleged implausibility of the recognizability condition derives from failure to distinguish between commitment and performance. X may fully believe that h without fully recognizing that h. X is committed to such full recognition, to full recognition of that full recognition, and so on. But clearly, X need not live up to these commitments. It is easy to say, in such cases, that X believes that h but does not recognize that she believes that h. I do not complain about this. But as long as the distinction between commitment and performance is retained and the recognizability condition is understood to be a constraint on doxastic commitment, there is no difficulty.

A more subtle version of the objection proceeds by probing the general constraints on commitment I have endorsed. Consider a deductively closed set of sentences (a corpus or theory), membership in which is not recursively decidable. Even if X had the computational capacity of a Turing machine, X could not determine via an algorithm for every sentence in $\underline{L}$ whether that sentence was in her corpus or not. Hence, failure to recognize a sentence's status as being in or out of the corpus (or being a serious possibility or not) cannot always be blamed on factors inhibiting calculation.

The elements of axiomatizable corpora are effectively enumerable, so that if X had the computational capacity of a Turing machine and time enough, she would recognize every element of her corpus as belonging to it. On the other hand, there is no algorithm to secure her recognizing sentences in $\underline{L}$ as not being in her corpus. But recognizing that "$\sim h$" is not in $\underline{K}$ is required for recognition that h is seriously possible.

Some such argument may suggest that we should not require clause (3) of the full recognizability condition, but only clauses (1) and (2).

If this view is endorsed, we can no longer use the standard for serious possibility condition to obtain for K^* the result that if $\Diamond h$, $\Box \Diamond h$. The axioms for S5 have to be weakened to S4.

This objection has already been discussed in Section 2.5. I repeat my responses here.

1. Although granting that the main impediments to living up to doxastic commitments are obstacles to computation such as emotional stress, limited memory, and computational ability, I do not think that we need restrict our commitments so that we could live up to them if we had the computational capacities of Turing machines. Thus, it is entirely plausible to claim that if we are committed to the truth of Peano's postulates, we are committed to Gödel sentences even if neither they nor their negations are theorems and, moreover, that we can recognize that such sentences are true if Peano's postulates are true.

2. Those favoring an S4-like conception of serious possibility concede that if X is certain that h, X is certain that X is certain. Suppose, however, that X judges that h as positively probable. Should he be committed to being certain that he judges that h as positively probable?

If X judges that *h* as positively probable, X judges it as seriously possible. Hence, anyone who (as I do) endorses an affirmative answer to the question should also concede that X is committed to being certain that he judges that *h* as seriously possible. Consequently, at least for that domain of doxastic propositions over which credal probabilities are allowed to be assigned positive credal probabilities (whether X does so or not), all elements of the domain ought to be judged seriously possible and X ought to be certain that they are. For this domain of doxastic propositions, at any rate, S5 conditions appear to prevail.

Thus, to the extent that S5 is relaxed to S4, there must be some important restriction on the domain over which credal probability is defined. Perhaps some reason can be offered in some cases for imposing such restrictions. However, it makes sense to assume as extensive a domain as is feasible pending good reasons to the contrary. This may leave too many loose ends to satisfy a careful logician. However, for the purposes of this discussion, it seems to me sensible to suppose that S5 conditions are operative unless good reasons to the contrary are offered for some specific class of doxastic propositions.

All things considered, therefore, when the distinction between commitment and performance is acknowledged, and the standard for serious possibility condition and the Recognizability Condition are understood as constraints on doxastic commitment, they seem to capture well the function that states of full belief are supposed to perform in deliberation and inquiry.

I have suggested representing doxastic performances as cases of fully recognizing *doxastic propositions*. Given the distinction between commitment and performance, this may seem to present a difficulty. Let "*h*" and "*g*" be any two logically equivalent sentences in <u>L</u> whose equivalence X does not fully recognize. There are two cases to consider:

Case 1: X fully recognizes that *h* and fully recognizes that ~*g*.

Case 2: X fully recognizes that *h* and judges with recognition that ~*g* is a serious possibility.

X might be in either a case 1 situation or a case 2 situation because of his failure to recognize the logical equivalence of "*h*" and "*g*." In case 1, for example, X might sincerely utter a sentence in his idiolect that we translate as "*h*" and do the same for a sentence we translate as "~*g*." Or, if it is a case 2 predicament, X may register doubt when asked about the translation of "*g*."

In the case 1 situation, we have two possibilities:

a. Both doxastic performances are fulfillments of X's doxastic commitment, which is, therefore, inconsistent. X's belief state is **0**.

b. We have misinterpreted X's linguistic behavior. At least one of his utterances has been misconstrued. Either one of the alleged doxastic performances is not a doxastic performance at all, or it is a doxastic performance fulfilling a commitment different from the one we have taken it initially to be fulfilling. That commitment is consistent, although X's doxastic performances are not.

The same two approaches are possible in case 2 situations.

a'. Both doxastic performances are fulfillments of X's doxastic commitments, so that X is committed to judging that h seriously possible and also impossible. Once more, the state of full belief is **0**.

b'. We have misinterpreted the agent. As before, either one of the utterances has been misconstrued as a doxastic performance or the doxastic performance has been misidentified.

Perhaps someone will worry that because the problem is omnipresent, we will be driven to conclude that every agent is in the inconsistent state of full belief **0**.

It would be foolish to rule out the possibility that X is inconsistent in some cases. As we shall see, it is possible for inquirers to stumble inadvertently but legitimately into inconsistency. Such situations provide one type of occasion for contraction. However, inquirers often appear inconsistent because they are subject to confusion and clearly lack perfect computational capacity and memory. We would do well to explain away such apparent inconsistency as due to failures of performance either because the inquirers themselves have misconstrued their doxastic performances or because they have engaged in failed attempts at doxastic performances. In addition, even if the inquiring subject is not confused, the interpreter can, for diverse reasons, misconstrue the inquirer.

Why should we favor this understanding of X's attitudes?

Suppose that X revealed her recognized full belief that h by uttering "h" with all the behavioral earmarks of sincerity, and her utterance was accompanied by efforts to convince us of the truth of the doxastic proposition that h. Suppose further that X uttered "$\sim g$" but did so after furnishing written proof deriving "$\sim g$" from "h" and other sentences in L that express propositions X gives signs of fully believing. We recognize the proof as faulty and conclude that X has made a mistaken inference. We account for X's doxastic performance in recognizing that $\sim g$ and, hence, that $\sim g$ as being due to this mistake. We can, therefore, explain why X failed to live up to the commitments generated by her full belief that h (commitments that she has partially fulfilled) without supposing that the commitments are inconsistent.

Should it be preferable to regard X's commitments as being consistent in this case even though X's doxastic performance is inconsistent? Inconsistency in performance is no more satisfactory than inconsistency in commitment.

The remedy for inconsistency is quite different in the two cases. Inconsistency in doxastic performance is to be removed by logical therapy. When we have a good indication of the presence of confusion and bad logical reasoning, such therapy promises to be most helpful. If, however, we do not think that the trouble is due to confusion, failure of memory, reasoning, or emotional storm and can, moreover, provide a sensible account of why X undertook an inconsistent doxastic commitment (a point to which I shall return later in this book), we may conclude that the trouble is in the inconsistent commitment. In that case, the remedy is to be found in a revision of doxastic commitment by contraction or giving up doxastic propositions.

Hence, even though inconsistency in doxastic commitment and inconsistency in doxastic performance are troublesome, the remedies are to be sought in different places.

It may be thought preferable to replace doxastic propositions as the objects of recognized full belief by sentences in the agent's idiolect. I do not see that there is any advantage to this.

We may say that X fully recognizes "h" to be true and fully recognizes "$\sim g$" to be true. However, if full recognition is an indicator of X's commitments and X is committed to all logical truths including logical equivalences, X is committed to an inconsistent set of sentences. To avoid inconsistency in commitment, we must conclude that X's recognizing either "h" to be true or "$\sim g$" to be true is a violation of X's doxastic commitment. Individuating doxastic performances sententially gains us nothing in such cases.

If there is any advantage to using sentences to individuate doxastic performances, it would appear to be in distinguishing different doxastic performances of the same type with the same doxastic proposition as object. X might recognize that h at time t by asserting a translation of "h" in his idiolect and recognize that h at t' asserting a translation of "g." But we can acknowledge this without being required to recognize sentences as objects of attitudes. We can distinguish between full recognition that h by having a disposition to utter "h" upon interrogation and full recognition that h by having a disposition to utter "g" upon interrogation. In this way, we can use sentences to distinguish between the two performances without taking sentences to be objects of propositional attitudes.

According to a sententialist veiw, if doxastic performances (full recognitions or failed attempts at such) are not evaluated in terms of whether they fulfill or violate doxastic commitments because no such commitments are undertaken, then either they are not criticized at all or the standards they are meant to satisfy are standards imposed on performances. Thus, the full recognizability condition would have to require that agent X fully recognize which sentences in L are in his corpus at t and which are not. According to the version of recognizability I favor, this condition applies only to commitments, not to performances. The version I favor does not impose excessive demands on the capacities of ordinary agents. But when it is construed as a constraint on performance, only rational angels could gratify its demands.

Some who understand principles of rationality as conditions on perfor-

mance rather than commitment defend the normative force of such principles as regulative ideals that we ought to strive to approximate. But we can
never come close to satisfying all of the demands of doxastic rationality we
have introduced here when they are construed as demands on performance.
We inevitably fail to have a system of recognized full beliefs representable by
a deductively closed set of sentences.

What shall we say about sentences entailed by those that we fully recognize
to be true but that we do not recognize to be entailed? Is their falsity a serious
possibility or not? If we say that they are not serious possibilities, then we
have to allow for sentences to be impossible even though we do not recognize
them to be such. But this reintroduces the distinction between commitment
and performance. If we say that they are serious possibilities because we
recognize that such sentences are not recognized to be consequences of what
we fully recognize to be true, we countenance as serious possibilities sentences that are logically inconsistent with what we fully recognize to be true.
Countenancing such sentences as serious possibilities need not discomfit us
as long as we do not recognize that they are inconsistent with what we
recognize to be true.

Observe that what we have done is to have regarded the corpus $\underline{K}$ to be the
set of sentences X at t fully recognizes as true and not those X is committed
to recognizing fully.[18] We have abandoned the requirement that the corpus
be closed under deduction or under any other stronger notion of consequence. Two sentences in $\underline{L}$ that are logically equivalent need not be expected to be co-members or co-nonmembers of $\underline{K}$. And we cannot, as we did
before, take doxastic propositions to be objects of propositional attitudes; for
there are no doxastic propositions if there are no doxastic commitments. Nor
can we use propositions or sets of possible worlds as the objects of doxastic
performances. We would need to acknowledge that X can fully recognize that
h and fully recognize that $\sim g$ where "h" and "g" are logically equivalent. If
propositions are the objects of doxastic performances, these performances
are inconsistent. If one wishes to prevent wholesale inconsistency, one will be
driven to suggest that X fully recognize as true sentence "h" and fully
recognize as true sentence "$\sim g$." As long as X does not recognize the logical
equivalence of "h" and "$\sim g$," this need not bother X.

This is, as I understand it, the view that I. Hacking took on this matter
over two decades ago (Hacking, 1967, pp. 311–25). I believe that Hacking's discussion is as clear an articulation as one might find of attitudes
that motivate much of H. A. Simon's (1972, pp. 161–72) concern with
bounded rationality, I. J. Good's (1983) preoccupation with type II rationality, and attitudes toward belief revision of the sort advocated by G. Harman
(1986).

In presenting this view, I have ignored a problem that, to my way of
thinking, ought to be most vexing to its advocates. Hacking, like Good before

him, addressed this problem and seems to have thought that he had satisfactorily answered it. I disagree.

One of the best-known versions of the problem concerns an agent X who is offered a bet on whether the integer 9 is in the billionth place in the decimal expansion of π. Because of lack of computational capacity, X does not recognize that 9 is that integer and does not recognize that it is not. According to Hacking's view, neither hypothesis is in the corpus of doxastic performances. X does not know that 9 is (is not) the integer in "the examiner's sense of knowledge" and, hence, both alternatives are "personal possibilities" – that is, serious possibilities. They may both be assigned positive credal probabilities.

However, if X is moderately literate in mathematics, X knows that the sentence "9 is (is not) the integer in the billionth place in the decimal expansion of π" is effectively decidable. Being convinced, as X is, of the truth of Peano's postulates and, hence, assigning them credal probability 1, X fully recognizes that one or the other of the hypotheses should receive credal probability 1. That is to say, X fully recognizes that if he assigns credal probability of, say, 1/10 to the hypothesis that 9 is the integer and 9/10 to its negation, he will be in violation of the canons of rational credal probability judgment.

The worry I am registering would not arise if X did not fully recognize that whether 9 is or is not the integer in question is effectively decidable, so that one or the other is a deductive consequence of what X fully recognizes to be true.

Hacking himself (1967, pp. 312–13) addresses the problem by considering the following two cases:

Case 3: Person Y is asked to bet on whether the product of one pair of five-digit binary numbers is greater than the product of another such pair. Y lacks the ability and the opportunity to calculate the products. Instead, Y assigns a credal probability of 0.2 to the hypothesis of equality and 0.4 to each of the hypotheses of inequality. Y accepts and rejects the bets accordingly.

Case 4: Person Z is asked to bet on whether there are more stops when traveling between Gloucester Road and King's Cross on the Picadilly line or on the Circle line. Z assigns a credal probability of 0.2 to the hypothesis of equality and 0.4 to each of the two hypotheses of inequality.

Hacking acknowledges that personalists of Savage's persuasion would regard Y as incoherent. On the other hand, Z can regard his three alternatives as serious possibilities and, hence, can assign them all positive credal probabilities. A Savage-type personalist must make a sharp distinction between cases 3 and 4.

Hacking wants to treat Y and Z on a par as both perfectly coherent. He thinks that this is to be done by jettisoning the distinction between a priori and a posteriori propositions. Indeed, part of the attraction of views such as his, I suspect, is that in this respect his position conforms to the attitude that Quine has rendered so fashionable in philosophy.

I myself do not understand the distinction between the a priori and the a posteriori or between the analytic and the synthetic, and find little illumination in the philosophical literature. So I have no more inclination than Hacking does to revive such distinctions. But I do not think that is the critical problem. In case 3, if Y has the same mathematical sophistication that X has, Y fully recognizes (Y "knows," in Hacking's "examiner's sense of knowledge") that exactly one of the three alternative hypotheses is a logical consequence of what Y fully recognizes to be true. This is not so in case 4. That is the critical difference between cases 3 and 4, and not any fancied distinction between the a priori and the a posteriori.

Why is this difference important? The problem to be faced is whether the sentence "The two products are equal" is to be judged a serious (i.e., personal) possibility or not. Its negation is not fully recognized to be true and, hence, it might appear that the sentence should be counted as a possibility. By the same token, the negation of this sentence should be considered a serious possibility. However, Y fully recognizes that at least one of these alternatives should not be judged a serious possibility. That is to say, Y fully recognizes that recognizing the sentence and its negation as serious possibilities violates the injunction to avoid judging a sentence a serious possibility when it is recognized to be inconsistent with what one recognizes to be true. Given this recognition, would it not be appropriate for Y, at the very least, to avoid assigning positive credal probability to more than one of the hypotheses? Perhaps we cannot advise Y as to which hypothesis (if any) to consciously assign credal probability 1; but given the constraints Y recognizes, this would appear to be the appropriate way to satisfy them all.

But this argument presupposes, in effect, acknowledgment of a distinction between commitment and performance. If Y recognizes that he should assign no more than one of the alternatives positive credal probability given what he recognizes to be true, what he is recognizing is that what he recognizes to be true generates a doxastic commitment.

Once the distinction between commitment and performance is acknowledged, we may say that Y is committed to assigning credal probability 1 to the alternative that follows from Peano's postulates – not because Peano's postulates are a priori true but because Y is committed to fully recognizing these postulates to be true. On the other hand, Y cannot fulfill his commitment unless he can actually calculate the two products. If he has the opportunity to do so without exhorbitant cost, that is precisely what he should do. If he does not have such an opportunity, we can say to Y that he should not assign positive credal probability to more than one of the alternatives. It would be best if Y could dodge the issue. If he cannot, at least he will not violate his commitments in a recognizable way if he assigns 1 as the credal probability to one of the alternatives and 0 to the rest. This will not guarantee that Y fulfills his doxastic commitments, but at least it will avoid guaranteeing that Y violates them.

As I understand Hacking's position (which recognizes no distinction between commitment and performance), Y's recognition that either it is mathematically demonstrable that the two products are equal or it is demonstrable that they are not is irrelevant to assessments of personal possibility and credal probability judgment. Hence, Y is not prohibited from assigning positive credal probability to both the hypothesis of equality and its negation.

One implication of Hacking's view is that Y's recognizing that the issue of the equality or inequality of the two products is decidable as a consequence of axioms Y recognizes as true does not place Y under any pressure to determine whether the two products are equal or not should he have the opportunity to do so.

Hacking disagrees. Citing an argument of Savage's and Good's that he thinks can be modified to suit his approach, Hacking contends that finding out whether the two products are equal or not must yield at least as much benefit as not doing so, as long as the new information is cost-free (1967, pp. 322–3).

The Good–Savage argument is not as powerful as Hacking suggests it is. In particular, to yield its results, the decision maker must be assured not only that the acquisition of new information is cost-free but also that there is no risk of error in the acquisition.[19] If one conducts experiments or makes calculations and there is a significant chance of error in the results, this might make it disadvantageous to acquire the new information even if there are no other costs. And if one allows for indeterminacy in credal probability judgment, new information may yield indeterminacy where determinacy initially prevailed.

However, we may gloss over these points. The Good–Savage argument presupposes a way of identifying a space of serious or personal possibilities. When Hacking invokes the argument, he presupposes that judgments of serious possibility should follow his recommendation and should ignore as irrelevant information like that already available to Y. So, on Hacking's view, having *that* information (namely, that either the equality or the inequality is effectively decidable and, hence, is exactly 1 is a logical implication of what Y fully recognizes to be true) is not a benefit. So if Y initially did not have it and had the opportunity to find it out cost-free, it would be no benefit to him to obtain it.

More to the point, having that information would not furnish Y with any special incentive to make the calculations required to decide the question of equality or inequality. The incentive to ascertain whether the two products are equal or not would remain exactly as it was before acquiring the information.

In any case, suppose that Y did not know of the Good–Savage theorem and, hence, did not recognize that it would be a benefit to him to find out whether the two products are equal or not. Yet imagine, as before, that he did recognize that the issue is arithmetically decidable. Does Y have any incentive to do the computations if there is an opportunity to do so at small cost?

In this variant of the predicament, Hacking must deny that Y has any reason to make the computations. On my view, Y is committed and, hence, rationally obligated to do so.

In the final analysis, therefore, Hacking's "more realistic" brand of personalism reduces the incentives one has to meet standards of rationality.

Hacking's proposal is distinguished from views like Simon's, Harman's and others in that he seeks to generate a system of norms applicable to humans, with their capabilities, that deviates as little as possible from ideal theory. That is why I have selected it for critical discussion. I have sought to show that even Hacking's subtle but conservative approach fails to give a fully satisfactory account of why we should spend so much on technologies and therapies that facilitate our computational capacities and our memories. Views, like Simon's or Harman's, that tailor our critical standards to fit our capacities more directly are deprived of the use of the Good–Savage argument and seem to be in an even more difficult position than Hacking's with respect to this question.

Central to Hacking's argument is his insistence on rejecting the analytic–synthetic and a priori–a posteriori distinctions as relevant to deliberation and inquiry. I have framed my response so as to minimize my disagreement with him. However, there is one respect in which disagreement is inescapable. Nothing in what I have said implies endorsement of the analytic–synthetic or a priori–a posteriori distinctions. However, the commitment–performance contrast and the distinction between changes in belief that are changes in commitment and changes that are changes in performance correspond to a traditional difference between substantive changes of view and changes in one's comprehension of the view one has.

This distinction is not to be confused with the analytic–synthetic distinction or the a priori–a posteriori distinction. Using it does not presuppose one of the other distinctions. I grant that I am relying on some notion of deducibility and truth-preserving consequence. But this does not require me to endorse notions of conceptual necessity, analyticity, a prioricity, and the like.

On my view, therefore, proving new theorems is to be understood as nonampliative elucidation of convictions to which one is already committed. There is a genuine change involved in such activity. One comes to fulfill more of the doxastic obligations one has undertaken. But it is not to be confused with a change in commitment.

Changes in commitment ought to be instituted through inquiry. Whether they are always so instituted is another issue. Changes in performance due to clarification of commitments are facilitated by therapy.

The critical distinction to which I am holding fast is a distinction between changes in doxastic performance and other attitudinal performances due to therapy aimed at improving our capacity to fulfill our commitments and changes in commitments. I am sure Hacking would reject it. I do not know how to refute him. Concerning such fundamental matters, the proof of the pudding is in the eating.

By insisting on these distinctions, I am not seeking to reinstate any theory of meaning or to draw a distinction between the analytic–synthetic or the a priori–a posteriori. Hacking and many others have presupposed too much in arguing from their rejection of these untenable dualisms to the untenability of other dualisms.

2.8 Commitment to the truth

According to Frege, the laws of deductive logic can be laws of thought only in the sense that they prescribe how we ought to think. I too have, in effect, suggested that a notion of logical consequence serves a prescriptive function. This conception characterizes the commitments to full recognition under-taken by agents given their states of full belief – commitments that such agents ought to fulfill insofar as this is feasible. There is, however, an impor-tant difference between the way Frege thought about the matter and the way I have been talking here. Frege (1967, p. 12) wrote:

It will be granted by all at the outset that the laws of logic ought to be guiding principles for thought in the attainment of truth, yet this is only too easily forgotten, and here what is fatal is the double meaning of the word "law." In one sense a law asserts what is; in the other it prescribes what ought to be. Only in the latter sense can the laws of logic be called 'laws of thought': so far as they stipulate the way in which one ought to think. Any law asserting what is, can be conceived as prescribing that one ought to think in conformity with it, and is thus in that sense a law of thought. This holds for laws of geometry and physics no less than for laws of logic. The latter have a special title to the name "laws of thought" only if we mean to assert that they are the most general laws, which prescribe universally the way in which one ought to think if one is to think at all.

According to Frege, there is no difference between the prescriptive force of a law of logic and that of a law of physics save the greater generality of the former. This must be so if the prescriptive force derives from the role of true laws as "guiding principles for thought in the attainment of truth." It seems clear that for Frege it is not the case that we ought to be committed to fully recognizing all doxastic propositions expressible by sentences that are deduc-tive consequences of sentences expressing doxastic propositions we fully recognize to be true. This is so only when the doxastic propositions in question are error-free or the sentences in L that represent them are true. The reason is that we should be committed to fully recognize all true (error-free) doxastic propositions.

On my view, X is or ought to be committed to fully recognizing all (doxastic propositions expressible by) sentences deducible from what he fully recognizes. Moreover, he is committed to the sentence in his meta-corpus $\underline{K}^t$ expressible in $\underline{L}^t$ stating that all sentences in his corpus $\underline{K}$ expressible in $\underline{L}$ are true in $\underline{L}$. That is to say, X at t is committed to fully recognizing that his current state of full belief is error-free.

However, I deny that X is committed to fully recognizing all true sentences in $\underline{L}$ (i.e., all error-free doxastic propositions).

The view I am attributing to Frege denies that there is any distinction between doxastic performances that entail no change in doxastic commitment and doxastic performances that do. All such performances are of the former kind because they are directed toward obtaining true belief. Whereas for Hacking there is no doxastic commitment to doxastic performances extending beyond our capacities, for Frege there is a single unchanging doxastic commitment of this kind. In spite of the difference, however, both views undermine a nontrivial distinction between doxastic commitment and doxastic performance, and with it a nontrivial sense in which laws of logic are laws of thought but laws of physics are not.

Frege's idea (and Carnap's occasional expression of similar views) seems to be that doxastic commitment ought never to change. We ought to be committed to the true, complete story all the time. To the extent that our state of full belief is neither free of error nor complete, we have failed to live up to our commitments. Any change in belief we make is a change in doxastic performance.

If the sole difference between the laws of logic qua laws of thought and the laws of physics qua laws of thought is the greater generality of the former, then changes in what is recognized to be true come solely from recognizing the deductive consequences of what is already recognized to be true and changes due to recognizing true laws of physics. Neither change is a change in doxastic commitment. For Frege, as for most analytic philosophers who followed him, there can be no distinction between doxastic commitment and doxastic performance. Once more, the distinction between therapy aimed at improving computational competence and inquiry undertaken to remove ignorance of the laws of physics is denied.

The distinction between logical therapy and inquiry cannot be delineated at the outset with any great precision. A clear head and computational capacity are prerequisites for sophisticated inquiry, and it is not easy to say precisely what virtues are peculiar to inquiry in advance of giving a systematic account of rationally conducted inquiry in general and belief revision in particular. Ultimately the best defense one can make for insisting on the distinction is the account of inquiry that can be based on it. In these remarks, the best I can do is to point to a distinction between those intellectual failures that are failures of computation and ratiocination that training and therapy can partially remedy and those intellectual failures that call for inquiry. On my view, the laws of logic are laws of thought in the sense that they characterize commitments undertaken in a state of full belief. As the state of full belief changes, so do the commitments, although the new commitments, like the old, are constrained by deductive closure requirements. In this sense, the true laws of physics are not laws of thought. If X fully believes that sentence "h" expresses a true law of physics, then she is committed to fully recognizing the deductive consequences of the doxastic proposition that h. But we do not judge X to have failed to live up to her commitments because we fully believe that "h" is false. To the extent, however, that X does not recognize some deductive consequence of "h," we do judge her to have failed.

Let us suppose, however, that the distinction between failures to believe the truth due to lack of logical omniscience and failures due to inadequate inquiry is conceded. Might not somebody insist still that what we are concerned with in the final analysis is finding out the truth as an ultimate aim of inquiry?

In this sense, commitment to the truth is not a doxastic commitment. Doxastic commitments are commitments to fully recognize doxastic propositions to be true. Such commitments, I have been assuming, are open to revision. Moreover, such revisions of commitment may be criticized in terms of how well they promote various goals. Agents can, therefore, be committed to revising doxastic commitments in ways that promote some long-term objectives. Such diachronic commitments undertake to revise synchronic doxastic commitments when such changes promote certain ends, but they are distinct from the synchronic doxastic commitments.

It is in this sense that C. S. Peirce and K. R. Popper advocated a commitment to the truth. This conception, as far as it goes, is compatible with allowing for a distinction between doxastic commitment and doxastic performance – in contrast to what I take to be the Fregean view.

What is to be understood by a quest for the truth? Even if we assume that we understand the concept of a true sentence or a doxastic proposition, the answer is by no means free of controversy.

Presumably someone engaged in a quest for truth is concerned to avoid error – that is, to avoid fully believing false sentences or, alternatively but equivalently, to avoid being in a state of full belief that is not in the ultrafilter of error-free potential states of belief.

However, a quest for *the* truth is not only a quest to avoid error. Someone who is committed to believe true only the elements of the minimal urcorpus will attain that goal; for the potential state of full belief corresponding to that corpus is the state 1 that is an element of the ultrafilter of error-free potential states of full belief, no matter which principal ultrafilter of the boolean algebra that happens to be.

I take it that authors like Peirce and Popper have had in mind that the ultimate aim of of inquiry is to attain a potential state of full belief that is (1) error free – that is, is an element of the principal ultrafilter of error-free potential states of full belief – and (2) maximal – that is, is the strongest element of some principal ultrafilter of potential states of full beliefs. The potential state of full belief meeting these two requirements is represented by a potential corpus expressible in L that is maximally consistent and error-free. It is the true and complete story of the world.

To be sure, to say that the story is complete must be relativized to the expressive resources of L or to the conceptual framework of potential states of full belief being deployed. It is doubtful whether either Peirce or Popper would have endorsed an absolute or unrelativized notion of a complete story of the world. In any case, I certainly do not intend to do so.

But the story must not only be complete. The aim is to find the true complete story of the world – that is, the complete story that is also error-free. Granting that the conception of a complete story is relative to a conceptual framework or a language used to represent potential states of full belief in that framework, how are we to understand truth or freedom from error *as an aim of inquiry?* I emphasize that we are concerned with truth as an aim of inquiry focused on revising doxastic commitments.

In characterizing potential states of full belief in an atomic conceptual framework, truth was represented by the elements of the principal ultrafilter of error-free states. These are the true doxastic propositions. This may not seem helpful as an explication of truth or avoidance of error as an aim of inquiry.

A state of full belief (or the corpus that represents it) is X's commitment to a standard for serious possibility for the purpose of making decisions and conducting inquiries. This commitment obligates X, insofar as he is able, to recognize his current state of full belief to be error-free. There is no serious possibility, according to X, that it contains error. That is to say, there is no serious possibility that any sentence in K is false in L.

Consequently, if X is concerned to avoid error, he is concerned to do so on the assumption that every item in K is true.

There are, of course, many philosophers who resist the idea that agent X, whose doxastic commitment at t is represented by K, is committed to full recognition that all sentences in K are true in L or, alternatively, that X is committed to full recognition as true of all doxastic propositions in the filter generated by his current state of full belief.

By way of contrast, I maintain that in his practical conduct and his inquiries, X is committed to dismissing the threat of a *melan genie* and to discount the worry that he is a brain in a vat. Not only is X committed to ruling out the logical possibility of wholesale deception in his firm convictions. He is committed to ruling out the logical possibility of there being even one error in his firm convictions.

This view I take to be an implication of Peirce's belief–doubt model made famous in his "Fixation of Belief" and endorsed not only by him but by Dewey. To endorse it, however, seems outrageous to many philosophers, who feel obliged to reject at least one of the assumptions on which it is based.

I take it that the chief objection is not to the use of a Tarskilike conception of truth, which seems innocuous enough. Rather, the complaint is about the characterization of "true in $\underline{L}$" according to which all sentences in $\underline{K}$ are true in $\underline{L}$.

Keep in mind that this characterization is intended to clarify the sense in which agent X is or ought to be committed to truth or avoidance of error as an aim of inquiry in which doxastic commitments are revised. I take it, therefore, that those who object to such characterizations do so because they object to the conception of truth as an aim of inquiry that emerges.

No matter what conception of "true in $\underline{L}$" is deployed in representing truth as an aim of inquiry concerned with revisions of corpora in $\underline{L}$, that conception will be represented in a corpus $\underline{K}^1$ of sentences in $\underline{L}^1$ where the metalanguage $\underline{L}^1$ contains $\underline{L}$. The set of sentences of $\underline{L}$ that are in $\underline{K}^1$ represent those sentences in $\underline{L}$ whose truth is presupposed by the agent when seeking to avoid error or obtain new true information in the sense of truth so characterized. Those who object to the view that all elements of $\underline{K}$ are true in $\underline{L}$ according to $\underline{K}^1$ may, perhaps, do so because they deny that when an agent is concerned with truth as a goal, he presupposes that everything he is currently committed to fully believing is true.

To come to grips with the rival views that may be entertained concerning this matter, four positions should be considered:

1. All and only sentences in $\underline{L}$ in the urcorpus $\underline{\iota}$ ought to be incorporated in $\underline{K}^1$.

2. All and only sentences in Y's corpus for $\underline{L}$ ought to be in X's metacorpus $\underline{K}^1$.

3. All and only sentences in the corpus for $\underline{L}$ of an omniscient god ought to be in X's corpus $\underline{K}^1$.

4. All and only those sentences from $\underline{L}$ in X's corpus $\underline{K}$ ought to be in X's corpus $\underline{K}^1$, as I have been advocating.

We started off being concerned with X's state of full belief and regarded X's corpus expressible in $\underline{L}$ as the set of sentences in $\underline{L}$ representing doxastic propositions X is committed to fully recognizing to be true. According to this view, all sentences in $\underline{L}$ consistent with $\underline{K}$ are seriously possible according to X's commitments at t. Alternatively, all doxastic propositions that are members of at least one principal ultrafilter of which X's state of full belief is a member are seriously possible according to X at t. Thus, $\underline{K}$ represents the standard for serious possibility to which X is committed at t. No sentence in $\underline{L}$ inconsistent with $\underline{K}$ is counted as possibly true (in $\underline{L}$) in the "serious" sense – that is, when X is engaged in either practical deliberation or scientific inquiry. Hence, there is no serious possibility that any sentence in $\underline{K}$ is false.

Hence, to endorse positions 1, 2, or 3 is tantamount to saying that even though, in all practical deliberation or in scientific inquiries, $\underline{K}$ is X's standard for serious possibility, when situations arise where X is concerned to avoid error, and, in particular, when he is concerned to do so in revising $\underline{K}$, the standard for serious possibility expressible in $\underline{L}$ that is used should not be $\underline{K}$ but should be the subset of $\underline{K}^1$ expressible in $\underline{L}$, as stipulated according to positions 1, 2, or 3. In other words, X is required to use a double standard for serious possibility: one for practical purposes and another for characterizing the theoretical concern to avoid error that is a desideratum in efforts to revise the first standard.

But how is the division of labor between the practical and the theoretical to be understood? Is the practical restricted to deliberation aimed at reaching decisions relative to practical goals, in contrast to the cognitive goals of inquiry? This would seem to suggest that the practical standard for serious possibility $\underline{K}$ does not identify those settled assumptions that serve as the background and evidence when efforts are made to revise $\underline{K}$ in order to avoid error. But whatever the corpus is relative to which efforts to avoid error are to be undertaken, the best way to minimize the risk of error would be to equate $\underline{K}$ with the corpus in question so that the double standard collapses into a single standard. If the single standard is according to position 1, X becomes a skeptic, refusing to fully believe true any sentences other than logical, set theoretical, and mathematical truths. If position 2 is in place, X seeks to agree with Y, and if position 3 holds, X seeks to agree with God. X may fail in these endeavors but only because X does not correctly identify Y's or God's views. So the ultimate aim of inquiry then becomes to ascertain the opinions of Y or of God.

An alternative version of the double standard grants that $\underline{K}$ is the standard for serious possibility not only for practical deliberation but for inquiry aimed at revising $\underline{K}$. However, another standard (as spelled out by position 1, 2, or 3) is used when one is engaged in philosophical reflection. According to this vision, the concern for truth and avoidance of error, as judged relative to the second philosophical standard, is irrelevant to either practical deliberation or scientific inquiry. At best, it serves as a reminder to X that there is a perspective relative to which his evolving doctrine either is false or might be false.

Thus, the double standard either collapses back into a single standard or ensures the irrelevance of the second standard for the purposes of practical deliberation or scientific inquiry. To say that it, nevertheless, has philosophical importance is to cast doubt on how important philosophical importance can be.

In sum, I see no acceptable way to furnish a Tarskilike characterization of "true in $\underline{L}$" so that avoidance of error is a desideratum of efforts to revise $\underline{K}$ and $\underline{K}$ is understood as representing X's standard for serious possibility or, what amounts to the same thing, to X's state of full belief without endorsing position 4. From the agent X's point of view at t, every sentence he fully believes true is true.

None of this implies that "true in $\underline{L}$" is confused with "believed true in $\underline{L}$."

From X's point of view, every sentence he fully believes true is true, but the converse does not hold. Truth is not truth relative to X or to what X believes. What is relative to X or what X believes is X's commitment to avoid error. X can seek to avoid error only relative to what he judges to be true and to be false. Moreover, the only revisions of attitude concerning which avoidance of error can be relevant are revisions in states of full belief; for it is only doxastic propositions and the linguistic representations of them that are free of error or immune from error. As a consequence, the concern to avoid error is relative to X's conceptual framework or the language $\underline{L}$ of truth value−bearing sentences used to represent linguistically potential states of full belief in X's conceptual framework.

From X's point of view, his corpus $\underline{K}$ is error-free. Moreover, according to X, there is no serious possibility that any sentence he fully believes true is false. The infallibility implied here is not a manifestation of arrogance but is an implication of what it is to be in a state of full belief understood as a standard for serious possibility. It does not imply the logical impossibility of X's current corpus containing error unless X is maximally ignorant, so that his current corpus is $\underline{1}$.

In addition, there is no suggestion in any of this that, from X's point of view at t, it is impossible that he will cease being certain of the truth of sentence "h" and, indeed, with good reason. X's corpus $\underline{K}$ of full beliefs or standard for serious possibility is corrigible or open to revision not only by adding sentences to it (expansion) but by removing sentences from it (contraction). Some readers will, no doubt, be puzzled as to how X can consistently recognize as seriously possible that he will in the future have good reason to revise his corpus by removing "h" when X is currently certain that it is true. One of the aims of this book is to offer a more detailed account of contraction than I have previously done, one that seeks to show how a consistent account of justified ceasing to believe is feasible even when $\underline{K}$ is taken to be a standard for serious possibility and all members of $\underline{K}$ are true in the sense in which avoidance of error is taken to be a desideratum of efforts to improve $\underline{K}$ by revising it.

There is, however, a conception of "commitment to the truth," as an aim of inquiries engaged in revising doxastic commitments, that precludes assuming that doxastic commitments construed as standards for serious possibility are revisable by contraction.

If the concern to avoid error is taken to be a dimension of the ultimate goal of reaching a true, complete story of the world, X can never be justified in ceasing to believe any sentence once he has become convinced of its truth. I suspect that many of those who think that infallibility, as implied by the claim that all elements of the corpus are true, and the thesis that the corpus is the standard for serious possibility jointly entail incorrigibility are gripped by this conception of the ultimate aim of inquiry. According to such messianic realism, if X is certain that h is true, by ceasing to be certain, he runs the risk of subsequently becoming certain of the truth of "$\sim h$," which he is currently certain is false. Concerned, as he is, to obtain the true, complete story of the world and, assuming as we are, that "true in $\underline{L}$" is characterized under assumption 4, he would be betraying his ultimate objectives by giving up his conviction that h is true.

We are faced with the following predicament: Either we give up assumption 4 and the thesis that the corpus is the standard for serious possibility (i.e., that the corpus represents the state of full belief), or we abandon the view that the standard for serious possibility or state of full belief is revisable or we give up seeking the true, complete story of the world as the objective of belief revision–that is, messianic realism. It is well known that Peirce's belief–doubt model and his messianic realism are in some tension – although the particular explanation of the tension just offered is not widely endorsed. And there is some indication that Peirce sought to relieve the tension by invoking a double standard for serious possibility. As we have seen, the double standard approach renders the concern to avoid error irrelevant to the revision of belief states and, hence, is self-defeating.

Dewey, as I understand him, retained Peirce's belief–doubt model and abandoned his messianic realism. I follow Dewey in this. Unlike Dewey, however, I do not favor abandoning realism altogether. For Dewey, truth and avoidance of error did not appear to matter at all. I have already suggested that this is an implication of messianic realism when it is supplemented with the double standard. The virtue of Dewey's approach is that the irrelevance of truth is frankly acknowledged. As a consequence, both messianic realism and the double standard are abandoned.

I favor a more "secular" realism according to which X should seek to avoid error in making the next revision he contemplates in his state of full belief or corpus. (In the past, I have called this *myopic* realism, but, perhaps, *secular* is more appropriate.) X should seek to avoid error at the next step on the assumption that every sentence in his corpus prior to revision is true. Once the revision is made, of course, his corpus is a different one, and now X should seek to avoid error on the assumption that every sentence in the new corpus is true. In this way, we can, so I shall argue, retain a form of secular realism without compromising the integrity of the belief–doubt model. In this way, the original insight of American pragmatism can be preserved intact.

I began this section by insisting on the importance of the distinction between doxastic commitment and doxastic competence and performance as it relates to the question of the commitment to the truth. Given this insistence, Frege's contention that the laws of deductive logic prescribe how one ought to think, in the same way that the laws of physics do, may be understood as denying the importance of the distinction. For this reason, Frege's conception is to be rejected. The laws of deductive logic characterize the commitment to recognized full belief generated by belief states and, in this sense, are prescriptive principles relevant to the criticism of our doxastic performances and competence. The true laws of physics are not laws of thought in this sense.

The only sense in which the true laws of physics may be thought of as regulative of our thinking is as characterizing the ultimate goal of inquiries aimed at revising our commitments. It may be said that our ultimate aim is to endorse a commitment to full belief that is a true, maximally consistent, or complete story of the world. If at the End of Days we should attain that goal, we would indeed reason in conformity with the true laws of physics as well as the true laws of logic. Any distinction between the two would collapse.

Although Peirce seems to have been wedded to some such version of messianic realism, I have been arguing that this view clashes with his belief–doubt model of inquiry. If we replace messianic realism by secular realism, then, even in this attenuated sense, Frege's contention that the laws of logic as laws of thought differ from the laws of physics only because of their greater generality seems profoundly wrong.

According to secular realism, the laws of logic do characterize (in part) the commitment to full belief of an agent at a time. Of course, the laws of logic alone do not do so. Unless X is in a state of maximal ignorance represented by $\underline{1}$, his commitments are characterized by the deductive consequences of extralogical assumptions that include generalizations, perhaps, that X takes to be lawlike and true. So X is committed to the consequences of those lawlike sentences that he is certain are true. The falsity of these sentences does not imply a failure on X's part to live up to his commitment. On the other hand, if X fails to live up to the true laws of logic, there is a failure of commitment.

Of course, X is not logically omniscient and, for this reason alone, fails to live up to his commitment. But, on the view endorsed here, the changes of view emerging from X's finding out more logical truths are to be regarded as significantly different from the changes of view emerging from finding out new physical laws. The latter change entails a change in commitment. The former represents not a change in commitment but an elaboration of commitments.

I cannot claim to have shown that this distinction is as fundamental as I am taking it to be. To sustain its importance, it would be necessary to offer sufficiently elaborate accounts of the growth of physical knowledge and of knowledge of mathematics to show how the revision of belief involved in both developments differs and why the differences are important. I will not and, indeed, cannot embark on such an undertaking.

In this discussion, I take for granted that there is an important distinction between doxastic commitment and competence, that the laws of logic are among the principles that define doxastic commitment, and that truth or avoidance of error is a value that ought to be taken into account in the revision of states of full belief.[20]

Avoidance of error is not the only cognitive aim of inquiry. In the chapters that follow, there will be occasion to consider other values relevant to the revision of doxastic commitments.

2.9 Types of belief change

In Section 2.2, four types of change of states of full belief were identified: expansions, contractions, replacements, and residual shifts.

Expansion: **K′** is an expansion of **K** if and only if **K′** is at least as strong as **K** (i.e., precedes **K** according to the consequence relation partially ordering the elements of the boolean algebra of potential states of full belief).

If **K** and **K′** are represented by the corpora $\underline{K}$ and $\underline{K}′$, respectively, $\underline{K}′$ is an expansion of $\underline{K}$ if and only if $\underline{K} \subseteq \underline{K}′$.

Our concern is to develop a coarse-grained taxonomy of changes or revisions of potential states of full belief or the potential corpora that represent them. In characterizing expansions, I have relied exclusively on the relations between the initial corpus and the expanded corpus representable within the framework of the boolean algebra of potential belief states. Hence, we may, if we like, call **K′** an expansion of **K** even when we are not contemplating a change from the latter belief state to the former. However, the intent is to use the typology proposed to offer an account of the conditions under which a change in belief is justified or otherwise legitimate. In doing so, it is desirable that we avoid building into our characterization of the typology conditions that distinguish legitimate from illegitimate changes above and beyond those we have already explicitly required by insisting that potential states of full belief constitute a boolean algebra. That is what has been done in the case of expansion, and the characterization of other sorts of change will be designed to meet the same requirement.

Contraction: **K** ($\underline{K}$) is a contraction of **K′** ($\underline{K}′$) if and only if a shift from the former to the latter is an expansion.

When **K** = **K′**, a shift from **K** to **K′** is both a degenerate expansion and a degenerate contraction. Aside from these degenerate cases, no contraction can be an expansion.

Replacement: **K*** is a replacement of **K** if and only if **K** $\wedge$ **K*** = **0** and both **K** and **K*** are distinct from **0**.

Residual Shift: **K**** is a residual shift from **K** if and only if **K**, **K****, and **K** $\wedge$ **K**** are all distinct from **0** and from each other.

As just announced, this classification of changes in states of full belief seeks to avoid prejudging which changes are legitimate and which are not. It does not do so entirely. By requiring the space of potential states of full belief to be a boolean algebra, the following condition is endorsed:

Commensurability Thesis: Given an initial state of full belief K_1 and another state of full belief K_2, there is always a sequence of expansions and contractions, beginning with K_1, remaining within the space of potential states of full belief and terminating with K_2.

The commensurability thesis is a consequence of the condition that the conceptual framework is a boolean algebra. Although it does not make any claims about how transitions between K_1 and K_2 actually do take place or should take place if they are to count as legitimate or justifiable, it asserts the *feasibility* of reaching the terminal state from the initial state via a series of contractions and expansions. I label this thesis a commensurability thesis because advocates of incommensurability appear to reject it. Thus, Kuhn and Feyerabend appear to deny the feasibility of suspending judgment between incommensurable theories. An advocate of one theory cannot contract by removing his theory from his belief state and suspending judgment between his view and the rival view. Hence, a conversion from one incommensurable theory to the other is an example of a replacement in the sense defined here that is not decomposable into a sequence of contractions and expansions. If the space of potential states of full belief is a boolean algebra, there are no incommensurable belief states in this sense and, hence, no incommensurable theories – at least within a given framework of potential states of full belief. And if, as I assume, every change in conceptual framework is from one boolean algebra to another that is either a subalgebra or a superalgebra of the first, commensurability is secured over conceptual changes.

As already stated, the commensurability thesis does no more than ensure the *feasibility* of restricting legitimate changes in belief states to those in which the final state is reached from the initial state by a sequence of intermediate changes each of which is a legitimate contraction or legitimate expansion. I call the condition restricting legitimate changes in this way *the commensuration requirement*.

The Commensuration Requirement: Every legitimate change in belief state from initial K_1 to K_2 is decomposable into a sequence of contractions and expansions each of which is legitimate.

The commensuration requirement asserts that there are two basic kinds of legitimate changes in belief states: legitimate contractions and legitimate expansions. There are other kinds of legitimate changes; but they are derivative and include derivatively legitimate contractions and expansions, as well replacements and residual shifts. There are no basically legitimate replacements or residual shifts.

Given the commensuration requirement, the task of an account of legitimate belief change reduces to giving an account of legitimate expansion and
contraction. Chapter 3 examines expansion and Chapter 4 discusses contraction. It should be emphasized, however, that the commensuration requirement that is controversial is not to be confused with the commensurability
thesis that is implied by the relatively uncontentious assumption that the
space of potential states of full belief is a boolean algebra. We could endorse
both the requirement that the conceptual framework be a boolean algebra
and the commensurability thesis while rejecting the commensuration requirement. This, in fact, seems to be the attitude of many students of belief
change, including Peter Gärdenfors, although the distinction between the
commensurability thesis and the commensuration requirement is rarely
made explicitly, so that interpretation of such authors involves some specula-
tive hermeneutics.

Peter Gärdenfors, along with several others, has deployed a somewhat
different classification of belief changes than I am using.[21] Gärdenfors focuses attention on changes in an initial belief state K (corpus $\underline{K}$) generated
by some doxastic proposition A (sentence $\underline{A}$) taken to be input. He considers
cases where propositions (sentences) serving as inputs are added or deleted
and where the output states of full belief are uniquely determined as functions from the input propositions operating on the initial states of full belief.
Given a state K of full belief, adding (deleting) doxastic propositions becomes a function from the doxastic propositions added (deleted) to new
belief states.

Gärdenfors does, for the most part, work with spaces of potential states of
full belief that are boolean algebras and clearly endorses the commensurability thesis that is a consequence of it. We may safely assume that there is no
difference between his position and mine in this respect.

Agreement between us runs still deeper than this. For Gärdenfors, every
basically legitimate change in belief state is induced by an input that is either
the addition or the removal of a doxastic proposition from the initial doctrine.
The commensuration requirement implies that every basically legitimate
change is either an expansion or a contraction. As it turns out, one can
represent every basically legitimate expansion as the addition of a doxastic
proposition to an initial belief state and every basically legitimate contraction
as the removal of a doxastic proposition from the initial belief state. Hence,
my position agrees with Gärdenfors's thesis that every basically legitimate
change is either the addition to or removal of a doxastic proposition from the
initial doctrine.

To see this, consider that for every expansion K' of K there is at least one
doxastic proposition A such that $K' = K \wedge A$. (Let $K' = A$.) Since a
transition from K' to K is a contraction, the doxastic proposition A added in
the expansion is deleted in the contraction. All of this can be said without

presupposing anything about legitimate changes in belief state other than the boolean algebra and commensuration requirements.

Observe, however, that although, given **K**, the value **K'** of **K** $\wedge$ **A** is uniquely determined without further assumptions,[22] the state of full belief obtained by deleting **A** from **K'** is not uniquely determined. As Gärdenfors explicitly recognizes and emphasizes, additional assumptions are needed to obtain uniqueness (Gärdenfors, 1988, pp. 53–4, 61, and ch. 4). I take the additional assumptions to be constraints on legitimate or justified changes in states of full belief, so that the assumption of uniqueness is to be understood as a constraint on legitimate or justified changes of this sort. In my judgment, when all relevant factors in a given context are taken into account, one change at most should be legitimate or justified. Hence, given the initial corpus **K** and *all other relevant factors* (whatever these may be), and given that adding or deleting **A** is legitimate or justified, the new belief state to which one shifts legitimately or with justification is uniquely determined.

This *uniqueness condition* is almost trivial. It is not completely trivial, for it does rule out the possibility that two or more contractions deleting **A** from **K** in a given context can be admissible. Although I do not think such a require-ment should obtain in other kinds of decision making, I am inclined to think that when two or more cognitive options (such as two contractions or expan-sions) are admissible given the goals of the inquiry, one should adopt a cognitive option that in some sense "suspends judgment" between the two. How such an attitude may be rendered precise is at least partially explained in Chapters 3 and 4. For present purposes, we need only observe that the uniqueness condition is, indeed, nearly trivial and is not a point over which Gärdenfors and I are in disagreement. Disputes over what constitute rele-vant contextual factors are suppressed.

The upshot of all of this is that the commensuration requirement, which I advocate, implies that all basically legitimate changes in belief state are determined by legitimate additions or deletions of doxastic propositions.

In spite of this substantial area of agreement between Gärdenfors's ap-proach and my own, there remain some philosophically important and interest-ing differences. The differences surface in the case of adding a doxastic proposition **A** to **K** when the complement ~**A** is a consequence of **K**. In that case, **K** $\wedge$ **A** = **0**. If one construes adding a doxastic proposition as construct-ing the meet of the initial state of full belief and the doxastic proposition added (or as forming the deductive closure of the union of the initial corpus and a strongest sentence added), such addition always yields an expansion in the sense in which I have defined that operation, and adding a doxastic proposi-tion to a state inconsistent with it leads to expansion into inconsistency.

If one adopts the position that expansion into inconsistency is never legiti-mate or justifiable (as Gärdenfors, 1988, p. 52 appears to do) when **A** is inconsistent with the initial state, adding **A** in a manner resulting in expansion is prohibited. Yet, it is widely thought (and Gärdenfors agrees) that some sort of change where **A** is added to **K** inconsistent with it should sometimes be legitimate. Making observations and coming to fully believe propositions incompatible with one's initial convictions is a case in point. Hence, it is thought that there are cases of basically legitimate addition of doxastic propositions that are not expansions. Gärdenfors seems to endorse such a view. However, he seems to restrict such additions to cases where **A** is in conflict with **K**. In such cases, the additions yield replacements. Otherwise, the additions result in expansions.

Gärdenfors calls the new state of full belief obtained by adding a doxastic proposition **A** to an initial state of full belief **K** when legitimate the *minimal revision* K_A^* *of* **K** by adding **A**. When A is consistent with **K**, the minimal revision is supposed to be an expansion. When there is a conflict, the minimal revision is supposed to be a replacement.

Thus, although Gärdenfors recognizes expansion as a type of change in belief state, from his viewpoint it is legitimate only if the resulting state of full belief is consistent – that is, if the expansion is also a minimal revision. According to Gärdenfors, all legitimate cases of adding doxastic propositions to an initial state of full belief are cases of minimal revision.

More crucially, in cases where **A** is added to **K** when ~**A** is a consequence of **K**, the addition is legitimate only if the result is a replacement. If such addition is basically legitimate, as Gärdenfors thinks it sometimes is, the resulting minimal revisions are not to be justified by identifying a sequence of legitimate contractions and expansions. Since, by hypothesis, the input is the addition of a doxastic proposition **A** to **K**, and since expansion into inconsistency is prohibited, the addition of A cannot be an expansion. It must be a replacement. Although Gärdenfors seems to endorse the commensurability thesis, he appears also to reject the requirement of commensuration.

I, by contrast, endorse the commensuration requirement (Levi, 1980a, p. 65). I contend that whenever adding a doxastic proposition to a state of full belief is legitimate, the result is an expansion even if the expansion is into inconsistency. As I explain in Chapter 3, such expansions is sometimes legitimate. Yet, it is always urgent to contract from an inconsistent state of full belief. The contraction will remove either **A**, ~**A**, or both. In the second case, the result will be a replacement. More likely, both A and ~A should be removed. If inquiry is then undertaken to adjudicate between these two alternatives and terminates with a subsequent expansion by adding A, the sequence of expansions and contractions results in a replacement. My contention is that no replacement is legitimate unless it can be rationalized as a sequence of legitimate contrations and expansions. According to those who prohibit expansion into inconsistency but allow addition of propositions to belief states inconsistent with them, this commensuration requirement must be rejected, just as it must by Kuhn and Feyerabend. Whereas Kuhn and Feyerabend must reject it because they deny the commensurability thesis,

Gärdenfors and others who appear to accept the commensurability thesis reject the commensuration requirement because they prohibit expansion into inconsistency.[23]

The commensuration requirement does not prohibit replacements. To the contrary, insofar as sequences of legitimate expansions and contractions are envisageable, some such sequences are likely to be replacements. The commensuration requirement denies that replacements are basically legitimate but allows that their legitimacy can be obtained derivately.

The same observation applies *mutatis mutandis* to residual shifts. For that reason, I have identified four kinds of changes in belief state, only two of which are basic. Neither Gärdenfors nor other writers on belief change who pursue programs akin to his have provided for residual shifts. I suspect that the reason for this is that Gärdenfors is primarily concerned with basically legitimate changes that, he and I agree, are to be construed as the result of adding propositions to or deleting them from the belief state. There does not seem to be any obstacle to analyzing legitimate residual shifts in terms of sequences of legitimate minimal revisions and legitimate contractions (where the minimal revisions are expansions).

Neither Gärdenfors nor I have demonstrated the impossibility of taking residual shifts as basically legitimate. But if they were so taken, one could no longer require basically legitimate changes to be the product of inputs that are either the addition of propositions or their deletion. At the very least, we would need a pair of inputs: the deletion of one proposition and the addition of another. I shall not explore that possibility here.

To sum up, for Gärdenfors, there are two fundamental kinds of legitimate change in belief states: minimal revisions resulting from adding a doxastic proposition to a belief state and contractions resulting from deleting a doxastic proposition from a belief state. Expansions by adding a doxastic proposition to a belief state consistent with the given proposition can also be legitimate, but they constitute a species of minimal revision. Expansions into inconsistency are never legitimate.

On my view, too, there are two basic kinds of legitimate change in states of full belief: legitimate expansions and legitimate contractions. Expansions into inconsistency are sometimes legitimate. The only basic legitimate minimal revisions are legitimate expansions. Other minimal revisions are replacements and, according to the commensuration requirement, are never basic legitimate revisions. They must be decomposed into sequences of legitimate contractions and expansions.

The philosophically central bones of contention involved in the differences between Gärdenfors's approach and my own concern the legitimacy of expansion into inconsistency and the commensuration requirement. In Chapter 3, I review the account of legitimate expansion I have proposed in previous work. I emphasize the conditions under which, in my judgment, expansion into inconsistency is legitimate. In Chapter 4, the topic of contraction is discussed. A by-product of this discussion should be an account of the kind of case Gärdenfors would regard as adding **A** to a belief state in conflict with it without ending up in contradiction. Such analysis will serve to illustrate the force of the requirement of commensuration.

I do not claim that my argument will demonstrate the superiority of my approach to that of Gärdenfors; but it should establish its coherence and, in addition, elaborate the philosophical perspective relative to which it clearly is superior.

3

Expansion

3.1 Routine and deliberate expansion

According to an influential tradition in epistemology that includes David Hume and W. V. Quine among its proponents, beliefs are either responses to stimuli or dispositions to such responses. As such they are not, in general, under the control of the believer. Inquirers cannot choose what to believe. Hence, suggesting that changes in belief ought to be evaluated according to principles of rational choice relative to appropriate cognitive goals rests on a misguided voluntarism. Epistemology should be engaged in explaining such responses to dispositions rather than in prescribing norms for choosing beliefs.

In Chapter 2, I indicated that I shall not be focusing on changes of beliefs construed as responses to stimuli or as dispositions to such responses. Such beliefs are doxastic performances that may or may not fulfill doxastic commitments and are not fully under the control of deliberating agents. The topic of this book is revision of doxastic commitments or undertakings. I contend that agents are able to choose how to revise their doxastic commitments and, in this sense, can deliberately change their beliefs.

Nonetheless, we should not conclude that agents always choose or ought to choose directly the changes in belief states (construed as doxastic commitments) they institute, even if they are able to do so. This is especially true in the case of expansions. Expansion may take place in one of two ways: deliberate and routine. In deliberate expansion, the inquirer chooses one of several expansions of his initial doctrine. In routine expansion, the inquirer expands according to a program for adding new information to his state of full belief or corpus in response to external stimulation. The agent's commitment to the program may itself be a product of nature or nurture, but it is also open to revision by deliberate choice when required.

Deliberate expansion is expansion via direct choice. The inquiring agent concerned to find an answer to some question has identified potential answers to the question of interest. (The task of constructing potential answers to a question is the task of abduction in the sense of Peirce. We shall return to this later.) The set of potential answers to the question recognized are, in effect, a set of optional expansions the inquirer recognizes to be relevant to his objectives in seeking an answer to the question. I assume that obtaining

new error-free information meeting the demands of the question under
investigation ought to be a common feature of the goals of such efforts.

The aims of such efforts are multidimensional. Gratifying the demand for
more information favors adopting the strongest expansion strategy, and this
tends to increase the risk of incurring error. Minimizing the risk of error
favors refusing to expand altogether. Consequently some sort of trade-off is
required. Omitting details, it is enough to note for the present that which of
the expansion strategies available for choice is adopted depends on the
following factors:

   1. The potential answers identified as cognitive options.

   2. The inquirer's evaluation of how well the various options satisfy the
demand for information occasioned by the question – the *informational value*
of the various potential expansions.

   3. The risk of error incurred by each of the options where the inquirer
takes for granted that his initial state of full belief or corpus is error-free and
assesses risks of error by means of judgments of subjective or credal probability relative to his initial state of full belief.

   4. A commitment to the relative importance of avoiding error as compared to acquiring an answer of informational value (reflected in the degree
of caution or boldness) exercised by the agent.

Notice that the contextual parameters involved here are those one might
expect in a decision problem where the goals are multifaceted, so that com-
promises among the several desiderata are necessary, and where considerations of uncertainty are relevant.[1]

Deliberate expansion rationalized along these lines is, in a sense, "inferential." But the inferences are not to be confused with deductive inferences. In
deductive inference from premises that an agent takes for granted, the conclusion inferred is an elaboration of a doxastic commitment the agent already
has undertaken in virtue of fully recognizing the truth of the premises. There
is no change in doxastic commitment. In expansion, the "conclusion" is a
change in doxastic commitment. Furthermore, it is misleading to think of the
justification of this conclusion of an expansion as grounded exclusively on
the premises (presumably the assumptions initially taken for granted) via
rules of inference. In addition to the initial corpus or state of full belief, the
potential answers, the informational value of these answers, the risks of error,
and the index of caution are relevant parameters that need to be taken into
account, along with these premises, in order to assess via the principles of
choice whether the conclusion is justified or not. Yet, the conclusion is based
on the total evidence – that is, the initial corpus – along with these other
parameters. In this sense, there is an inference from premises to conclusion.
Such expansion may be called *inferential* as well as *deliberate.* Moreover, since
the inference is ampliative in the sense that new information is added to the
initial doctrine, it might be regarded as *inductive* expansion.

Once the agent has expanded his state of full belief or corpus via inductive expansion, he might consider deploying the expanded corpus to justify further deliberate or inductive expansions. There is no principled objection to doing so as long as appropriate requirements for justified deliberate expansion are satisfied. However, there is a limit to the amount of new information that might be obtained by what I have previously called *bookkeeping* procedures (Levi, 1967, pp. 151 and 1980a, ch. 2, sec. 6).

To acquire new information when these techniques have played out calls for another kind of expansion strategy that enables the inquiring agent to exploit external sources of information. Such sources often include making observations (sometimes of the outcome of deliberately designed and instituted experiments) and consulting witnesses and experts. The structure of such routine expansion strategies is quite different from that of deliberate (= inferential = inductive) expansion.

Implementing a program for routine expansion resembles consulting an oracle or using a measuring apparatus. The inquiring agent initiates some process (by making an observation, by designing and conducting an experiment and then observing the result, or by consulting a witness or expert), just as one connects a measuring apparatus to what is to be measured. The agent presupposes that trials of the kind initiated are capable of resulting in one of several responses by the agent, just as the measuring apparatus can yield one of several readings on being hooked up to the object of measurement. In response to sensory stimulation, the observer makes a report. The liquid in the test tube looks red, or the witness makes some remarks. These reports are reactions by the inquirer to external stimuli that are often automatic. Mere reactions to stimuli need not, however, be reports. For such a reaction to be a report, the inquirer must interpret the reaction as a sign that something is the case. The inquirer reports that the liquid is red, or that the witness says that she saw Jones do the dastardly deed. For the most part, there will be some default interpretation of the report that the inquirer adopts as a matter of course. Sometimes, however, the inquirer may have difficulty interpreting what he observes or what the witness says, and may have to engage in a side inquiry to settle the hermeneutic difficulty.

No matter how the content of the report is identified, reporting that h is not coming to fully believe that h – at least not in the sense in which belief is doxastic commitment. The inquirer may not trust the witness or his own color sight and may, for this reason, be reluctant to convert his report into an expansion of his corpus.[2]

However, if the inquirer has committed himself in advance of observation, experimentation, or consultation of the witness to adding the content of the report he makes in response to the observation, experiment, or consultation to his state of full belief or corpus, he is obligated to do so, as he is with any other undertaking.

Consulting oracles in this manner can be a more sophisticated process.

The inquirer who is sensitive to his partial color blindness might make corrections to his color reports and add these to his evolving doctrine. Programs for using reports or data as inputs whose outputs are expansions of the state of full belief or corpus can become quite sophisticated. The programs for such *routine expansion* are often acquired by either nature or nurture and are unreflective. But they, like other commitments, are subject to criticism and revision. When such revision is required, the inquiring agent faces another sort of decision problem.

Routine expansion, like deductive inference, involves implementing a commitment antecedently endorsed. However, unlike deductive inference, the commitment is not a doxastic commitment or state of full belief. Rather, it is a commitment to revise doxastic commitments in response to external stimuli according to a certain procedure.

However, assuming that the inquiring agent is concerned in expansion to obtain new error-free information, the agent who deploys a program for routine expansion presupposes not only that the routine will yield information of the sort desired but that the routine is reliable – that is, bears a sufficiently low chance or statistical probability of yielding error. If he has questions as to its reliability, he ought not deploy it.

Thus, routine expansion does begin with certain assumptions or premises – namely, assumptions about the reliability of the program. But the expansion adopted is not inferred from these premises. The agent must implement the routine and respond by making a report that he converts via the program into an expansion.

It may, perhaps, be suggested that the datum that a report that *h* was made in response to external stimulation is an additional premise that, together with the assumption of reliability, constitutes the basis for an inference to a conclusion as to which expansion to adopt. This view, however, is misleading, for its suggests that first the datum is added to the state of full belief or corpus as a premise and then a deliberate or inferential expansion is deployed to reach the conclusion. But then an account must be given of the preliminary expansion of the corpus to which the datum is added. This would call for a prereport that a report that *h* was made, and we are well on our way to an unacceptable infinite regress.

Routine expansion is needed precisely because new information is not to be had via inferential expansion from the available information. The inquiring agent either unreflectively or deliberately adopts a program for routine expansion in which the reports made are inputs and the outputs are expansions.

In such a setting, the inquiring agent does not choose an expansion – although he may (if the matter was not already settled) have chosen beforehand a program for routine expansion. In this respect, routine expansion preserves an important element of the Hume–Quine view. Beliefs are not impressions or dispositions to assent or other behavior. They are commitments. But in routine expansion, changes of such commitments are not chosen. They are themselves reactions to programs for using data as input. In this respect also, routine expansion is not inferential but "immediate," even though – counter to some classical empiricist views – it is not presupposition-free. Commitment to using a program for routine expansion brings with it commitment to full recognition that the routine is sufficiently reliable.

The difference between the classical empiricist view and this account of routine, noninferential expansion runs even deeper than this. It has been common among empiricists to draw some relatively fixed distinction between information accessible via observation and information that can only be obtained via inference.

On the view being proposed here, however, routine expansion includes consulting witnesses. If these witnesses are assumed sufficiently trustworthy, consultation can furnish information that is often considered highly theoretical and nonobservational. Indeed, most students of the sciences spend the early stages of their careers retrieving the testimony of their teachers and textbooks, and cannot reach a stage where they can engage in sophisticated inquiry unless the bulk of their early learning was of this nature.

But even if we ignore the consultation of experts and witnesses and focus on the testimony of the senses, programs for routine expansion can lead to adding information that, according to the empiricists, would be assumed to be highly theoretical. Dudley Shapere's example of efforts to observe directly features of the chemical composition of the core of the sun is a case in point (Shapere, 1982; Levi, 1984). The use of techniques of confidence interval estimation along the lines pioneered by Peirce and developed by Neyman and Pearson can lead to the addition of information concerning statistical magnitudes and other theoretical parameters associated with them. Such techniques represent highly sophisticated programs for routine expansion, as I have argued elsewhere (Levi, 1980a, ch. 17).

Thus, it is conceivable that, in some contexts, information may be added via routine expansion that in other settings could legitimately be obtained via inference.

It may, perhaps, be suggested that the only legitimate mode of expansion should be reliable routine expansion.[3] From this perspective, not only is routine expansion required in order to exploit sources of new information that would not be accessible to inference in a given context, but it could allow us to dispense with inferential expansion altogether.

Such a conclusion is unwarranted. In inferential expansion, respect for the demand that error be avoided forbids the inquiring agent from ever expanding into the contradictory state of full belief **0**. This is not true in the case of routine expansion. Because routine expansion can inject inconsistency into the evolving doctrine, it can create the kind of difficulty that calls for contraction (in order to remove inconsistency). Such contraction may call into question the background assumptions that clash with the results of routine expansion, as well as these results. To settle the doubts that are thereby generated, efforts at expansion will be undertaken, including efforts to assess or reassess the reliability of the routines that produced the conflict. New information will have to be acquired. Although some programs for routine expansion may be available whose reliability has not been brought into question, such programs will not, in general, be powerful enough to furnish answers to the questions of interest. Deliberate or inferential expansion will also be required.

Suppose that I am walking on 72nd Street and Columbus Avenue and see someone who is a dead ringer for Victor Dudman. I am sure that Dudman is safely ensconced in Sydney, New South Wales. But my initial confidence in my eyesight and in Dudman's appearance is reflected in a commitment to add the doxastic proposition that Dudman is on 72nd and Columbus to my state of full belief. I have expanded into inconsistency. Or consider the case of Michelson, who was certain that he would not obtain a null result in his Potsdam experiment and yet reported that he did. He stumbled into inconsistency.

I am not suggesting that such a result should be accepted with equanimity. To the contrary, such situations furnish one of the occasions that justify contraction through coming to doubt the information obtained via routine expansion or some other item in the initial corpus or, as I think is normally sensible, both.

For example, in the confrontation with the Dudman look-alike, I would look again. This would make little sense if I took for granted the deliverances of my first observation or if I remained convinced that Dudman is in Sydney. Looking again reveals that I have contracted by questioning part of my initial background assumptions as well as the testimony of my senses.

Similarly, the null result of Michelson brought into question both classical assumptions and the design of Michelson's experiment.

Both cases call for contraction from 0.[4]

Thus, routine expansion is conflict injecting in a way in which deliberate expansion is not. To be sure, someone might end up with inconsistency in deliberate expansion due to confusion or failure of memory and computational capacity. But if one is living up to one's commitments, one cannot legitimately expand into inconsistency via deliberate expansion. On the other hand, routine expansion can and sometimes does lead to inconsistency even when all commitments are fully met.

Prior to undertaking a commitment to a program for routine expansion on a specific occasion, the inquiring agent should not expect that she will, as a result, end up contradicting herself. She might conceivably be sure that she will not or, if (as should be more likely) she does not assume that her program is perfectly reliable but contains a small chance of error, she might judge it sufficiently unlikely that she will end up in error that she feels justified in taking the risk.

When routine expansion injects inconsistency into the inquirer's doctrine, contraction from the inconsistent state is required. An inconsistent state of full belief or corpus fails as a standard for serious possibility for the purpose of subsequent inquiry and for practical deliberation. Such contraction will, so I contend, not only call into question elements of the initial state of full belief but may also raise doubts about the program for routine expansion and about how well it was implemented.[5] Once the reliability of the program is called into question, however, that issue becomes a question for inquiry. The investigation into the reliability of the program and alternatives to it will, if successful, lead to subsequent expansions. But it is not to be expected that one will be able to rely exclusively on programs for routine expansion that have not yet been called into question in order to do so. Deliberate or inferential expansion will be required.

My contention is that we need both deliberate and routine expansion to obtain new information. Neither alone can furnish sufficient resources to enable us to obtain new information in a manner that respects the concern to avoid error.

I mentioned that, in deliberate expansion, the inquirer must first undertake the abductive task of identifying potential answers to the problem being investigated. The fruits of his efforts are the cognitive options (the potential expansions) he recognizes as available to him relevant to his question. The need to undertake the abductive task is not eliminated in routine expansion. A program for routine expansion specifies for each of a set of reports that are possible outcomes of a "trial" of a certain kind (making an observation, conducting an experiment, consulting an expert or a witness, etc.) an expansion that is to be implemented. If the program has already been adopted, there is no need for specifying expansions to be adopted in response to the possible outcomes of the trial. That has already been settled prior to the inquiry. But when a program is being designed, the inquirer will have to identify the potential answers that he wishes to have as responses to his question, as well as specifying which answers to adopt in response to which reports. And even in cases where programs for routine expansion have already been designed, the inquirer will need to elect a program suited to his problem, and this too will require consideration of the abductive task.

Charles Peirce, who did so much to emphasize the importance of abduction as a task in inquiry, conceived of induction as the task of eliminating potential answers from among those identified via abduction. Although he called both abduction and induction species of inference along with deduction, he became quite clear in the last years of his career that they are "inferences" in quite different senses. The "conclusions" of abductions are conjectures that are potential answers to questions. Deduction elaborates on the implications of assumptions already taken for granted or of conjectures when they are taken, for the sake of the argument, to be true. Induction weeds out for rejection some conjectures, leaving the survivors for further consideration.

The chief difference between the account I am offering here and Peirce's in this respect is that Peirce thought of induction as a species of routine expansion. Peirce's account of quantitative induction, which is the version of induction he presented with greatest precision, is an anticipation of the Neyman–Pearson approach to confidence interval estimation (Levi, 1980b, in press). The rationale that Peirce offered for this approach [and the rationale that Neyman and Pearson (1933) offered for their views] is best understood as a rationale for routine expansion or, more generally, routine decision making.

I have no principled objection to calling routine expansion a species of induction. It does, after all, add new information to the evolving doctrine and is, therefore, ampliative, which is often taken to be characteristic of induction.[6]

However, as Neyman and Pearson pointed out, routine expansion lacks some of the salient properties of inference from premises. They suggested calling it *inductive behavior* rather than *inductive inference.* Unfortunately, this term suggested (to others and apparently sometimes to them) that the outputs of routines are to be interpreted as policies or acts aimed at practical objectives.

Although it is true that routine expansion is a species of a more general category of routine decision making that includes not only cases where the results are changes in doxastic commitments but can also be other kinds of acts, I deny that revisions of doxastic commitments are reducible to other kinds of behavior or that the aims of revisions of doxastic commitments are practical, moral, political, economic, or aesthetic goals. Nor do I think it is essential to the pragmatist tradition of Peirce and Dewey, with which I ally my own views, that such a reduction be endorsed. What is "pragmatic" about pragmatism is the recognition of a common structure to practical deliberation and cognitive inquiry in spite of the diversity of aims and values that may be promoted in diverse deliberations and inquiries.

Since I think that the term *inductive* is reserved for a species of expansion, and since customarily it is understood to be inferential, in contrast to expansion via observation or consultation with experts or witnesses, I am inclined to think of deliberate expansion as inductive, in contrast to routine expansion.

On the other hand, if one focuses on the *task* that Peirce relegated to induction, routine expansion, like deliberate expansion, qualifies as a species of induction.

Furthermore, as I have already emphasized, deliberate expansion is not inferential in the sense in which deductive reasoning is. The truth of the matter is that neither deliberate expansion nor routine expansion qualifies as inference from premises to conclusion, although they fail to do so in different ways.[7]

I have, nonetheless, used both *inferential expansion* and *inductive expansion* as alternative tags for deliberate expansion because there is an important parallel between the traditional epistemological contrast between information obtained immediately or directly and information obtained via inference, and the contrast between routine expansion and deliberate expansion. Immediate acquisition of information is typically seen as a response to external signals, whereas inference is not. And this facet of classical views is preserved in the distinction I have proposed. For this reason, I have called deliberate expansion *inferential* and *inductive,* in contrast to routine expansion, which is *direct* or *immediate.* However, it should be firmly kept in mind that the distinction I am deploying denies that routine expansion is immediate in any sense that implies that it is presupposition-free.

I have suggested that the aim of both routine and deliberate expansion ought to be the acquisition of new error-free information. In the sections that follow, I elaborate on the import of these suggestions.

3.2 Informational value

All inquiry aimed at changing states of belief and, in particular, all changes by expansion ought to seek to avoid error. In expansion, the concern to avoid error is combined with an interest in acquiring new information of value. In contraction, the concern to avoid error is vacuous. The reason is that no new information is being imported into the belief state and, hence, no risk of error is incurred. I cannot claim that this view of avoidance of error as a common feature of goals of diverse inquiries is required as a minimal condition of rational coherence. Nor is this constraint on cognitive goals noncontroversial. Instrumentalists and critical empiricists deny that avoidance of error is a desideratum in efforts to settle on potential answers to certain kinds of questions. And some authors see convergence on the truth as an ultimate goal of inquiry while apparently regarding avoidance of error as irrelevant as a proximate aim of expansions, except insofar as it promotes the ultimate goal. I lack a decisive argument for removing controversy concerning the aims of inquiry. I can only invite the skeptic to consider the consequences of proceeding in conformity with the view I propose as compared with the consequences of alternative conceptions of the aims of inquiry.

I shall not undertake such a comparison here. My intent is to explain the content of the thesis I am advancing about the common features of the goals of cognitive inquiries – that is, inquiries concerned with revisions of states of full belief. This section elaborates on the claim that the common feature of the proximate aims of efforts at expansion is the concern to obtain new error-free information as a result of that expansion.

This thesis does not deny what is, after all, obvious – to wit, that different inquiries aim to solve different problems and, in this sense, have different objectives.

Moreover, the thesis is a claim about the common features of the *proximate* goals of efforts to revise states of full belief via expansion. Many epistemological and methodological discussions of cognitive aims focus instead on the topic of progress in inquiry toward some ultimate end and understand the proximate aims of specific revisions as regulated by how well they promote such progress. Although I do not endorse such a perspective, I do not mean to rule it out of consideration. But we should not beg the question the other way by presupposing that the proximate aims of inquiry are controlled by some set of goals that defines our conception of scientific progress. It is best, therefore, to focus on characterizing general features of the immediate outcomes of revising states of belief in general and of expansions in particular that are the objects of epistemic affection. It may be that the common feature is conduciveness to promoting progress toward the true, complete story of the world or to promoting progress understood in some other way. So the advocates of the centrality of conceptions of scientific progress are not excluded from the discussion. At the same time, points of view like the one I favor, which demotes the concept of scientific progress from the center of attention, can also be represented. The particular thesis I am advancing is that the proximate aim of all efforts at expansion ought to be to obtain new error-free information as a consequence of such expansion.

My thesis concerns the proximate aims of expansions. When discussing contraction in the next chapter, we shall be in a better position to identify the properties both types of basic change share and to indicate the extent to which changes of states of full belief are justified by reference to how well such changes promote progress and the extent to which reference to progress is irrelevant.

With this much understood, I discuss informational value in this section and turn to avoidance of error in Section 3.3.

According to Peirce, the sole end of inquiry is removal of doubt. By the end of "Fixation of Belief," Peirce qualified this claim by insisting on the claims of truth. Nonetheless, there are many philosophers who ignore or reject concerns to avoid error in inquiry, at least in contexts of so-called theory choice, if not in making observations. For many such authors, curiosity remains a strong motive. The inquiring agent seeks information he or she does not have.

In Section 2.2, a state of full belief was characterized as a standard for serious possibility. Every potential state or doxastic proposition in a proper ultrafilter to which the current state of full belief belongs is seriously possible relative to that state. Alternatively a doxastic proposition is seriously possible, according to a state of full belief, if and only if its complement or negation is not in the filter generated by the state of full belief. Such serious possibilities are consistent with the given state of full belief. In effect, it separates the potential states into those that are serious possibilities, from the point of view of the agent, and those that are not. The agent is in doubt as to which of the serious possibilities is true (without error) and is sure that the serious impossibilities are false. The more doxastic propositions are ruled out as impossible, the more information the current state of full belief carries.

"Information" does not mean "true information." Some authors equate the two, and some (e.g., Dretske, 1981) make a great point of it. Although wishing to avoid tedious logomachy, I do mean to insist on the right to speak of false information without contradiction.

William James (1897), borrowing a theme already found in Peirce in 1865 (1982, p. 285), contended that we should "shun error" and "seek truth" as two competing desiderata. To seek truth in James's sense may mean to seek information in Dretske's sense. If so, seeking truth is seeking true (i.e., error-free) information. So construed, it already represents an accommodation of the tension between seeking more information as I understand it and seeking to avoid error. James's insistence on the tension between shunning error and seeking truth becomes mystifying on this reading. Perhaps, however, seeking truth meant seeking information, whether true or false, in the sense I favor.[8]

Once it is understood that information is not the same as true information, it should not be too difficult to appreciate the implication that the inconsistent doxastic proposition **0** carries maximum information. If in expansion we sought to maximize the amount of information carried by a potential answer, we should expand into **0** – the inconsistent state. What deters us from doing so is the concern to avoid error. Relative to any consistent potential state of full belief, expansion into **0** is expansion that is certain to import error.

To avoid another kind of misunderstanding, information as I understand it is not indexed by a decrease in entropy. One potential state of full belief carries more information than another if the second state is a consequence of the first in the partial ordering of potential states of full belief according to the boolean algebra. Another way to put the point is that one doxastic proposition carries more information than another the more logical possibilities (maximally consistent potential states of full belief or *atoms*) it rules out. Entropic measures are intended, in the first instance, to make comparisons between probability distributions over a given field of possibilities. If they are to be used to make comparisons of potential states of full belief with respect to informational value, informational value has to depend not only on the state of full belief but also on the credal probability distribution over a set of elements in some partition of the space of possibilities relative to that state. (If the boolean algebra of potential states is atomic, the set of atoms will serve.) But then it can happen that a strong state can carry less information (i.e., greater entropy) than a weaker state. Information, as I propose to construe it, is independent of the credal probability distribution relative to the state of full belief and agrees with the partial ordering with respect to strength characterizing the boolean algebra of potential states.

On this view, not all doxastic propositions or states of full belief are comparable with respect to information carried.

When X is in a state of full belief **K** and is seeking to expand her state, the relevant concept is new information. In this case, minimal information is carried not by **1** but by **K**; for if X fails to expand at all, she acquires no new information. The only other potential states in the partial ordering with respect to new information are the nondegenerate expansions of **K** including the expansion into inconsistency **0**. Such nondegenerate expansions are partially ordered according to the restriction of the partial ordering of the potential states to the filter generated by **K**.⁹

When an inquirer expands with an interest in new information, her interest in new information is typically restricted, with more or less definiteness, to information of relevance to a given problem. The inquirer is not interested just in gratifying her curiosity by strengthening her doctrine, but in doing so in certain respects.

Consequently, when representing the agent's interest in new information, we cannot say that if one potential state carries more new information than another, it gratifies the agent's interest in new information more than than the other and, in this sense, is more valuable to her.

On the other hand, if the agent is seeking new information, she should not regard a potential state that carries more new information than another as less valuable to her as far as informational value is concerned. Perhaps acquiring the new information is a nuisance or inconvenience, and she would rather not have it. But if it is an inconvenience, it is because of goals other than seeking new information that it is so. We are attending to the value of information as if it were the sole desideratum of concern to the inquirer. I do not claim that it is or ever ought to be the sole desideratum. But in order to bring out the content of the claim that new information is one (but not the only) desideratum of inquiry, it is useful to proceed in this fashion.

With this understood, it becomes clear that we should distinguish *informational value* from *information*. Just as someone seeking more money need not take the utility of money as a linear function of the amount of money held, so that a distinction between amount of money and value of money is made, so too we may distinguish between new information carried and the value of the new information carried.

Having said this, however, we may impose (hopefully, noncontroversially) the following condition on the notion of the value of information:

Weak Monotonicity: If doxastic proposition **A** carries at least as much new information as doxastic proposition **B** relative to **K**, **A** carries at least as much informational value as **B** relative to **K**.

The weak monotonicity condition yields a quasi-ordering of potential expansions with respect to new informational value. The inquiring agent may seek to complete that quasi-ordering and, indeed, might seek to assign numerical values or *utilities* to the value of new information.

To do this, it will be necessary to invoke considerations additional to the partial ordering with respect to strength that characterizes information or the quasi-ordering with respect to informational value generated in accordance with the monotonicity condition. I am not suggesting that the quasi-ordering is always extended to a complete ordering or to a numerical representation, but it does appear to be the case that inquirers do compare some potential expansions with respect to informational value even though the expansions compared are not comparable with respect to strength or new information carried.

Thus, rival theories are often compared with respect to explanatory power, predictive power, simplicity in some sense or other, or their conformity to some paradigm for an adequate theory, even though they are not comparable in the boolean lattice with respect to information carried relative to the background information **K**. I suggest that all such comparisons are or ought to be regarded as attempts to extend the quasi-ordering partially or completely with respect to informational value.

The considerations that enter into an evaluation of information value are diverse, often competing, and heavily context dependent. Different kinds of inquiries impose different demands for new information, so that it is not to be expected that evaluations of informational value will meet the same requirements in all contexts. And inquiries addressing the same issues may be committed to different research programs generating different demands for information.

Discussion of what I am calling *informational value* in this extended sense is widespread in the literature of the philosophy of science. I do not care to enter into this discussion here. I am, however, suggesting something that some participants may not want to endorse. I regard the various requirements of simplicity, explanatory power, and the like as considerations that complete, to some degree, the quasi-ordering with respect to informational value generated by the monotonicity condition from the partial ordering with respect to information carried. This rules out taking seriously the notion that a weaker potential answer is simpler, in the sense relevant to assessing informational value, than a stronger answer. Such conceptions of simplicity play no role here.[10] The same applies (perhaps less controversially) to explanatory power. In efforts at expansion, more informational value in a sense satisfying the monotonicity condition is better than less – provided that the risk of error is the same or may be ignored.

A cardinal representation of informational value for a range of potential expansions should have the properties of a utility function unique up to a positive affine transformation. However, I do not assume that an inquirer's evaluation of informational value will be representable by such a utility function unique up to a positive affine transformation.[11]

Are there any additional constraints that may be imposed on evaluations of informational value?

I am inclined to think that there is no single system of constraints applicable to all contexts in which assessments of informational value become relevant. Broadly speaking, I think that there are two kinds of assessments of informational value. *Probability-based* evaluations of informational value are relevant in the assessment of potential expansions. In the context of contraction, however, both probability-based assessments and another kind derived from measures initially developed by G. L. S. Shackle for another purpose (Shackle, 1949, 1961), and that I shall, therefore, call *Shackle-based*, will prove relevant. I shall defer discussion of Shackle-based measures until Chapter 4 and focus for the present on probability-based measures.

Consider the set E of potential expansions of the initial corpus **K**. E is a boolean algebra relative to the partial ordering of its elements with respect to strength. The maximum is **K** and the minimum is **0**. Hence, any measure satisfying the requirements of a finitely additive probability defined over E will generate an ordering of its elements whose inverse satisfies the requirements of the weak monotonicity condition. If, in addition, the only element of the lattice receiving o probability is **0**, the inverse of the ordering with respect to probability preserves the partial order with respect to strength. Potential expansions strictly increase in probability with a decrease in strength.

The point is a familiar one. Probability varies inversely with strength and, more generally, with informational value. This suggests that utility functions that are inverse functions of probability measures satisfy the requirements of the monotonicity condition for a numerical evaluation of informational value. Many authors have endorsed this suggestion. Given a probability $M(\mathbf{A})$ defined over potential expansions of **K**, the question then arises as to which inverse function to use. Several such functions qualify – for example, $1 - M(\mathbf{A})$, $1/M(\mathbf{A})$, and $-\log[M(\mathbf{A})]$. The first of these, often called a measure of "content," $Cont(\mathbf{A}) = 1 - M(\mathbf{A})$, has two attractive properties. Its range of values is finitely bounded, so that there is no need to consider expansions bearing infinite informational value. If one regards expansions bearing o M-value as carrying infinite informational value, when one seeks to weigh the relative importance of avoiding error against the importance of new informational value, expansions carrying such informational value cannot be valued less, all things considered, than expansions carrying finite new informational value even if the former carries error and the latter is error-free.[12]

Moreover, it is "additive" in the sense that if $\sim\mathbf{A}$ and $\sim\mathbf{B}$ are exclusive given **K**, $Cont(\mathbf{A} \wedge \mathbf{B}) = Cont(\mathbf{A}) + Cont(\mathbf{B})$. This latter property is especially attractive. Expansions increase information and, hence, informational value by ruling out additional belief states as serious possibilities. So increments of information depend on the initially serious possibilities that are ruled out. The additive property suggests that the dependency is of a special kind. Suppose that the inquirer is in doubt between $\mathbf{T}_1, \mathbf{T}_2, \ldots, \mathbf{T}_n$ but takes for granted that exactly one of them is true and each is a serious possibility. Any potential expansion answering the question as to which is true will reject some subset of these alternatives. The informational value of a potential answer will be at least as great for an answer ruling out more as compared to a potential answer ruling out fewer $\mathbf{T}_i$'s. The additive property implies that increments in informational values are the sums of the increments obtained from rejecting each of the T_i's alone. Moreover, the incremental value of ruling out an additional T_i as a serious possibility is the same no matter how many others and which others are eliminated as well (Levi, 1984, ch. 5).

Two qualifications of this account of probability-based evaluations of informational value need to be made.

Advocates of probability-based evaluations of informational value often assume that the probability measure used to define an assessment of informational value should be either a logical probability measure conditional on the evidence K or a subjective or credal probability. I do not make any such assumption. I have argued elsewhere that such views have embarrassing consequences (Levi, 1984, ch. 5). But without addressing these matters, I suggest that the use of probability measures to represent degrees of confidence or belief that agents have in conjectures is a different use of probability measures than their use in assessing the informational value of adding these conjectures to the settled doctrine. Explanatorily attractive hypotheses may be improbable as well – but this need not and will not always be so. What is true is that a stronger hypothesis cannot be more probable than a weaker one, and it cannot be less informationally valuable.

Measures of credal probability or, if there be such, measures of logical probability are relevant to assessing the risk of error in expansion. This is a quite different task than assessing informational value, and there is no reason why the one should be the inverse of the other in general.

The second qualification concerns the assumption that assessments of informational value applying to all potential expansions are represented by a probability-based measure.

The inquiring agent asking a given question may or may not have a very precise conception of what would be a complete, consistent answer to his question, but it would not be an expansion into a maximally consistent state of full belief in his conceptual framework. In investigating the structure of DNA, Watson and Crick did not consider information about the state of the economy of Poland in the year 2000 as relevant and hence as informationally valuable. The doxastic proposition that per capita income in Poland will be higher that year than in East Germany and the doxastic proposition that it will not would have added 0 informational value to their settled assumptions relative to the inquiry they were attending to. Not only are these doxastic propositions not relevant potential answers, but adding either one of them to a potential answer would not improve the informational value of such potential answers.

But if probability-based assessments of informational value apply to all potential expansions of the agent's state of full belief, this commonplace condition cannot be satisfied.

Consequently, probability-based assessments of informational value need to be restricted to a subset of potential expansions.

I have suggested elsewhere (Levi, 1967, 1984, ch. 5) that this be done as follows:

Given the demands for information that occasioned the inquirer's problem and the results of his efforts to devise potential answers via abduction, the inquiring agent has identified what I have called an *ultimate partition*. Using doxastic propositions rather than sentences in $\underline{L}$, as I have done elsewhere, the ultimate partition consists of a set of potential expansions of K such that the truth (freedom from error) of K presupposes that exactly one element of this set is free of error (i.e., true).

The *relevant* potential expansions of K are all expansions that are joins of some subset or other of the ultimate partition. This includes the degenerate expansion where the inquirer refuses to expand beyond K. That is represented by the join of all the elements of the ultimate partition. The empty set represents expansion into 0, and each unit set represents a strongest consistent relevant potential expansion.

Informational value is assessed probabilistically for potential expansions belonging to the set of relevant potential answers, so that the information determining probability measure M is defined over these.

Credal probability measures relative to K may be used to assess risks in decision problems different from the particular problem of expansion under consideration and should not be supposed automatically to be restricted to the domain over which M is defined.

Informational value can be assigned to other potential expansions. However, if C is a potential expansion that is not a relevant one, its informational value is to be determined by identifying the smallest subset of the ultimate partition whose join is a consequence of C and assigning C the same informational value.

The ultimate partition is the range of strongest consistent potential answers recognized by the agent as relevant to his problem. It is, I take it, the identification of such a list of potential answers that is the first task of abduction. In some contexts, the elements of the ultimate partition may be a conjecture and some hypothesis incompatible with it given the initial background information. Or two or more hypotheses may be compared, along with a *residual hypothesis* specifying that all the others are false. Or the ultimate partition may be infinite and, indeed, nondenumerably infinite. Special technical problems arise in representing informational value in some of the infinite cases. For many purposes, these are not insuperable and will not detain us here (see Levi, 1980a).

Given the ultimate partition and the initial corpus K, it is to be emphasized that the evaluation of relevant potential answers with respect to informational value is not necessarily representable by a utility function unique up to a positive affine transformation. It can be a nonempty convex set of such functions. Such a convex set is probability based (over the domain of relevant potential answers) if all elements of the set are probability based.

The account of informational value just outlined will appear to some to be too subjective to meet the requirements of a cognitive value appropriate for scientific inquiry. The only general constraint I have imposed on it is the weak monotonicity condition. In the context of expansion, I have also required that it be probabilistic relative to an ultimate partition and, indeed, that it be a content measure relative to an ultimate partition. However, the choice of an ultimate partition depends on the interests of the inquiring agent and his or her imagination in constructing potential answers to the question under investigation. Different inquirers can, relative to the same evidence or state of full belief and confronting what initially looks like the same problem, identify potential answers relative to different ultimate partitions.

Even if, however, they somehow come to some agreement on an ultimate partition, they may differ with respect to how they assess the informational values of elements of the ultimate partition and, hence, of other potential answers as well.

These contextual relativities will seem excessive to many who hold to an exacting standard of scientific objectivity as requiring freedom from context dependence.

The only response one can make to demands for such hyperobjectivity is to resist them on the grounds that such requirements can be met only by restricting beliefs to trivia. One can seek to ameliorate the confrontation by pointing out that when agents do differ in their demands for information but need to engage in joint inquiry, they can undertake to proceed relative to their shared agreements. If they differ in their ultimate partitions, they can shift to an ultimate partition consisting of the consistent meets of the doxastic propositions belonging to pairs in the cartesian products of their respective partitions.

However, they may still assess informational value differently for the elements of the consensus ultimate partition. To obtain consensus on this point, we may consider all utility-of-information functions in the convex hull of the sets of such functions representing the assessments of each party to the consensus. There are fine points of technical detail to iron out, but these need not detain us here (Levi, 1984, ch. 6; 1980a, sect. 8.6).

The point to be emphasized is that disagreements in demands of information do not preclude inquirers from resolving disputes from a non-question-begging point of view with respect to the truth of the issues under dispute. To this extent, scientific inquiry is objective. Objectivity in this sense will not satisfy the requirements of those who lust after a hyperobjectivity that requires the appeal to a standard correct way to assess informational value. Nonetheless, those who abandon the requirements of hyperobjectivity need not fear that they are abandoning themselves to epistemic anarchy.

I am denying that inquiry can proceed without appeal to some point of view (state of full belief, demands for information, judgments of credal probability, etc.). I am also denying that there is some standard, objective point of view to which appeal may always be made. But I fail to see that these denials lead to cognitive licentiousness. Enough objectivity remains available to provide for reasoned inquiry that avoids question-begging confrontation. We may always identify a consensus as shared agreements relative to which inquiry may begin.[13]

3.3 Avoidance of error in deliberate expansion

The demand for potential answers carrying new informational value is a technical expression of the truism that in inquiry we seek to gratify our curiosity. We seek to rule out more serious possibilities, thereby converting them into impossibilities. This is true both in deliberate expansion and in routine expansion. But our curiosity is or should be tempered by our concern to avoid error. Again, this is true both in deliberate and in routine expansion. But how avoidance of error contributes as a desideratum differs in the two types of expansion. In this section, I focus on deliberate expansion.

If the quest for new informational value were the sole consideration motivating efforts at deliberate expansion, the best thing to do would be to expand into inconsistency. State 0 carries more information than and at least as much informational value as any other potential state of full belief.

Few of us (including ardent advocates of "falsificationism") are prepared to bite this bullet. We do not think deliberate expansion into the inconsistent state 0 is to be recommended. This means that we cannot be committed exclusively to maximizing informational value in deliberate expansion. On the other hand, maximization of informational value in conformity with the weak monotonicity condition does seem to capture an aspect of our concern when expanding a state of full belief. We need a characterization of the aims of expansion that does justice to the desideratum of informational value while taking into account our resistance to expansion into inconsistency.

One possible answer is to endorse a qualified version of the weak monotonicity condition that restricts its application to potential states of full belief other than 0 and ranks 0 below all other expansion strategies. This suggestion seems unsatisfactory. It fails to explain why an exception is made to the recommendation to maximize informational value in the case of expansion into inconsistency.

Another explanation might be that 0 is not serviceable as a standard for serious possibility. On the one hand, every state of full belief is ruled out as impossible on the grounds that the complement or negation of every doxastic proposition is in the filter generated by 0. On the other hand, every state of full belief or doxastic proposition is counted as certain and, hence, possibly true because it is in the filter generated by 0.

On the basis of this consideration, one might argue that an expansion into 0 should be excluded from the assessment of informational value to begin with. We should be restricting attention to potential states of full belief that are viable standards for serious possibility. If we must rank all potential expansions, whether they are viable standards or not, the nonviable ones should be ranked below all others.

Why, however, should 0 be considered nonviable as a standard for serious possibility? To be sure every doxastic proposition is counted as both a serious possibility and an impossibility. And such judgments of serious possibility are incoherent. But this need not disqualify 0 as a standard for serious possibility.

Someone seeking to maximize informational value without regard for other values (cognitive or noncognitive) should not care that 0 is an inconsistent standard for serious possibility. What matters is that it carries maximum informational value. A consistent standard for serious possibility is needed for practical deliberation and scientific inquiry when the inquiring agent is in doubt and needs to distinguish, therefore, between what is seriously possible and what is not. In state 0, the need for such distinctions has dissipated. The inquirer has succeeded in acquiring maximum informational value.

Simply asserting that an exception ought to be made of inconsistency in assessing informational value according to the weak monotonicity condition is no substitute for the absence of an explanation of why an inquirer seeking to maximize informational value should make an exception of 0.

Anyone who insists on defending the view of the aims of expansion under consideration may deny the need for any such rationalization. I lack a decisive objection to this reaction. However, it is possible to offer an attractive account of why expanding into inconsistency is to be resisted that acknowledges the relevance and importance of maximizing informational value.

Instead, however, of keeping the injunction to maximize informational value as the sole desideratum qualified by the unexplained exception in the case of expansion into inconsistency, the alternative approach understands the problem of expansion as a multiattribute decision problem where the alternatives are evaluated differently according to several different desiderata and then the several evaluations of the alternatives are somehow aggregated.

According to this approach, maximizing informational value is a desideratum in expansion but not the sole one. As a desideratum, no qualification is made. The best expansion strategy relative to the interest in maximizing informational value is to expand into inconsistency.

But there is another competing desideratum relative to which expanding into inconsistency is the worst expansion strategy. That desideratum characterizes the aim of avoiding error. Prior to expansion, the inquiring agent is committed to full belief that 0 contains error. Insofar as the inquirer is concerned to avoid error, he has a motive for refusing to expand into inconsistency.

To be sure, this consideration is at odds with his interest in promoting informational value. But what is at odds with promoting informational value is not merely a restriction of the domain of appraisal to all potential states except **0**. Avoidance of error is a desideratum that is relevant to other expansion strategies aside from expanding into inconsistency. If the inquiring agent is concerned to avoid error, the various potential expansion strategies would be evaluated with respect to the agent's expectation prior to expansion of importing error. Prior to expansion, the inquirer recognizes as a serious possibility that implementing a nondegenerate expansion strategy will introduce error into the evolving doctrine. Different expansions will vary with respect to how probable it is that they will inject error. These probability assessments may be more or less indeterminate. But if the inquiring agent cares whether a potential answer or expansion strategy carries a large or small probability of importing error, then avoidance of error is a relevant consideration in his value structure. And if, all else being equal, he prefers less probability of error to more, that is a sign that the inquiring agent is concerned to avoid error.

Thus, the concern to avoid error, when considered in isolation from the other cognitive desiderata in expansion, yields an evaluation of potential expansion strategies. Probability of error becomes risk of error (because importing error is a disutility) that the rational inquirer will seek to minimize.

Expansion into inconsistency will, from this perspective, incur a maximum risk of error and, for this reason, will be resisted.

Thus, we have two ways of assessing potential expansion strategies relative to **K**: with respect to informational value and with respect to risk of error. Risk of error must satisfy a requirement that is the inverse of the weak monotonicity condition. Risk of error increases with increase in strength. For this reason, concern to avoid error is at odds with concern with new informational value. The concern to avoid error argues in favor of refusing to expand altogether so as to reduce risk of error to o. The concern to obtain new informational value argues in favor of expansion into inconsistency.

We have the beginnings of an account of why we are concerned to avoid inconsistency that does a little more than just declare it a brute fact that we are concerned to avoid inconsistency. It relates the concern to avoid inconsistency with the more general concern to avoid error.

If asked why we should be concerned to avoid error in expansion, I have no further response to offer. I can, however, point out that avoidance of error is nearly as noncontroversial a desideratum in inquiry as avoidance of inconsistency.

Controversy may, however, break out with respect to how I understand the concern to avoid error.

An inquiring agent's concern to avoid error, like all other practical or cognitive goals that he might have, generates evaluations of serious possibilities relative to the agent's current state of full belief. According to agent X's current state of full belief **K**, no doxastic proposition in the filter generated by **K** is possibly false. They are all certainly error-free.

Consequently, from X's point of view prior to expansion, there is no serious possibility of error in X's current state of full belief. The only way X can incur a risk of error, from X's point of view, is by expanding his current doctrine. X cannot import error via contraction since, from X's initial point of view, there is no serious possibility of error in a contraction of his doctrine.

Some may insist that an inquirer should be concerned to avoid error in his current state of full belief. Let us grant the concern in the sense that it would be a good thing to remove error from the current doctrine. But there is, from X's point of view, no serious possibility that error is present. Hence, there is no risk of error in endorsing that state of full belief.

I grant, of course, that unless $K = 1$, there will be a logical possibility of error in the current doctrine. But risk of error is assessed relative to credal probability judgments based on a space of serious possibilities – not on a space of logical possibilities.

To take this position does not imply that truth or falsity is relative to what the inquirer fully believes. What the inquirer judges true or false is relative to what the inquirer fully believes. And when an inquirer is concerned to avoid error, he can proceed only relative to the judgments of truth available to him.

It may, perhaps, be objected that what Ron is committed to fully believing to be true, George may be committed to fully believing to be false. And Nancy may be in doubt concerning the issue. Consequently, the import of a concern to avoid error will differ for Ron, George, and Nancy.

This is true, but it is no objection. Ron, George, and Nancy share the concern to avoid error. But given their different views of what is true, their assessments of the risk of error will differ. Far from being objectionable, countenancing such situations is countenancing the commonplace.

Of course, the questions of when it is desirable to resolve such disagreements and how they are to be resolved, given that it is desirable to do so, remain vexing. I assume that if the dispute is to be resolved without begging questions, Ron, George, and Nancy should all contract to a set of assumptions they share in common. Whether they should do so is related to the general conditions under which contraction is legitimate. For the present, our attention is focused on expansion, so that further reflection on these matters must be deferred. My present purpose in mentioning the question is to point out that the phenomenon of disagreement concerning truth and the problem of resolving such disagreement pose no insuperable obstacle to the conception of avoidance of error as a common feature of proximate aims of expansion.

The introduction of avoidance of error as a desideratum of expansion additional to the quest for new informational value is the first step in explaining why inconsistency is not to be recommended as an expansion strategy. To complete the account, we still need to indicate how the two competing desiderata of avoidance of error and new informational value are to be aggregated into a single evaluation of the expansion strategies.

In Section 3.2, I suggested that informational value is to be represented by a utility function that is a positive affine transformation of $Cont = 1 - M$ or by a nonempty, convex set of such content measures. Expansion strategies, when evaluated relative to the concern to avoid error, come in two varieties: those that avoid error and those that do not. We may assign 0 as the utility of failure to avoid error and 1 as the utility of avoiding error.

In this book, I focus on cases where informational value is evaluated in a manner representable by a unique content measure.[14]

If the inquirer is engaged in deliberate expansion so that the available expansions are options for him, his predicament may be represented as follows:

The agent is in an initial state of full belief **K**. He has identified via abduction an ultimate partition U that is a set of strongest consistent potential expansions of **K** that furnish new information of value to the inquirer. Given U, one can identify a set of potential expansions relevant to the demands for information of the inquirer.

Relative to **K** and U, an information-determining probability M is defined over doxastic propositions that are joins of elements of subsets of U. For any such potential answer **A**, the informational value of **A** is $Cont(\mathbf{A}) = 1 - M(\mathbf{A})$.

Relative to **K**, a belief or credal probability Q is defined over all potential expansions of **K**, including all potential answers generated by U. For every potential answer **A**, the risk of error incurred by adopting it is $1 - Q(\mathbf{A})$.

Each of these evaluations orders the potential answers but does so differently. To maximize according to the content measure will recommend expanding into inconsistency. To minimize the risk of error will yield a refusal to expand at all – that is, remaining with **K**.

I have suggested elsewhere that when an inquirer recognizes two or more such desiderata, a potential resolution of the conflict should be a weighted average of the utility functions representing the desiderata.[15]

In particular, this means that a potential resolution should be representable as $\alpha Q(\mathbf{A}) + (1 - \alpha)Cont(\mathbf{A})$ or some positive affine transformation thereof, and that this index should be maximized in choosing an expansion strategy.

Divide the weighted average by α and subtract from the result $q = \alpha/(1 - a)$. The result will be $Q(\mathbf{A}) - qM(\mathbf{A})$. This is a positive affine transformation of the weighted average, and, hence, maximizing this index is equivalent to maximizing the weighted average.

We have thus far not fixed the value of α or of q. One constraint can be imposed on this value that ought not to be controversial. No case of importing error should ever be preferred to any case of avoiding error. In particular, importing error for sure should never be preferred to avoiding error for sure. Hence, expanding into contradiction should not be strictly preferred to refusing to expand. But this means that q should never be greater than 1.

The result of all of this is that one should choose an expansion to a potential state of full belief A such that relative to K and U, $Q(A) - qM(A)$ is a maximum where $0 < q \leq 1$.

It is possible that there will be more than one potential answer that bears maximum expected epistemic utility in this sense. I contend that if expanding to A and expanding to B are both optimal in this sense, so is expanding to $A \vee B$.[16] More generally, the join of all optimal expansions must also be optimal. Hence, one may invoke a rule for ties as a secondary criterion and recommend that one should adopt the weakest optimal expansion (Levi, 1967, sect. 5.4).

When the ultimate partition is finite, this leads to the convenient result that one should reject every element H_i of the ultimate partition such that $Q(H_i) - qM(H_i)$ is negative and suspend judgment between the rest.

Consequently, even when $q = 1$, one should choose to suspend judgment and refuse to expand rather than to expand into inconsistency. Expansion into inconsistency is precluded, therefore, by (1) recognizing the concern to avoid error as one of the desiderata in expansion, along with the concern to obtain new error-free information; (2) recognizing the concern to avoid error as sufficiently important, so as to never prefer an erroneous expansion to one that avoids error; and (3) the rule for ties.

This sketch presupposes that there is no indeterminacy in evaluations of informational value and that a definite value for the index q has been fixed. However, just as inquirers may differ with respect to the ultimate partitions they deploy, so too they may differ in their assessments of informational value and in the degrees of caution they exercise. If they are to engage in joint inquiry, they need to identify their shared agreements concerning these matters and judge expansion strategies accordingly. This introduces technical complications that are discussed elsewhere (Levi, 1984, ch. 7; 1980a, sect. 8.6).

Once an inquirer has expanded his state of full belief via deliberate expansion, his new state of full belief is his standard for serious possibility. He is committed to full belief in every doxastic proposition implied by the new state of full belief. Elements of the ultimate partition U that represented his initial list of potential answers have been eliminated as serious possibilities. In the new state of full belief, however, he may still regard more than one element of the original ultimate partion as seriously possible and may wish to ascertain which of these conjectures is true. Given the new state of full belief K_1 and truncated ultimate partition U_1, the inquirer may seek to expand still further by deliberate expansion.

Even if the inquirer continues to use assessments of informational value consistent with those he used initially, adopts the same index q, and updates his credal probabilities via conditionalization and Bayes's theorem, it may be possible for him to reject still more elements of the original ultimate partition. Elsewhere, I have called such reiterated deliberate expansion *bookkeeping* (Levi, 1967). It is not, in general, possible to deploy such techniques to answer every question as completely as we wish. The account of deliberate expansion just sketched cannot supply a complete story of how new information is obtained.

That is not surprising. The acquisition of new information requires appeal to external sources, both through observation and by consulting witnesses and experts. In Section 3.1, I contended that routine expansion that proceeds differently is needed to supplement deliberate expansion even though, as in deliberate expansion, the inquiring agent ought to be concerned with the acquisition of error-free information.

In Section 3.1, I noted that routine expansion can induce inconsistency into a state of full belief and that when this happens, we have good reason for contraction and subsequent inquiry aimed at expansion to recover information value lost at the contraction stage. In the next section, I consider why the concern to avoid error does not preclude expansion into inconsistency in routine expansion, as it does in deliberate expansion.

3.4 Avoidance of error in routine expansion

Inquirers seeking new error-free information should not deliberately expand into inconsistency. Doing so injects error into the state of full belief for certain when options are available that carry a lower risk of error.

The situation is different with routine expansion. The decision maker engaged in routine expansion does not have expansion strategies as options. Instead, the inquirer lets the outcome of her following a program to which she is committed in advance of expansion determine the expansion she adopts. The program involves conducting a "trial" (such as conducting an experiment or making an observation or obtaining testimony from a witness); reacting to the trial by "reporting" the outcome of the experiment, the contents of an observation or the testimony of a witness; and expanding the state of full belief by adding new information in conformity with some instruction for converting the reports into expansions. The instruction can stipulate that when the report that h is made as a result of the trial, the doxastic proposition that h is to be added to the initial state of full belief. However, another procedure might recommend adding weaker information. Thus, if one weighs a piece of meat and obtains a reading of 5 pounds, one might expand by concluding that the meat weighs 5 pounds, give or take 3 ounces. Or the instruction might require correcting the report. A person driving through the Holland Tunnel might report that he is still descending and correct his judgment by coming to believe that he is driving horizontally.

Implementing such routines can lead to inadvertent expansion into inconsistency. The need to extricate himself from this embarrassment, then, calls for questioning erstwhile settled assumptions and, hence, for contraction. Contraction coerced by inadvertent expansion into inconsistency is not the only sort of contraction that may be justified, but it is a common type.

Whenever we receive testimony from individuals whose views we respect on some subject, or use the testimony of our senses in settings where we judge them reliable and such testimony yields information inconsistent with our settled assumptions, a pressure arises to question some of those settled assumptions, the reliability of the testimony of the witnesses or our senses, or all these things. For these reasons, it is important to see how routine expansion in the service of obtaining new error free information can generate the sorts of conflict that coerce contraction.

The trial that initiates a routine expansion may consist of making an observation, conducting an experiment and reporting the result, or interrogating a witness or expert. The inquirer presupposes that that the trial has a system of possible outcomes belonging to a *sample space* Ω. The *points* in the sample space are descriptions of events that, the inquirer takes for granted, it is possible for him to obtain on a trial of the kind in question and where the inquirer also takes for granted that exactly one will be instantiated on any given trial of the kind in question.

The notion of possibility used here is that of objective possibility, or ability of an object or system to do something or have something happen to it in an experiment of some kind. This notion of objective possibility is the dual of the notion of a sure fire disposition. x has the ability to respond in manner R on a trial of kind T if and only if x lacks the (sure) disposition to fail to respond in manner R on a trial of kind T. It is not to be confused with the notion of serious possibility that is relative to the agent's state of full belief. Whether a coin has the ability to land heads on a toss or not does not depend on the convictions of any inquirer.[17] Consequently, when an inquirer identifies a sample space Ω relative to a trial of kind T, the inquirer is committed to full belief in the truth of doxastic propositions. The inquirer is certain that it is objectively possible for him on a trial of kind T to obtain a result of kind R. According to the inquirer, there is no serious possibility that on a trial of kind T, he is constrained to fail to obtain such a result.

Suppose that the inquirer who takes for granted that the sample space of reports on a trial of kind T is Ω adopts a program representable by a function f from Ω onto a set Θ of conditions and fully believes that for every condition θ in Θ, whenever that condition is satisfied and a trial of kind T is conducted, a report in f^{-1} is made. In such a case, if $f(\omega) = \theta$, the inquirer is sure that whenever a report of type $\omega \; \varepsilon \; \Omega$ is made on a trial of kind T, a condition of type θ obtains. As far as he is concerned, his program for routine expansion is perfectly reliable.

Anyone who is convinced of the perfect reliability of her color sense or the infallibility of the pope when speaking ex cathedra has at her disposal such programs for routine expansion. I am not endorsing attitudes of this sort. However, it is useful to note that reliance on such programs for routine expansion can be conflict injecting.

Suppose that X judges her color sight to be perfectly reliable. She is convinced, in advance of looking, that the color of the liquid is not blue, but is otherwise in doubt as to what its color is. She then looks and relies on her color report, which is that the color is blue. She expands into inconsistency.

It might be suggested that if X is certain that the liquid is not blue, she should modify her program for routine expansion so that if she reports that the color is blue, she will not come to fully believe that the liquid is blue and expand into inconsistency.

But this will not do. Recall that X is also certain that her original program is fully reliable. She is convinced that whenever she looks at the color of an object, she reports that it is blue if and only if it is blue. Since X is certain that the particular liquid in question is not blue, she is certain that if she looks at its color, she will not report that it is blue.

Consequently, there can be no benefit, as far as X is concerned, in modifying the program she initially adopted for the case where blue is reported. From X's point of view, there is no serious possibility that this case will arise.

Furthermore, even if she does make the modification, she will not escape difficulty. Suppose that she follows a program for routine expansion that does not expand to full belief that the liquid is blue if the report is made that it is blue. Some other response will be made instead. But given the assumption of perfect reliability made previously, no recommendation can be made except failure to add any information about color. So if X looks at the color and reports that it is blue, she will fail to expand by adding information about color. But if the inquirer has decided to implement such a program beforehand, she is committed to being certain that she will implement it and, hence, to being sure that if she fails to expand, she has reported the color to be blue.[18] But X will find that she has not expanded, and given that she knows the program she is following, she will conclude deductively that she reported blue or some other precluded color. And this will contradict X's antecedent convictions. To extricate herself from inconsistency, X will need to call into question whether she had actually run the trial, whether the background assumption that the liquid is not blue is correct or whether the program for routine expansion used is perfectly reliable, as hitherto supposed.

Thus, X will not avoid injecting inconsistency into her state of full belief by modifying the program in the manner indicated.

Perhaps, it may be thought that if X avoids presuming perfect reliability of her program for routine expansion, the injection of contradiction into her beliefs can also be avoided. To see whether this is so, we shall review the general case where perfect reliability need not be assumed.

The inquirer committed to a program for routine expansion presupposes a sample space Ω of reports as possible results of a given kind of trial T. He is also committed to there being some well-defined statistical probability or chance distribution over the sample space Ω and that the distribution depends on which one of a given set Θ of conditions obtains on the occasion of a trial of kind T.[19] In a special case, the inquirer might be able to partition the elements of Ω into subsets such that given a condition θ from Θ, the inquirer fully believes that a report will be made from exactly one subset in the partition. If that is the case, the inquirer can construct a perfectly reliable routine for expansion that is also informative in the sense that the output is a firm belief that the condition obtaining is characterized by a definite element θ of Θ.

In general, perfect reliability will not obtain. It is possible that given any element θ, all elements of Ω are realizable on a trial of kind T. That is to say, it is possible for each report in Ω to be made on a trial of kind T when conditions of type θ obtain. In that event, the only perfectly reliable routine is one that yields no expansion regardless of what report is made. As in the case of deliberate expansion, the inquirer needs to make a trade-off between informational value and risk of error.

Thus, if X wants to ascertain the color of a liquid, she may look at it under suitable conditions. That is the trial of kind T. The sample space Ω consists of the various kinds of color reports the inquirer makes in response to such a trial. The chance distribution will depend on the color of the liquid. If the color of the liquid is red, for example, then the chance of reporting that it is red will be relatively high and the chance of reporting that it is green rather low.

Θ consists of all the colors for which X assumes a chance distribution over Ω on a color observation.

A program for routine expansion utilizing the trial of kind T to obtain information as to which of the conditions in Θ obtains in a specific case is representable by a function f from Ω to boolean combinations of elements of Θ. If the inquirer adopts the program, then he is in a position to determine a chance distribution for the expansions selected by the function f given each condition in Θ.

Moreover, for each expansion selected, the inquirer can specify whether it is with or without error, given that a specific condition in Θ obtains. Hence, for each condition in Θ, the inquirer knows the chance of avoiding error and of importing error on adopting the program represented by f. When the inquirer is certain that the routine is to be applied, and is also certain that the chances of avoiding and of importing error on adopting the program represented by f remain the same in the presence of the other circumstances he knows obtain, the chance of avoiding the avoidance of error can be converted into a credal probability concerning the importation of error in the specific case (Levi, 1980a, chs. 12, 13, and sect. 16.6; 1984, ch. 13). Let this credal probability be Q.

Furthermore, given the initial state of full belief **K**, the inquirer assigns an informational value to each expansion obtained by adding to **K** a doxastic proposition that is an instantiation of a boolean combination of elements of Θ. Hence, given any condition in Θ, an expected increase in informational value may be determined. This expected increase in informational value is equal to 1 minus the expected M-value, where this value is the information determining probability. Let the expected M be $\Sigma(M)$. When informational value and risk of error are taken into account along the lines sketched in Section 3.3, the expected epistemic utility accruing from following the program for routine expansion conditional on θ being the true value of Θ should be $Q - q\Sigma(M)$.

All of this assumes that the inquirer's question concerns which condition in Θ obtains on the particular occasion of use of the program. Insofar as the inquirer faces a decision problem, he is concerned to evaluate alternative programs for routine expansion that apply to questions of the kind he is addressing. To make such comparisons, he will need to consider the expected epistemic utilities of the alternative programs conditional on each θ in Θ.

To illustrate unrealistically, suppose that Θ consists of the conditions that a liquid is red, white, or blue. Ω consists of reports that a liquid is red, white, or blue. The chance distribution over these reports on an observation given that the liquid is red is 0.99, 0.009, and 0.001, respectively. For white the distribution is 0.001, 0.99, and 0.009, and for blue it is 0.009, 0.001, and 0.99.

It is clear that we can devise a routine for expansion that guarantees (from the agent's point of view) avoidance of error – namely, a program recommending failure to expand no matter which report is made. But if one is seeking new information, this will not be satisfactory. Suppose that the information determining probability assigned to all three elements of U is $1/3$. Then the program represented by the following function has an expected epistemic utility of $0.99 - q/3$ no matter which of the three colors is the true one:

$$f(\text{report the color as } C) = \text{accept that the color is } C.$$

Suppose that $q = 0$, so that the inquirer is maximally cautious. Then the expected epistemic utility of the program is 0.99. If the agent had adopted a program that suspended judgment between all three colors no matter what report she made, her expected epistemic utility would have been 1. So she should not pursue the program just suggested. If q is positive, the recommendation always to suspend judgment carries expected epistemic utility of $1 - q$. Hence, if q is greater than 0.015, the routine matching colors with color reports will be preferable to always suspending judgment. But there is a third routine that recommends suspending judgment between red and white if red is reported, between white and blue if white is reported, and between blue and red if blue is reported whose expected value is $0.999 - 2q/3$. This will be better than the routine matching colors with color reports unless q is greater than 0.027. For values greater than 0.027, the routine matching colors with color reports is better no matter what the true color is.

Even so, there are three programs to be considered that bear comparison with the program matching colors with color reports even in the case where q is greater than 0.027. These are programs that recommend expanding to a specific color no matter what report is made.

For example, the program recommending expanding to red no matter what report is made will yield expected epistemic utility of $1 - q/3$ if the true color is red and $- q/3$ if the true color is blue and if it is white. Expanding to red, come what may, is better, therefore, than the program that matches colors with color reports when the true color is red but is inferior to that program otherwise. There is no way to make a comparison in expected utility between this program and the one matching colors with color reports, except by invoking prior credal probability distributions over hypotheses concerning the true color and calculating unconditional expected epistemic utilities for each of the programs for routine expansion. If and only if the prior credal probability that the true color is red is greater than 0.99 is the new program superior to the one matching colors with color reports. But in that case, there is no need to employ a routine for expansion. One could deliberately expand and reach the conclusion that the color is red without making observations – at least when q is greater than 0.027.

However, if the prior credal judgments are not sufficiently skewed to warrant expansion, the program matching colors to color reports will not be beaten by such programs with respect to expected utility. There are two possibilities: Either the prior credal probability judgments will be sufficiently determinate to allow comparisons of routines with respect to unconditional expected utility and the matching program will be better, or probabilities will be too indeterminate for comparisons to be made. In the latter case, we can appeal to the fact that the minimum conditional expected utility accruing from following the matching program is higher than the one recommending the conclusion that the color is red no matter what report is made to favor the program matching colors to color reports.[20]

So on the assumption that routine expansion applies only insofar as deliberate expansion can no longer be exploited, when the inquiring agent is moderately bold in making trade-offs between informational value and risk of error, the program recommending matching colors will be recommended.

Let us now turn to cases where some values of Θ are ruled out as serious possibilities but not others. Consider a situation where the inquirer fully believes that the liquid is not blue but is in doubt as to whether it is red or white. However, the inquirer remains convinced of the conditional chance distributions specified before for the reports in Ω conditional on the color of the liquid being red, white, or blue, respectively – that is, conditional on the true θ in Θ. Such cases are of interest to us because we might want to continue employing the programs for routine expansion that we favor using when all values of Θ are serious possibilities. We should explore, therefore, how well such programs fare.

The inquirer is sure under these conditions that the chance of reporting the color to be blue is no greater than 0.009. If asked to predict the report she would make, she would deliberately expand to the conclusion that she will not report the color to be blue even if she used a fairly low value for the index q (any value greater than 0.0027). If she were so cautious that she would refuse to rule out her reporting the color to be blue as a serious possibility, she would not be prepared to adopt the program matching colors to color reports in the first place. So let us assume that the inquirer takes for granted that the report that the color is blue will not be made. Only the reports that the color is red or that it is white are serious possibilities.

If the color is red, the inquirer now supposes that the chance of a report that the color is red is $0.99/(0.99 + 0.009) = 0.991$. The chance of a report that the color is white is 0.009. If the color is white, the chance of a report that the color is white is $0.99/(0.99 + 0.001) = 0.999$. The chance of red is 0.001.

Consider how the original program, which assigned matching colors to all three kinds of color reports. The expected epistemic value conditional on red is now $0.991 - 0.5q$, and the expected epistemic value conditional on white is now $0.999 - 0.5q$.[21] With one exception, it is superior to every other E-admissible program with respect to security – that is, minimum conditional expectation. The exception is assigning matching colors to color reports other than the report that the color is blue. When the report is that the color is blue, remain in suspense concerning whether the color is red or white. Since the inquirer is sure that the report will not be made, from her perspective this program has the same merit in this instance as the original matching program.

If the inquirer adopts the original program matching color reports to corresponding colors and reports the color to be blue, she will (inadvertently) expand into inconsistency. Precisely the same happens if she adopts the modified program; for if she adopts this program, she will know it (or be committed to knowing it). If, in addition, she reports the color to be blue, she will come to be sure that she has failed to expand in response to implementing the program. Hence, she will be committed to the view that she did report blue. But this is inconsistent with her antecedent conviction that she would not do so. So inconsistency is injected after all, just as in the case of perfect reliability.

To obtain this result, we needed to suppose that the inquirer deliberately expanded before invoking the routine to rule out her reporting the color to be blue as a serious possibility. Someone may argue that there need be no interest on the part of the inquirer in what report she made. She is interested in the color of the liquid. Moreover, inconsistency is something to be avoided. For the sake of avoiding inconsistency, therefore, she should not have deliberately expanded prior to observing the color.

If the inquirer does not make the preliminary deliberate expansion ruling out her reporting the color to be blue, the program according to which the inquirer suspends judgment in response to reporting that the color of the liquid is blue will carry higher conditional expected epistemic utility than the original matching colors program whether the color is red or white. Given her conviction that it is not blue, the inquirer could plausibly endorse this routine and in this way avoid expanding into inconsistency in case she reports that the color is blue.

Refusing to make the preliminary deliberate expansion cannot be a satisfactory way, however, of preventing inadvertent routine expansion into inconsistency. I have been supposing throughout that inquirers ought seek new error-free information in expansion. Given a suitable index q, the probability of reporting blue erroneously is sufficiently low for the agent to be willing to incur the risk of error for the information to be gained by deliberately expanding prior to implementing the routine. To be sure, the inquirer recognizes that in so doing, there is the possibility that subsequently she will expand into inconsistency; but the probability of that happening is already taken into account in reckoning the risk of error. Hence, prior to implementing the routine for expansion, the question as to whether the report that the color is blue could very well be an issue for the inquirer, and if her index q is greater than 0.027, she will expand by ruling out as impossible that the report she will make will be that the color is blue.

But even if the inquirer refuses to rule out her reporting the color to be blue as a serious possibility prior to making an observation and adopts the program that avoids injecting inconsistency if the inquirer reports that the color is blue, the desirability of contraction will not be avoided. If the inquirer reports the color of the liquid to be blue and suspends judgment as to the color in response, she has an anomaly on her hands. The presence of such an anomaly will provide as good a reason for contraction as retrenching from inconsistency.

Suppose that the inquirer reports that the color is blue and fails to draw any conclusion as to the true color by remaining in suspense between red and white. Not only has the routine failed in its purpose, but, given the inquirer's background assumptions, it has yielded a very surprising result – that is, one that the inquirer would have ruled out if she had used a rather small (= 0.027) index q of caution. Perhaps the inquirer has elected to be more cautious than that. Even so, the result is unexpected and surprising.[22] Such an anomalous result might justify contraction even if the inquirer has not inadvertently stumbled into inconsistency. But even if no contraction is made, the inquirer may try to implement the program for routine expansion again if feasible. Suppose that the report is again that the color is blue. Again the inquirer has failed to obtain the information sought, and now the anomaly is even more serious. There is an 0.000081 chance of failure on two such tries if they are independent, and the inquirer would have to have been hypercautious to refuse to reject such an eventuality before the fact.

It will not make sense for the inquirer to abandon the program as long as she continues to be convinced that the chances are as specified earlier and remains convinced that the color of the liquid is not blue. She may continue to be highly confident that on the third trial she will obtain the desired information. But if she fails, the anomaly deepens.

Even if it is not impossible given the agent's feelings, such a result is highly surprising and might call for an explanation. But the best available explanations are, according to the agent's convictions, certainly false – to wit, that the color of the liquid is blue or, if that explanation is unacceptable, that the chances of making reports that the agent took for granted on making observations are not as she assumed them to be. Upon reflection, the inquirer may end up living with the anomaly; but prior to doing so, she should want to consider whether her initial assumption that the color of the object is not blue is correct and whether the chance distributions are as she had taken them to be. To do this, she will have to open up her mind by contracting her state of full belief even if, after some inquiry, she returns to the position she initially endorsed.

The point is that if the observation of the color as blue does not inject inconsistency into the evolving doctrine, as it can when the observer is convinced before observation that she will not make that report, it does inject anomaly. Moreover, the anomaly should not be one that the inquirer finds it easy to rest content accepting. As I argue in Chapter 4, the presence of anomaly is often a good reason for contracting, just as the presence of inconsistency is. If this is right, the proposed strategem will not avoid the need to contract. The desperate refusal to countenance the initial deliberate expansion does not bring the dividends promised.

Thus, whether the inquirer regards a routine for expansion to be perfectly reliable or not, if the routine is capable of furnishing new informational value on application, situations can arise where it leads to inconsistency. Yet, in routine expansion, the agent does uphold, from his initial point of view, the concern to obtain new error-free information. There is no deliberate expansion into inconsistency or, for that matter, into anomaly. It is entirely inadvertent, although the risk of inadvertent inconsistency is incurred.

Such inadvertence provides one of the main occasions for legitimate contraction. Because the inquirer has inadvertently expanded into inconsistency via routine expansion, he is compelled to contract. This is what I call *coerced contraction*. Not all contractions are coerced. But whenever an experimenter obtains results that are in conflict with background theory or an expert offers testimony that contradicts settled assumptions, we have occasions where coerced contraction is called for.

The circumstance that routine expansion has this critical edge may be one of the reasons why appeals to the testimony of the senses have seemed fundamental to many epistemologists. If one thinks an epistemological foundation is needed, it should have a critical edge.

There is, however, nothing foundationalist about the account given here.

First, routine expansion can appeal to the testimony of other agents, as well as to the testimony of the senses. Neither the testimony of the senses nor that of witnesses is foundational. Second, the fact that routine expansion has such a cutting edge is a weakness in such methods that is to be avoided if possible. We put up with the weakness because routine expansion is a means for obtaining new information with a prospect of its being error-free where deliberate expansion cannot do so and still respect the demands that error be avoided.

Both deliberate and routine expansion seek to obtain new error-free informational value. The assessment of risk of error is relative to the way the inquiring agent judges truth when his state of full belief is **K**; and what he considers to be new informational value is relative to that same state of full belief (among other things). When the inquiring agent has changed his state of full belief, whether by expansion or contraction, he judges truth differently than he did before and, hence, his assessment of risk of error is also changed. What is new informational value will also be modified.

In this sense, the inquirer's concern to obtain new error-free information changes with changes in his doctrine. This does not imply that truth and error have become relative to belief. Whether the inquirer succeeds in avoiding error is not relative to what he believes. But the inquirer's judgment that he has avoided error is relative to what he believes. In the conduct of inquiries aimed at avoiding error, it is avoidance of error as judged relative to the evolving doctrine that is relevant to the critically self-reflective conduct of inquiry aimed at avoiding error.

3.5 Duhem's thesis

The view attributed to Pierre Duhem that there are no crucial experiments has become a cornerstone of contemporary discussions of scientific methodology. The outcome of experimental investigations cannot decide for or against a given hypothesis, or between rival hypotheses, because tests of a hypothesis always presuppose various auxiliary assumptions that can be questioned should the results of experiment seem to go against the hypothesis, so that the hypothesis may survive unrefuted.

At best, the data of an experiment may refute the hypothesis-cum-auxiliary-assumptions that, in the more extreme exploitations of the idea, may include all of the inquirer's beliefs of the moment. We then obtain the vision, made fashionable from the writings of Quine, that the body of scientific theory as a whole is tested by the data.

Such a view is at odds with the approach to inquiry grounded in the Peircean belief–doubt model that I am deploying. According to that view, at any given stage of inquiry, a distinction needs to be made between what is conjecture and what is settled. That distinction is subject to revision over time, but at any given stage the inquirer is committed to some version of it.

Sometimes the new information obtained via routine expansion concerning the results of some experiment is taken to constitute a test of a conjecture or a pair (or n-tuple) of rival conjectures. We may think of the set of conjectures being subject to test as constituting an ultimate partition in the sense of Section 3.3 – that is, either as a set U of doxastic propositions that are consistent expansions of **K** such that one and only one element of U is true (free of error) if **K** is, or as a set $\underline{U}$ of sentences in $\underline{L}$ representing the doxastic propositions in such a set (when such linguistic representation is feasible).

It is important to emphasize that the elements of U are conjectures, whereas **K** is not. In linguistic terms, the sentences in $\underline{K}$ are taken for granted as certainly true, whereas the elements of $\underline{U}$ are hypotheses whose truth (and falsity) is seriously possible. We imagine that an experiment is designed so that, via routine expansion, some new information will be added to **K** (new sentence added to $\underline{K}$). Given the new information added to the initial corpus $\underline{K}$, the inquirer is justified in rejecting some subset of the elements of $\underline{U}$ either by deduction or by deliberate expansion. The experiment is crucial if the possible outcomes of experimentation are doxastic propositions that eliminate all but one element of U via deliberate expansion and where, for every element U, there is at least one such outcome. One might strengthen the requirement to stipulate that the various possible outcomes of an experiment when added to **K** must entail the truth of exactly one element of U. The weaker version is preferable, however, because it allows inductive and statistical considerations to play a role.

Usually attention is focused on crucial experiments testing a specific hypothesis. In that event, the ultimate partition is taken to be that hypothesis and its negation given **K**.

Whether one deploys the stronger or the weaker conception of a crucial experiment, and whether or not the ultimate partition is restricted to a hypothesis and its negation, Duhem's point was that the experiment selected an element of U only on the assumption that **K** (or its linguistic representation the corpus $\underline{K}$) is held fixed. But if one maintains, as Duhem apparently did, that all background assumptions (except, perhaps, phenomenal ones, whatever these may be) are conjectural, assumptions in $\underline{K}$ are always open to question. We may, if we like, introduce a notion of a crucial experiment relative to $\underline{L}$; but the relativity is of little interest since – in opposition to Newton and to Peirce – background assumptions are always conjectural.

According to the position I have been defending, this argument does not refute those who insist that there are or at least can be crucial experiments. To have a crucial experiment, one needs a state of full belief or a corpus of settled assumptions and an ultimate partition representing the relevant conjectures. If the results of an experiment contradict the elements of the ultimate partition, then they are eliminated as false. That is because the results of an experiment are added to the settled assumptions by routine expansion.

If $\underline{K}$ is the initial corpus of sentences and $\underline{E}$ is added by routine expansion as a result of observing the outcome of an experiment, the new corpus $\underline{K}_{\underline{E}}^+$ automatically rules out the elements of $\underline{U}$ incompatible with it as impossibilities. It is, of course, logically possible that some sentence in $\underline{K}$ is false. But this does not mean that the inquirer has any warrant for questioning such settled assumptions. Duhem, however, takes for granted that unless a sentence asserts the occurrence of a phenomenon, it is open to question. The denial of the feasibility of crucial experiments is a consequence of Duhem's phenomenalist epistemology. If one gives up this epistemology in favor of an approach that takes the main task of epistemology to be to give an account of principles for revisions of states of full belief, Duhem's argument against crucial experiments no longer appears compelling.

Yet, there is a kernel of truth in Duhem's thesis. Sometimes the results of experiment and observation do lead us to question background assumptions initially taken for granted. This happens, however, when routine expansion injects inconsistency into the state of full belief or corpus.

Observe, however, that such inconsistency is inadvertent. The inquiring agent is not seeking to test any item among the settled assumptions. If he were doing so, it would not be a settled assumption but a conjecture.

Furthermore, the outcome of routine expansion does not, in general, yield a rejection of some erstwhile settled assumption as false – at least not initially. If the routine expansion leads to inconsistency, *contraction* is required. The kernel of truth in Duhem's observation is that logical considerations alone cannot determine what that contraction should be. Given the initial corpus $\underline{K}$ entailing $\sim\underline{E}$, the addition of $\underline{E}$ via routine expansion does not automatically lead to rejection of $\sim\underline{E}$ as false. It may, instead, lead to rejection of the information $\underline{E}$ added by routine expansion or, as is more likely, to suspension of judgment concerning the truth of $\underline{E}$ and $\sim\underline{E}$. Detailed examination of this matter is deferred to Chapter 4.

On this view of the matter, Duhem's observations about crucial experiments are misplaced. They do not apply to crucial experiments but to experiments that lead to the injection of inconsistency into the background assumptions.

Thus, Michelson's attempts to ascertain the velocity of the earth relative to the luminiferous ether in the experiments initiated at Potsdam in 1881 were not designed to test classical mechanics cum electromagnetic theory. Michelson took that for granted. But the null results he obtained injected inconsistency into his background assumptions, which led to questioning of items in the background as well as the design of his experiment and, hence, to questioning of the correctness of the data obtained via routine expansion.

Contemporary textbooks are not concerned to address students of physics who share Michelson's background convictions in 1881. They speak to beginning students for whom the classical theories and the theory of special relativity may have the status of conjectures. In such a setting, the reports of the experiments with the interferometer may be presented as a crucial experiment. T. Kuhn and others argue fallaciously from the correct claim that the legitimacy of a revision of doctrine in science is heavily context dependent to the conclusion that textbook presentations misrepresent scientific reasoning. What is true is that the textbook presentation of the Michelson and Michelson and Morley experiments as testing classical doctrine misrepresents the position of Michelson and his colleagues in the 1880s. But it does not necessarily misrepresent thc epistemic predicament of the consumers of contemporary textbook physics, and the arguments used need not, in that setting, be bad arguments at all. What was not a crucial experiment for Michelson may be a crucial experiment for a physics tyro, and legitimately so.

3.6 The "comparative statics" of expansion

Peter Gärdenfors (1988, p. 47) introduces a distinction between the statics and the dynamics of belief.[23] The statics of belief specifies the equilibrium conditions in a state of full belief. In the terms I have been using, such equilibrium conditions are the conditions an agent would be in were the agent fully living up to the commitments undertaken by being in a given state of full belief. An inquirer in a state of full belief K is committed to fully recognizing all doxastic propositions in the filter generated by K. An inquirer is in doxastic equilibrium only if he lives up to this commitment. If one represents a state of full belief linguistically by a deductively closed set $\underline{K}$ of sentences in $\underline{L}$, the commitment is a commitment to recognizing all elements of $\underline{K}$. Equilibrium is attained when all sentences in $\underline{K}$ are recognized to be true.

Of course, equilibrium so construed, in contrast to the notions employed in mechanics, thermodynamics, and economics, is intended to be a normative notion. Given the agent's doxastic commitment, it is the condition he ought to realize insofar as this is feasible. Dynamics, as Gärdenfors understands it, focuses on changes in states of full belief or in the corpora (in Gärdenfors's terminology, the *belief sets*) that represent them. *Dynamics* does not seem to be an appropriate term for what Gärdenfors has in mind – at least if one means to take the analogy to physics or economics seriously. Dynamics, as I understand it, focuses on explanation of change. But Gärdenfors does not discuss explanation of changes in doxastic commitment. In passing, he suggests that "the most common causes of such changes are observations and the information provided by other people." Gärdenfors does not elaborate on how observation and the testimony of witnesses cause expansion. But even if he had offered an account, it would not be an explanation of how, starting in one state of doxastic performance falling short of doxastic equilibrium characterizing the initial commitment, one ends up in a state of doxastic performance with a commitment to another doxastic equilibrium. I would have thought that a dynamics of belief would have had to address that issue.

I sympathize with Gärdenfors's avoidance of the causal mechanisms involved in expansion. I do not address the dynamics of belief any more than, so I think, Gärdenfors does. I am concerned with conditions under which changes in doxastic commitments are legitimate. The concern is prescriptive, not explanatory.

However, even taking this into account, the question is not a normative analogue of a dynamic question. A normative dynamics would presumably prescribe the steps one should take in shifting from one commitment to another. I am concerned only with the conditions under which a change in commitment is legitimate or justified, without any particular interest in how one implements a change in commitment.

I see my own concern as a normative analogue of a question in *comparative statics*, where one begins with an equilibrium state of full belief should be when appropriate inputs are present (such as the demands for information, ultimate partition, degree of caution, credal state, and so on).

Gärdenfors's interest also seems to be in an aspect of such normative comparative statics.[24] However, as his discussion of expansion reveals, his approach differs from the one sketched in this book.

As noted earlier, for Gärdenfors, the common types of belief changes where a doxastic proposition is added to the belief state are through observation and the testimony of witnesses. He does not think of induction as a form of belief change (at least not of the kind in which he is interested) because, for him, expansion is a process of coming to equilibrium – that is, coming closer to living up to one's commitment. It involves no proper change in commitment at all. Thus, Gärdenfors does not consider induction to be a species of belief change.

I have suggested that the process of adding information via the testimony of the senses or of witnessess should satisfy three conditions:

1. The result of the process should be an expansion.

2. Initiating the process is legitimate, according to the inquirer, if the inquirer is convinced prior to starting the process that the expansion resulting from the process is the outcome of a reliable program for routine expansion.

3. The process can lead to the injection of inconsistency into the evolving doctrine.

Gärdenfors, as I pointed out in Section 2.9, thinks that expansion into inconsistency is never legitimate. State 0 is "epistemic hell" (Gärdenfors, 1988, p. 51). He thinks that when observation or testimony leads to adding a doxastic proposition inconsistent with the initial belief state, the resulting belief state is what I call a *replacement*. Only when the new information is consistent with the initial belief state is it an expansion. Hence, Gärdenfors's conception of how observation and testimony lead to changes of belief entails rejection of conditions 1 and 3. On his view, the basic shift involved is a revision that is legitimate only if it is minimal. (See Section 2.9.)

Although Gärdenfors claims that observation and testimony are sources of input propositions for minimal revision, he does not, to my knowledge, discuss the conditions under which such inputs are legitimately added. By way of contrast, not only do I think it important to sketch an account of the presuppositions of routine expansion, I also consider deliberate expansion where there is a demand for justifying the choice of adding one doxastic proposition rather than another. Induction, so I claim, is belief change of this sort. For Gärdenfors, induction cannot be expansion because induction involves no change of commitment, but rather a move to equilibrium.

Hence, for Gärdenfors, expansion is not a basic form of belief change in the sense of Section 2.9, although legitimate, consistent expansions are a species of minimal revision and minimal revision is a form of basically legitimate belief change. For me, on the other hand, minimal revision is not a basic type of legitimate belief change, although expansion is; and expansion into inconsistency can be legitimate when it is the product of a reliable routine. It is true, according to the approach I favor, that expansion into inconsistency is prohibited when such expansion is inductive or deliberate. But this prohibition does not extend to all forms of legitimate expansion. In particular, it does not apply to expansions in response to the testimony of the senses or of witnesses. As I have already argued, routine expansion of this sort can be conflict injecting. From this perspective, Gärdenfors's prohibition against expansion into inconsistency reflects confusion between what is a legitimate prohibition in the case of deliberate or inductive expansion and an inappropriate prohibition in the case of routine expansion together with a denial of the propriety of deliberate expansion.

Even though Gärdenfors does not regard expansion as basically legitimate, he does find it useful to have a formal characterization of the conditions characterizing legitimate expansion. That is to say, given that one is going to expand $\underline{K}$ by adding $\underline{A}$, what conditions *should* the new corpus satisfy?

In previous work, I answered Gärdenfors's question by characterizing an expansion of $\underline{K}$ by adding $\underline{A}$ as the deductive closure of $\underline{K} \cup \underline{A}$. And in this book, I take the expansion of the doxastic proposition $\mathbf{K}$ by adding A to be $\mathbf{K} \wedge \mathbf{A}$. Gärdenfors's own discussion is in terms of belief sets that are essentially sets of sentences in a language $\underline{L}$ meeting a closure condition on a consequence relation. When the consequence relation is deducibility in a first-order language, his characterization of belief set is essentially equivalent to mine. And given this understanding of the consequence relation, he ends up with a characterization of expansions essentially equivalent to the one I have favored.[25]

However, his discussion has the virtue of deriving the characterization of an expansion of a corpus given earlier from certain postulates about expansion.

We are taking for granted that the expansion of a corpus is itself a corpus, and if it is an expansion by adding $\underline{A}$, $\underline{A}$ is in the expansion. Gärdenfors enshrines these in two postulates:

(K$^+$1) $\underline{K}_A^+$ is a corpus (belief set)

(K$^+$2) $\underline{A} \varepsilon \underline{K}_A^+$

Gärdenfors adds to these requirements four additional postulates:

(K$^+$3) $\underline{K} \subseteq \underline{K}_A^+$. (Expansion)

(K$^+$4)   If $\underline{A} \ \varepsilon \ \underline{K}$, then $\underline{K}_A^+ = \underline{K}$.

(K$^+$5)   If $\underline{K} \subseteq \underline{H}$, then $\underline{K}_A^+ \subseteq \underline{H}_A^+$. (Monotonicity)

(K$^+$6)   For all corpora $\underline{K}$ and sentences $\underline{A}$, $\underline{K}_A^+$ is the smallest corpus that satisfies (K$^+$1) $-$ (K$^+$5).

Gärdenfors then points out that an "expansion function" satisfies these six postulates if and only if the expansion $\underline{K}_A^+$ is the closure under consequence of the union of $\underline{K}$ and $\{\underline{A}\}$.

Gärdenfors thinks of his six postulates as constraints on the "epistemic change" that "follows *learning* something – the epistemic attitude toward some sentence $\underline{A}$ is changed from indetermined to accepted" (1988, p. 48). There is no doubt that the linguistic representation of expansion [except in the degenerate case of no change that Gärdenfors also allows as (K$^+$4) indicates] involves a change of some sentence from "indetermined to accepted." But so do replacement and residual shifting, to which some of the postulates listed earlier do not apply. The only settings in which the six postulates are constraints on belief are where expansion is justified. Otherwise, they are not. And Gärdenfors clearly does not want to say that when X learns that the doxastic proposition A is true, expansion is always justified. For example, if $\sim$A is in the initial belief state, the constraint (K$^+$3) can be satisfied only if the shift is to an inconsistent belief state – which Gärdenfors explicitly disallows.

Gärdenfors seems to think that the postulates need some sort of vindication or justification. But the only claims that seem to me in need of serious defense are claims that expansion as characterized either by the six postulates or as the closure of $\underline{K} \ \cup \ A$ is justified. Yet, Gärdenfors fails to identify conditions under which expansion so understood is warranted, except to say that it is the product of observation or reliable testimony when the doxastic proposition learned does not conflict with the initial belief state.

Gärdenfors is interested in emphasizing the theme that at least some of the postulates – in particular (K$^+$3) – are motivated by a "heuristic criterion" of *informational economy* (1988, p. 49):

The key idea is that, when we change our beliefs, we want to retain as much as possible of our old beliefs – information in general is not gratuitous, and unnecessary losses of information are therefore to be avoided.

That information carries value relevant to evaluating changes in belief states is a point I have belabored in various ways since the 1960s. When changing belief states, we should seek to maximize new informational value and minimize losses of old informational value.

But this desideratum argues against giving up any old beliefs – that is, against contraction, replacement, and residual shifting. If, nonetheless, such changes are sometimes legitimate, it must be because of special incentives that warrant incurring losses of informational value. These matters are explored in Chapter 4. But when these incentives are absent, the only legitimate sort of belief change ought to be one that avoids giving up old beliefs altogether. Under such circumstances, the only legitimate form of belief change is expansion.

Furthermore, unless one has special incentives for incurring losses of old information, the injunction against giving up old information argues for the legitimacy of expanding into inconsistency rather than against it. Gärdenfors tells us that inconsistency is hell, and I suppose it is; but in a principled account of change of belief, we need to identify the goals and values that urge us to avoid it.

In the previous discussion, I have argued that expanding into inconsistency is expanding into certain error. If, as I assume, inquirers should be concerned not only with promoting informational value but also with reducing the risk of error, one should not deliberately expand into error. I have also tried to show that expansion into inconsistency may, nonetheless, be legitimate provided that it is the inadvertent result of deploying a reliable program for routine expansion. To say this is compatible with admitting that the result is hell and that one should extricate oneself from the inconsistency. But prior to the inadvertent expansion into inconsistency, the prospect of doing so following the routine was judged to be remote, so that the risk of doing so was justifiable.

Gärdenfors insists that such expansion into inconsistency is never legitimate and that we should instead think of it as a form of replacement. But, as I argue in Chapter 4, when conflict is injected into a belief state by observation or the testimony of witnesses, one does not always end up replacing doxastic propositions that are consequences of the initial belief state with the new input proposition. In such cases, it is often sensible to question both the testimony of the senses and of witnesses, as well as the background information and theory. When that is the case, the proposition A that is "learned" is then "unlearned." If we are going to obtain a systematic account of legitimate belief change that will shed light on the considerations that decide when conflict situations yield such a result rather than a replacement and when they yield a replacement, deploying the requirement of commensuration seems more promising as a means of yielding a fine-grained analysis than taking minimal revision as basic.

Moreover, it seems to me that the requirement of commensuration gives expression to an ideal of cognitive probity preferable to one that legitimizes revision in Gärdenfors's sense as a basically legitimate type of change in belief.

In short, although I have no quarrel with Gärdenfors's axioms for expansion as constraints on the comparative statics of expansion, I do have doubts about the status of expansion in his account of the conditions under which changes of belief state are legitimate.

What benefit, then, is to be reaped from characterizing expansion by means of the six postulates and then producing a representation theorem? There is one useful implication. (K^+3) or expansion and (K^+5) or monotonicity are clearly violated by residual shifting and replacement, and this fact sheds some light on the differences between these two types of revision and expansion.

There is, moreover, a related deeper benefit to be obtained from looking at these two postulates. It concerns the way modal judgments are to be addressed and how this impinges on the commensuration requirement.

3.7 Modality, monotonicity, and expansion

A conceptual framework is a boolean algebra of potential states of full belief or doxastic propositions together with a distinction between error-free states and those carrying error where the former are required to be members of a single proper ultrafilter. A doxastic proposition **A** is seriously possible relative to a given state of full belief **K** if and only if **A** is a proper ultrafilter containing **K**. Equivalently, **A** is seriously possible relative to **K** if and only if the complement of **A** is not a member of the filter generated by **K** (i.e., is not a consequence of **K** according to the boolean algebra).

On this account of judgments of serious possibility, when X judges that h to be seriously possible, the judgment locates the doxastic proposition that h in the conceptual framework relative to X's state of full belief. It is tempting (and many have been tempted) by the view that when X judges that h to be seriously possible, X fully believes that it is seriously possible that h. On this view, "that it is seriously possible that h" represents a doxastic proposition that is a consequence of X's current state of full belief.

Hence, in a rich enough regimented language, it should be possible to construct a set of sentences that represents the state of full belief and includes modal sentences like "It is seriously possible that h." In Section 2.5, the language $\underline{L}^*$ that contained the first-order language $\underline{L}$ and all truth functional compounds of sentences containing arbitrarily large but finite modal prefixes were suggested. A corpus $\underline{K}^*$ was required to be closed under the principles of sentential S5 modal logic. More crucially, given the set $\underline{K}$ representing the corpus expressible in $\underline{L}$, the corpus $\underline{K}^*$ expressible in $\underline{K}^*$ is uniquely determined, and conversely.

Consequently, when seeking to represent linguistically the potential state of full belief **K**, both $\underline{K}$ and $\underline{K}^*$ are equivalent. There are, however, some important differences in the way these sets represent **K**. For the language $\underline{L}$, I assumed the existence of a function Φ from sentences in $\underline{L}$ to doxastic propositions satisfying the deducibility preservation condition. The doxastic proposition represented by "h" is also represented by the closure under first-order deductive consequence of "h" and all sentences in the minimal or urcorpus $\underline{1}$. In effect, "h" represents the doxastic proposition that is represented by the expansion $\underline{1}^+_{"h"}$ of $\underline{1}$ by adding "h". If "h" is already in $\underline{1}$, the expansion is degenerate and is identical to $\underline{1}$; otherwise not.

Consider, then, the urcorpus $\underline{1}^*$ for $\underline{L}^*$ yielding the equivalent representation of $\mathbf{1}$ as $\underline{1}$ in $\underline{L}$ and the corpus $(\underline{1}^+_{"h"})^*$ in $\underline{L}^*$ that is equivalent to the expansion of $\underline{1}$ by adding "h." Unless "h" is already in the urcorpus $\underline{1}$, $(\underline{1}^+_{"h"})^*$ is not the expansion of $\underline{1}^*$ by adding "h." It violates the expansion condition (K^+3). $\underline{1}^*$ contains "it is seriously possible that $\sim h$." $(\underline{1}^+_{"h"})^*$ does not.

The monotonicity condition (K^+5) is also in trouble, not because it is violated but because it is trivialized. Let "h" and "g" be two consistent sentences in $\underline{L}$ that are mutually consistent and where neither sentence is in $\underline{1}$. $\underline{1}$ is a subset of $\underline{1}^+_{"h"} = \underline{K}$. $(\underline{1}^+_{"g"})^*$ is not a subset of $(\underline{K}^+_{"g"})^*$. Monotonicity is not violated because $(\underline{1})^*$ is not a subset of $(\underline{K})^*$. Indeed, no corpus in $\underline{L}^*$ is a proper subset of any other distinct corpus in $\underline{L}^*$.

Thus, if we seek a linguistic representation of the expansion of one state of full belief by adding a doxastic proposition that meets Gärdenfors's monotonicity condition for expansions of belief sets nontrivially and satisfies the expansion condition, we cannot do so by means of those sets of sentences in $\underline{L}^*$ that furnish representations of states of full belief equivalent to those representable in $\underline{L}$. In $\underline{L}^*$, if we restrict potential corpora or belief sets to those that are equivalent representations of states of full belief to potential corpora in $\underline{L}$, there can be no nondegenerate expansions of potential corpora.

This situation arises because of the requirement that the corpus expressible in $\underline{L}^*$ should be closed under S5 propositional modal logic. The motivation for this requirement is that this corpus represents the inquirer's *commitments* with respect to judgments of *serious possibility*, as opposed to his *performances*. If the focus of concern were performance rather than commitment or if some conception of possibility other than serious possibility were at stake, a different result would ensue.

Assuming that our concern here is with commitments, the critical question concerns the status of modal judgments. Even if it is granted that there are judgments of possibility that are not judgments of serious possibility, my contention is that commitments to judgments of serious possibility are undertaken when an agent is in a state of full belief. In this sense, judgments of serious possibility are unavoidable. On the other hand, a judgment that a doxastic proposition $\mathbf{A}$ is seriously possible is not itself a doxastic proposition or potential state of full belief. In this sense, the inquiring agent cannot be certain that $\mathbf{A}$ is seriously possible, cannot be in doubt as to whether it is true or regard its truth as a serious possibility. Consequently, it is not surprising that there can be no expansions (or, for that matter, contractions or residual shifts) of corpora in $\underline{L}^*$. Insofar as expansions are thought to involve adding doxastic propositions to the state of full belief or adding sentences representing doxastic propositions to a corpus, the corpus of concern is the corpus expressible in $\underline{L}$ – not $\underline{L}^*$.

Another way to approach this point appeals to the circumstance that expansion incurs a risk of importing error from the inquiring agent's point of view. In the case where a corpus $\underline{K}$ is expanded by adding a sentence $\underline{A}$ and forming the deductive closure, from the inquirer's point of view an error will be imported if and only if $\underline{A}$ is false. But the question of error arises only for sentences in $\underline{L}$ that are added. On the view I have taken, it is only avoidance of error with respect to such sentences that characterizes the inquirer's concern to avoid error. One may, if one likes, supply semantics for sentences in $\underline{L}^*$ that provide truth conditions for judgments of serious possibility. But avoidance of error in this sense is not of concern to the inquiring agent except insofar as this concern reduces to a concern to avoid error with respect to the nonmodal part of $\underline{L}$. Thus, one might say either that judgments of serious possibility lack truth values or, alternatively, that insofar as truth conditions can be provided for such judgments, avoidance of error with respect to the truth of such judgments is not a desideratum in inquiry.[26]

These remarks apply to judgments of serious possibility. I contend that such judgments are generated by states of full belief and in this sense are unavoidable. It remains an open question whether one has to operate with a conceptual framework that allows for other types of judgments of possibility that are doxastic propositions.

I am inclined to the view that we do need judgments of ability. Coins are able to land heads on tosses but are not able to melt on being tossed. We may distinguish between sentences that are provable in a given axiom system and those that are not. But we should distinguish between the possibility *for* some thing or system to respond in a certain way under appropriate circumstances and the possibility *that* some doxastic proposition is true. Serious possibility is a species of possibility that.

If this is right, then, insofar as we are prepared to acknowledge that nondegenerate expansions are sometimes justifiable, we should focus on expansions of corpora expressible in $\underline{L}$ that contain no *de dicto* modal connectives. One can, if one likes, represent expansions in the modal language $\underline{L}^*$ by characterizing expansions in terms of the nonmodal part of $\underline{L}^*$, but that, of course, amounts to focusing on changes in the corpus expressible in $\underline{L}$.

Of course, one could proceed without considering nondegenerate expansions altogether. Every change in corpus expressible in $\underline{L}^*$ is a replacement. One might offer an account of rational belief change exclusively in these terms.[27]

From the perspective of those who reify judgments of possibility by equating judgments of serious or epistemic possibility with full belief in the truth of statements representing doxastic propositions of objective possibility, my insistence that expansion and not revision should be a basic type of legitimate change in belief state must look unattractive. Indeed, such authors must also deny that contractions are a basic type of legitimate change. The *only* kind of change in belief state that is a basic type of legitimate change or, indeed, is even a derived type of legitimate change is a replacement or revision. (The only legitimate revisions are replacements.)

A still more radical claim may be made. If we take as our notion that one belief state is a consequence of another, one that is represented by entailment within an S5 system of modal logic of the sort required for $\underline{L}^*$, *no* belief state can be a consequence of any other. *Every* belief state will be a replacement for every other belief state.

I do not mean to suggest that those who take seriously the idea that judgments of possibility and necessity carry truth values are committed to the reification of judgments of serious possibility along lines that yield these remarkable results. However, skeptics about various versions of modal realism are entitled to point out that judgments of *de dicto* modality that are needed in inquiry and practical deliberation may be construed as judgments of serious (or epistemic) possibility, so that the pressure from presystematic precedent for endorsing some form of modal realism may be defused. This is important, since many advocates of the usefulness of possible worlds semantics for the purpose of explicating judgments of possibility and conditionals appeal to examples that may be given a straightforward epistemic or, in the case of conditionals, belief-change treatment. Those who make this appeal ought to consider how they are to finesse the charge that they have indulged in the reification of epistemic modalities while still sustaining the cogency of their appeal to presystematic precedent.[28]

My contention is that changes of corpora expressible in $\underline{L}^*$ consist of four kinds: expansions, contractions, replacements, and residual shifts of corpora in the *nonmodal* part $\underline{L}$ of $\underline{L}^*$. That is to say, this is so as long as the modality involved is serious possibility. According to the commensuration requirement, a change of a corpus expressible in $\underline{L}^*$ is legitimate if and only if it can be decomposed into a sequence of changes each of which is a legitimate expansion or legitimate contraction in $\underline{L}$. The substantive dispute between those who focus on minimal revisions of a corpus expressible in $\underline{L}^*$ and the approach to belief change I favor is not over whether changes in the corpus expressible in $\underline{L}^*$ are decomposable into expansions and contractions of corpora expressible in $\underline{L}^*$. As we have seen in the case of expansion (and since contractions are inverses of expansions, this must be true of them as well), there can be no nondegenerate expansions (or contractions) of corpora in $\underline{L}^*$ (and there can be no nondegenerate residual shifts either). Every change in corpus in $\underline{L}^*$ is a replacement (or, in Gärdenfors's terminology a revision). The critical question is whether legitimate changes of such corpora are to be rationalized in terms of changes of the nonmodal part of such corpora along the lines I have suggested, or whether some alternative notion of a minimal revision is to be deployed that is not equivalent to the requirements I am proposing.

3.8 Choosing true

Legitimate expansions are sometimes responses to inputs in conformity with reliable programs for routine expansion. Such expansions are not directly chosen by the inquirer. At other times, the inquirer does decide which one of alternative expansion strategies to implement in order to obtain new error-free information relevant to the question under consideration. In such cases, the inquirer chooses the expansion strategy to implement, but her choice does not ensure that the expansion strategy avoids error. Nor does the inquirer think that it does from her vantage point prior to implementing the expansion strategy.

There is a third type of expansion, different from routine and deliberate expansion, that ought, for the sake of completeness, to be mentioned. Suppose that X is deciding whether to see Woody Allen's movie *Crimes and Misdemeanors* or Michael Roehmer's movie *The Plot Against Harry*. X is convinced at the outset that it is under her control whether she sees one movie or the other. That is to say, she is certain that if she decides to see Allen's movie, she will see it, and if she decides to see Roehmer's, she will see it. Often we do not think of ourselves as being in such complete control of our destinies. We may think we can increase the chances of seeing one movie rather than the other. But if that is so, strictly speaking, we do not have the option of seeing Allen's movie and seeing Roehmer's movie, but rather of increasing our chances of our seeing one movie or the other. The point is that if X judges it optional for her to make it true that $\underline{A}$, she takes for granted that if she chooses to make it true that $\underline{A}$, $\underline{A}$ is true.

Suppose then that X decides to make $\underline{A}$ true (e.g., chooses to see Roehmer's movie). Once she decides to do it, X becomes certain that $\underline{A}$ is true. It is no longer a serious possibility that $\underline{A}$ is false (Levi, 1986, sect. 4.2). X's decision is accompanied by an expansion of X's state of full belief. This expansion is not the outcome of the implementation of a program for routine expansion. It does resemble deliberate expansion to the extent that such expansion is implied by the implementation of a deliberate choice. But in deliberate expansion, the inquiring agent chooses the expansion strategy without choosing to make true that it be error-free. In the type of expansion now under consideration, the inquiring agent chooses to make a doxastic proposition true, and by so doing adds the doxastic proposition to the consequences of her state of full belief. In implementing the expansion strategy, she is making it error-free.

The agent who expands by choice in this way does not betray the concern to avoid error. If prior to deciding to go to Roehmer's movie X is certain that if she decides she will go, X is confident that adding "X goes to Roehmer's movie" to her corpus will avoid error if X decides to go to Roehmer's movie. Hence, there is no risk of error to avoid in expanding.

Like deliberate expansion, expansion by choice cannot legitimately lead to expansion into inconsistency. If X is certain, prior to reaching her decision that she will not go to Roehmer's movie, then going to Roehmer's movie is not optional for her. And if she is not certain and she decides to go, expansion by adding the information that she will go to the movie cannot lead to expansion into inconsistency. To be sure, X may subsequently fail to go to the movie. (The subway may break down, or X may suffer a heart attack or may be called away on business.) On the account I have been proposing, X's realization of this will be the result of expansion into inconsistency via routine inadvertently followed by coerced contraction followed by expansion into a different view. Expansion by choice will not itself inject the inconsistency.

The account of optionality and choosing that underlies this view has important ramifications for decision theory. It is not my concern to address these ramifications here (Levi, 1991). For the sake of completeness, however, it is necessary to recognize that expansion by choice is often legitimate and that its rationale is different from that of routine or deliberate expansion.

4

Contraction

4.1 Two kinds of contraction

According to the view proposed in Chapter 3, one can never justify a deliberate expansion into inconsistency. Respect for the desideratum that error be avoided in changing states of full belief requires this. One can, however, legitimately though inadvertently expand into inconsistency via routine expansion.

Although routine expansion into such inconsistency may be legitimate in the sense that programs for routine expansion that can inject inconsistency are legitimately adopted even when they incur a risk of leading to inconsistency, it is, nonetheless, clear that an inconsistent result calls for contraction. I call such contraction *coerced contraction* because it is mandated by the inadvertent expansion into inconsistency and the urgency of retreating from inconsistency.

Contraction does not have to be coerced to be legitimate. One may be justified in ceasing to be certain that a doxastic proposition is true even though one is not retreating from inconsistency. Uncoerced contraction may be justified because someone has proposed a conjecture that, given the current state of full belief, is certainly false. The inquiring agent may be justified in incurring the loss of information that must result from such contraction in order to obtain a cognitive benefit. The contraction is not imposed as the remedy for the inadvertent expansion into inconsistency but is deliberately chosen as best for the purpose of realizing the inquirer's cognitive goals.

Uncoerced contraction is illustrated by situations where investigators are confronted with unexplained anomalies. The presence of the anomalous phenomenon is consistent with the rest of what is taken for granted. However, the phenomenon is anomalous because no explanation compatible with the current doctrine has been furnished that merits admission to the state of full belief. This circumstance may exert pressure to seek such an explanation, and it may result in identifying a potential explanation inconsistent with the current doctrine. If someone proposes an attractive potential explanation that, nonetheless, is inconsistent with presently held views, the inquirer may regard it as worthwhile to give the new doctrine a critical hearing. But the proposal cannot be given a hearing without begging the question against it if the explanatory hypothesis is taken to be false. Consequently, the inquiring agent needs to modify his current state of full belief or corpus so that the new hypothesis becomes a serious possibility.

Let us suppose that the potential explanation consists of the doxastic proposition **T** and that the current state of full belief **K** has as a consequence ~**T**. Clearly, it will be necessary to remove ~$\underline{T}$ from the corpus $\underline{K}$. But this itself does not require contraction. One might shift to a corpus containing $\underline{T}$ via a replacement. However, if the inquiring agent is concerned to avoid error, he should not deliberately replace a claim (~$\underline{T}$), which in his view is certainly true, with another claim ($\underline{T}$) he takes to be certainly false. To replace one claim with another is to do violence to the concern to avoid error.

Contracting the initial doctrine by removing ~$\underline{T}$, so that the inquirer comes to be in suspense as to the truth of $\underline{T}$, avoids this difficulty. From the point of view prior to contraction, no error can be injected by contraction. To import error, information needs to be added. But in contraction, information is never added. To the contrary, it is removed.

Of course, this raises a new difficulty for the inquirer interested in new error-free information. There must be some inducement to incur the loss of information and, perhaps, of valuable information entailed by contraction. Roughly speaking, I suggest that the inducement is the possibility of obtaining valuable information through subsequent inquiry that compensates for the information lost. This suggestion will be explained later on in this chapter. For present purposes, it is sufficient to note that uncoerced contraction to give a potential explanation of an anomaly a hearing not only avoids begging the question *against* the initially settled assumption ~$\underline{T}$ but avoids begging the question *in its favor.* The adjudication of the merits of the old theory and the new proposal may be undertaken from a "neutral" perspective. It is the desirability of regarding this as a condition on legitimate change in belief state that is the ultimate motivation for advocating the requirement of commensuration.

In addressing the topic of justifying contraction, three problems must be examined. One of these problems concerns both coerced and uncoerced contraction, whereas the other two are relevant to only one of these kinds of contraction.

A. *Whether to Contract:* In the case of coerced contraction, there is no question that some form of contraction is required. In the case of uncoerced contraction, however, one needs to justify contracting the corpus to give an erstwhile impossibility a hearing.

B. *What to Remove:* In the context of uncoerced contraction, one is given a hypothesis $\underline{T}$ that is incompatible with the current corpus $\underline{K}$. If one is to contract at all [that is the question addressed under (A)], one must contract by removing ~$\underline{T}$ from $\underline{K}$.

In the context of coerced contraction, however, the situation is more complicated. The corpus is $\underline{o}$, and the inquirer reached it by adding some claim $\underline{A}$ via routine expansion when the corpus $\underline{K}$ prior to routine expansion contained $\sim\underline{A}$. Because $\underline{o} = \underline{L}$, there is a problem in specifying which sentence ought to be removed in contraction. For every sentence $\underline{C}$ in $\underline{L}$ $\underline{C}\&\sim\underline{C}$ must be removed. And this means that for every sentence, either $\underline{C}$ or $\sim\underline{C}$ must be removed.

The issue can be simplified somewhat by considering the fact that the inconsistency was injected by adding $\underline{A}$ to $\underline{K}$. Presystematically, we would consider questioning the results of expansion via routine (i.e., by observation, experiment, or the testimony of others) and, hence, by removing $\underline{A}$ or by questioning the background information and, hence, by questioning $\sim\underline{A}$ or conceivably by questioning both.

Questioning the results of expansion via routine alone may be due to doubts as to whether the program for routine expansion was properly implemented or whether the program was reliable after all. The first alternative may be represented as a contraction from $\underline{o}$ to $\underline{K}$.

Questioning the reliability of the program may be represented as a contraction $\underline{K}_1$ of $\underline{o}$ constructed as follows:

i. Contract $\underline{K}$ by removing the assumption that the given routine for expansion is reliable according to the chance distribution given.

ii. Expand the result of the contraction given in (i) by adding the information that the program for the routine was started and a report that, according to the routine, requires adding $\underline{A}$ was made.

iii. Do not expand by adding $\underline{A}$.

Questioning the background information can be viewed as a contraction $\underline{K}_2$ of $\underline{o}$. It is obtained as follows:

i'. Contract $\underline{K}$ by removing $\sim\underline{A}$.

ii'. Expand the result of the contraction given in (i') by adding the information that the program for the routine was started and a report that, according to the routine, requires adding $\underline{A}$ was made.

iii'. Expand the result of (ii') by adding $\underline{A}$.

To question both the background and the results of expansion is to contract from $\underline{o}$ to the intersection of $\underline{K}_1$ and $\underline{K}_2$.

This issue does not arise in connection with uncoerced contraction, as we have seen.

C. *How to Contract:* In the case of coerced contraction, it is an open question what is to be removed, even though it is clear that some contraction is required. There is another question, however. If one is going to contract by shifting to $\underline{K}_1$ through removing the assumption of the reliability of the routine from $\underline{K}$, or by shifting to $\underline{K}_2$ through removing $\sim\underline{A}$ from $\underline{K}$, the contraction from $\underline{o}$ is characterized by considering a contraction of $\underline{K}$ by removing some specific sentence. But there is no unique way to undertake such a contraction from a consistent corpus $\underline{K}$. So we must choose between contraction strategies that remove the given assumption.

In uncoerced contraction, where there is no doubt that $\sim\underline{A}$ is to be removed if contraction is justified at all, the same problem of choosing between contraction strategies arises.

Thus, the problem of how to contract is common to both coerced and uncoerced contraction.

Gärdenfors and those who have participated in the discussion of contraction along the lines he has developed have focused on question (C), which concerns how to contract given that one is going to remove a specific sentence. But just as Gärdenfors and his colleagues neglect the distinction between routine and deliberate expansion, they overlook the distinction between uncoerced and coerced contraction and, with it, the problem of whether to contract facing uncoerced contraction and the problem of what to remove facing coerced contraction.

In Sections 4.2–4.6, I discuss the question of how to contract from $\underline{K}$ by removing $\underline{A}$. In Section 4.8, I consider coerced contraction and the topic of what to remove and, in Section 4.9, uncoerced contraction and the topic of whether to contract.

4.2 How to contract: The available strategies

There is no parallel to the problem of how to contract arising in connection with expansion of a belief state K by adding a doxastic proposition A or with expansion of a corpus $\underline{K}$ by adding a sentence $\underline{A}$. We need to address the questions of whether to expand and, if so, what to add, just as questions of whether to contract and what to remove may prove relevant in contraction. But there is no issue concerning how to expand. *The* expansion of K by adding A is $K \wedge A$, and the expansion $\underline{K}_{\underline{A}}^{+}$ of $\underline{K}$ by adding $\underline{A}$ is the deductive closure of $\underline{K} \cup \underline{A}$. There is no problem of choosing among alternative strategies for adding $\underline{A}$ to $\underline{K}$. In deliberate expansion, there is a question as to what sentence is to be added to $\underline{K}$ or whether expansion should be undertaken at all. Whether to implement a program for routine expansion may be a question for deliberation; but once that decision is made, whether $\underline{A}$ is added is the result of implementing the routine and not a matter for deliberate choice. Once it is settled, either deliberately or by routine, that $\underline{A}$ is to be added to $\underline{A}$, there is no further issue concerning how to expand. That is because the expansion of $\underline{K}$ has been characterized as the closure of $\underline{K}$ and $\underline{A}$.

If $\underline{K}_2$ is an expansion of $\underline{K}_1$, $\underline{K}_1$ is a contraction of $\underline{K}_2$. Suppose that $\underline{K}_2 = (\underline{K}_1)_{\underline{A}}^{+}$. $\underline{K}_2$ is uniquely determined by $\underline{K}$ and $\underline{A}$. And, as just noted, $\underline{K}_1$ is a contraction of $\underline{K}_2$. Furthermore, it is a contraction of $\underline{K}_2$ by removing $\underline{A}$. However, $\underline{K}_1$ is not uniquely determined as *the* contraction of $\underline{K}_2$ by removing $\underline{A}$.

Example: Suppose that $\underline{K}_1$ = the closure of $(\underline{A} \supset \underline{B})$. $\underline{K}_2$ = the closure of $\{\underline{A} \supset \underline{B}, \underline{A}\}$ = the closure of $\{\underline{A}, \underline{B}\}$. $\underline{A}$ is logically equivalent to $(\underline{B} \supset \underline{A}) \& (\sim\underline{B} \supset \underline{A})$, and $\underline{B}$ is logically equivalent to $(\underline{A} \supset \underline{B}) \& (\sim\underline{A} \supset \underline{B})$. $\underline{K}_2$ is the closure, therefore, of the three material conditionals ingredient in the two conjunctions. (I am taking the logically equivalent conditionals $\sim\underline{B} \supset \underline{A}$ and $\sim\underline{A} \supset \underline{B}$ to be the same.) Removing $\underline{A}$ from $\underline{K}_2$ entails removing $\underline{B} \supset \underline{A}$, or $\sim\underline{B} \supset \underline{A}$. In addition, one can remove $\underline{A}$ by removing both material conditionals. Moreover, regardless of whether one removes exactly one of the conditionals or both, one is free to remove $\underline{A} \supset \underline{B}$ as well. Hence, as long as we focus on sentences in $\underline{L}$ that are truth functional compounds of $\underline{A}$ and $\underline{B}$, there are six possible contraction strategies removing $\underline{A}$ from $\underline{K}_2$ that yield distinct contractions. The one recommending the removal of both $\underline{B} \supset \underline{A}$ and $\sim\underline{B} \supset \underline{A}$ but retaining $\underline{A} \supset \underline{B}$ results in $\underline{K}_1$.

Thus, the inquirer needs to determine which of the six contractions removing $\underline{A}$ to implement even if she has already concluded that she should remove $\underline{A}$. The problem of how to contract once it is settled that $\underline{A}$ is to be removed from $\underline{K}$ should be considered a decision problem in its own right. We need to identify the available options or strategies for contraction by removing $\underline{A}$ and then examine the goals and values that ought to be promoted in order to decide among them. In this section, I discuss the available options. In Sections 4.3 and 4.4, I consider alternative views of what the goals and values might be, and in Section 4.5 I indicate some of the important implications of our discussion.

Let $C(\underline{K},\underline{A})$ be the set of contractions of $\underline{K}$ by removing $\underline{A}$. Among these contractions are all *saturatable* contractions. A contraction of $\underline{K}$ by removing $\underline{A}$ is saturatable if and only if the result of adding $\sim\underline{A}$ to this contraction is maximally consistent in $\underline{L}$. $S(\underline{K},\underline{A})$ is the set of all saturatable contractions of $\underline{K}$ by removing $\underline{A}$.[1]

As long as we restrict attention to a language containing truth functional compounds of $\underline{A}$ and $\underline{B}$, the saturatable contractions of $\underline{K}_2$ by removing $\underline{A}$ are as follows:

1. The consequences of $\{\underline{B} \supset \underline{A}, \underline{A} \supset \underline{B}\}$. $\sim\underline{B} \supset \underline{A}$ is removed from $\underline{K}_2$.
2. The consequences of $\{\sim\underline{B} \supset \underline{A}, \underline{A} \supset \underline{B}\}$. $\underline{B} \supset \underline{A}$ is removed from $\underline{K}_2$.
3. The consequences of (1) once $\underline{A} \supset \underline{B}$ is removed.
4. The consequences of (2) once $\underline{A} \supset \underline{B}$ is removed.

The two nonsaturatable contractions are (5) = the meet of options 1 and 2 (which is $\underline{K}_1$ of example 1) and (6) = the meet of options 3 and 4 (which is $\underline{1}$ in the language $\underline{L}$ restricted to truth functional compounds of $\underline{A}$ and $\underline{B}$).

Of course, with a richer language $\underline{L}$, the set of potential contractions of $\underline{K}_2$ by removing $\underline{A}$ is larger still, as is the set of saturatable contractions. Thus, the inquirer would have to decide whether to remove $\underline{C} \supset \underline{A}$ or $\sim\underline{C} \supset \underline{A}$ given that she has to remove $\underline{A}$. In a saturatable contraction, she must remove one and only one of these. If the saturatable contraction also calls for removal of $\underline{B}$ (as option 1 does), the inquirer will also have to decide whether to remove $\subseteq \supset \underline{B}$ or $\sim\subseteq \supset \underline{B}$ or both. No matter which of these alternatives is adopted, the contraction remains saturatable.

Although some contractions by removing $\underline{A}$ from the initial corpus are nonsaturatable, all contractions $C(\underline{K},\underline{A})$ of $\underline{K}$ by removing $\underline{A}$ are meets of subsets of $S(\underline{K},\underline{A})$. Hence, we may abstractly characterize the class of all contractions of $\underline{K}$ by removing $\underline{A}$ as meets of sets of saturatable contractions that remove $\underline{A}$.

Hence, if we are to determine how to contract, we need to determine the subset of saturatable contractions whose meet is to be contracted.

Keep in mind that in removing $\underline{A}$ from the initial corpus $\underline{K}$, a loss of information will be incurred (if $\underline{A}$ is in $\underline{K}$). Given this constraint, the inquirer should be concerned to keep the loss of informational value incurred to a minimum. At least, this should be so as long as the inquirer's goal is to avoid error and obtain valuable information. Consequently, the inquiring agent should evaluate the various contraction strategies available to her with respect to the loss of informational value incurred and should choose a contraction strategy that minimizes the loss of informational value if a minimizing strategy exists.[2]

Consequently, an identification of admissible contraction strategies removing a given sentence $\underline{A}$ requires consideration of how the available contraction strategies are to be evaluated with respect to loss of informational value. This is the topic to which I now turn.

4.3 How to contract: Probability-based informational value

In Chapter 3, the proximate aim of expansion was taken to be the acquisition of error-free informational value, and this was understood to entail a compromise between two desiderata: avoidance of error and informational value. Each of the two desiderata was represented by an epistemic utility function, and the utility function representing the quest for error-free information was taken to be a weighted average of these.

We are now focused on the problem of choosing among the available contraction strategies in $C(\underline{K},\underline{A})$ involving the removal of $\underline{A}$ from the corpus $\underline{K}$. The idea we are exploring is that in choosing a contraction strategy from this set, we should minimize the loss of informational value incurred.

Informational value, in general, was understood to be constrained by the weak monotonicity condition formulated in Section 3.2. In the setting of expansion, assessments of informational value were also taken to be probability based relative to an ultimate partition, an information-determining probability measure M, and K. The information-determining probability M relative to K used to represent informational value should be distinguished from an expectation-determining probability measure representing the agent's credal probability judgment or some standard confirmation measure of the sort examined by authors like Carnap or Jeffreys (Levi, 1980a, p. 48; 1984, ch. 5). Given the set of potential expansions generated by the ultimate partition, each of them is assigned an M - value and the informational value was represented by a content measure $cont(\underline{A}) = 1 - M(\underline{A}$.

This content measure does not define the informational value of potential expansions obtained by adding a sentence $\underline{B}$ that is not equivalent given $\underline{K}$ to a sentence asserting that some element of a subset of the members of the ultimate partition is true. According to the account given in Section 3.2, the informational value of such an expansion is equal to the informational value of the strongest sentence entailed by $\underline{B}$ given $\underline{K}$ asserting that some element of a subset of the members of the ultimate partition is true. Thus, even in the context of expansion, assessments of informational value are not fully probability based, but only relative to the given ultimate partition. This, I contend, is as it should be given the familiar fact that, when seeking to answer a question, not all new information is relevant to the question being asked. This is, perhaps, the chief of several reasons why measures of informational value ought to be carefully distinguished from measures of information.

We are assuming that in choosing among contraction strategies in $C(\underline{K},\underline{A})$, the inquirer should minimize loss of informational value. The question that needs to be addressed in the context of determining how to contract from $\underline{K}$ by removing $\underline{A}$ is to what extent may losses of informational value that are to be minimized be evaluated in terms of a probability-based measure of informational value.

In order to explore this question, let us begin by supposing that we are given an information-determining measure M defined over all doxastic propositions in the conceptual framework or over all sentences in $\underline{L}$ that represent such doxastic propositions. In this way, the doxastic proposition $\mathbf{K}$ or the corpus $\underline{K}$ may be assigned a content value, as will all potential contractions of $\underline{K}$ by removing $\underline{A}$. Losses in informational value incurred by adopting various elements of $C(\underline{K},\underline{A})$ can be assessed by taking the differences between the content of $\underline{K}$ and the contents of the several contractions.

This suggestion, however, stands in need of qualification. Just as in expansion some increments of information carry no value, so too it is to be expected that in contraction some losses carry no value. We have just noted, in the case of expansion, the possibility that adding $\underline{A\&B}$ to $\underline{K}$ fails to yield more informational value than just adding $\underline{A}$ to $\underline{K}$, and that the same is true for adding $\underline{A\&\sim B}$ to $\underline{K}$. The information concerning the truth value of $\underline{B}$ may be of no interest or relevance to the inquiry. By the same token, contraction from $\underline{K}^{+}_{A\&B}$ (and from $\underline{K}^{+}_{A\&\sim B}$) to $\underline{K}^{+}_{A}$ may incur no loss of informational value. In that case, as far as informational value is concerned, it will not matter to the inquirer whose corpus is $\underline{K}^{+}_{A\&B}$ and who is going to give up $\underline{A}$ whether he also gives up $\underline{B}$.

To take this into account, we may introduce a *basic partition* consisting of a set of doxastic propositions exclusive and exhaustive relative to the minimal belief state $\mathbf{1}$, or a system of sentential representations of these doxastic propositions, and consider all boolean combinations of these doxastic propositions. The M function will be defined over the elements of the basic partition and all boolean combinations. The M value of any other doxastic proposition will be equal to the M value assigned the strongest doxastic proposition in the algebra generated by the basic partition that the given doxastic proposition entails.

The idea of a basic partition may be used not only in the context of contraction but in the context of expansion as well. If the inquiring agent were concerned to expand his corpus $\underline{K}$ relative to a given basic partition, he would rule out as impossible those elements of the basic partition that are inconsistent with $\underline{K}$. The truncated basic partition would then correspond to the ultimate partition. The M function relative to the ultimate partition would be the M function relative to the basic partition normalized over elements of the ultimate partition (or, in other words, the conditional M function given that an element of the ultimate partition is true).

The advantage of using the basic partition for both contractions and expansions arises in those cases where, in ongoing inquiry, the inquirer's demands for information remain fairly stable (which need not always be the case) and where a series of changes through contraction and expansion are made. When expansions are examined in isolation, use of the ultimate partition to represent demands for information remains more convenient. But when the focus is on contractions, the basic partition is required.

Although I take the position, both with respect to expansion and with respect to contraction, that demands for information are relative to a basic partition that need not coincide with the set of maximally consistent corpora expressible in $\underline{L}$, in the discussion that follows, those who wish to think of the basic partition in this way may do so without altering the main conclusions.

Given the qualification relativizing the probability-based evaluations of informational value to a basic partition, the core of the probability-based index of informational value and of losses of informational value remains in place. The question before us is whether, given this qualification, probability-based measures of informational value are suitable for use when assessing rival contractions of a corpus by giving up $\underline{A}$ with respect to losses of informational value. I argue that they are not.

To make the case, an examination of the implications of probability-based evaluations of losses of informational value is undertaken. Although, in the context of expansion, I deploy probability-based measures that are content measures, in this section very little depends on the use of content measures and similar results obtain if one uses any measure according to which informational value varies inversely with the M value.

Given a corpus $\underline{K}$ that bears a given M value, we assume that any contraction of $\underline{K}$ that removes $\underline{A}$ from $\underline{K}$ incurs a positive loss of informational value. We also suppose that a contraction yielding a minimum loss exists, although, in principle, there need not be such a contraction. The question before us is what sort of contraction will yield a minimum loss.

Recall the definition of a saturatable contraction by removing $\underline{A}$ from $\underline{K}$. Such a contraction is saturatable if and only if the result of adding $\sim\underline{A}$ to the contracted corpus is maximally consistent in $\underline{L}$. This means that for every sentence $\underline{B}$ in $\underline{L}$, either $\sim\underline{A} \supset \underline{B}$ or $\sim\underline{A} \supset \sim\underline{B}$ is in the saturatable contraction, so that when the contraction is expanded by adding $\sim\underline{A}$, either $\underline{B}$ or $\sim\underline{B}$ will be added as well. (The result will be consistent because, by hypothesis, at most one of these truth functional conditionals is in the saturatable contraction.)

Consider, then, any nonsaturatable contraction removing $\underline{A}$ from $\underline{K}$. It is nonsaturatable because, for some sentence $\underline{B}$, neither $\sim\underline{A} \supset \underline{B}$ nor $\sim\underline{A} \supset \bar{\underline{B}}$ is in the contraction. It must, therefore, be weaker than a saturatable contraction obtained from it by adding, for each such $\underline{B}$, one of these truth functional conditionals and forming the deductive closure. Hence, by the weak monotonicity condition, for every nonsaturatable contraction, there is at least one saturatable contraction that carries at least as much informational value as it does.

If the index of informational value is probability based, we may make a stronger statement: If the doxastic proposition $\mathbf{A}$ represented by sentence $\underline{A}$ is a boolean combination of elements of the basic partition (for doxastic propositions), for every nonsaturatable contraction, there is at least one saturatable contraction that carries more informational value than it does.[3]

From this consideration, we may conclude that (1) if informational value is probability based and (2) removing $\underline{A}$ incurs a positive loss of informational value no matter which contraction from $\underline{K}$ doing so is adopted, minimizing loss of informational value requires choosing a saturatable contraction.

We may go one step further. Saturatable contractions come in two varieties. There are some that meet the condition that if $\underline{B}$ is in $\underline{K}$, so that not only $\sim\underline{A} \supset \underline{B}$ and $\sim\underline{A} \supset \sim\underline{B}$ but also $\sim\underline{B} \supset \sim\underline{A}$ is in $\underline{K}$, $\sim\underline{B} \supset \sim\underline{A}$ remains in the saturatable contraction. There are others that fail this condition for some $\underline{B}$ in $\underline{K}$.

Contractions that pass this test are what Gärdenfors calls *maxichoice* contractions by removing $\underline{A}$ from $\underline{K}$. A maxichoice contraction removing extralogical $\underline{A}$ from $\underline{K}$ is a saturatable contraction that, for every $\underline{B}$ that is in $\underline{K}$ but not in the contraction, contains $\underline{B} \supset \underline{A}$.[4]

It is clear that for every saturatable but non-maxichoice contraction, there is a stronger maxichoice contraction removing $\underline{A}$ from $\underline{K}$. But weak monotonicity does not require the stronger maxichoice contraction to carry greater informational value. If $\sim(\underline{A} \supset \underline{B})$ carries positive M value, we could argue that maxichoice contractions carry more informational value than the weaker saturatable contractions. But even when we assume that all contractions removing $\underline{A}$ incur a loss of informational value, we are not driven to such an assumption. Of course, if it does hold, the best contractions must be maxichoice contractions. Still, using probability-based measures does not require the choice of maxichoice contractions under all circumstances. However, it does require the use of a saturatable contraction as long as every contraction, by removing $\underline{A}$, incurs a loss of informational value.

Nonetheless, contractions removing $\underline{A}$ from $\underline{K}$ that minimize loss of informational value must include at least one maxichoice contraction even though other saturatable contractions may minimize loss of informational value as well. The question arises as to which contraction to adopt when two or more contractions minimize loss of informational value. I suggest that we should invoke the principle that the weakest of these contractions should be adopted. The suggestion is motivated by the idea that when there are several optimal contraction strategies, the inquiring agent should be in doubt as to which to implement. But to be in such doubt is, in effect, to shift to the corpus that is the intersection of optimal contraction strategies.

This idea works well when there is a weakest contraction strategy minimizing loss of informational value; for, in that case, the weakest contraction must be an intersection of the other optimal contraction strategies. However, it is possible for two or more saturatable contractions to be optimal even though their meet is nonsaturatable and, hence, suboptimal. Thus, the maxichoice contraction removing (1) and the maxichoice contraction removing (2) could both minimize loss of informational value, but the intersection of the corpora resulting will not only fail to be maxichoice but will fail to be saturatable as well. Hence removing both (1) and (2) cannot minimize loss of informational value.

Should we give up the procedure for breaking ties by urging suspension of judgment in favor of choosing one of the saturatable contractions by some extra criterion? Or should we say that all the optimal saturatable contractions are admissible to use? Neither of these suggestions can be satisfactory. As Alchourròn and Makinson (1982) have observed, if inquirers were obliged to choose a maxichoice contraction, then if, in subsequent inquiry, $\sim\!\underline{A}$ is added, the result is a maximally consistent corpus. The inquiring agent is in a position to come to a complete view on every issue expressible in $\underline{L}$ by contracting and then replacing what is removed by its negation. The same is, of course, true of saturatable contractions that are not maxichoice. This result is clearly unacceptable. Thus, any result suggesting the mandatory choice of a saturatable contraction should be rejected.

Alchourròn, Gärdenfors, and Makinson (1985) argue that the meet or intersection of optimal maxichoice contractions should be adopted. I think that the meet of optimal saturatable contractions is to be recommended. The significance of the difference between these views will be explained later. What is clear, however, is that neither recommendation can be endorsed as long as informational value is probability based and as long as the recommendation is to minimize loss of informational value.

This result suggests that when contractions of $\underline{K}$ by removing $\underline{A}$ are evaluated with respect to the losses of informational value incurred with an eye to minimizing that loss, evaluations of such losses cannot be probability based. In Section 4.4, I argue for an alternative structure to impose on assessments of losses of informational value that will avoid the difficulties confronting the use of probability-based evaluations of losses of informational value.

4.4 How to contract: Damped informational value

The set of all potential contractions of $\underline{K}$ by removing $\underline{A}$ is identifiable by beginning with the set $S(\underline{K},\underline{A})$ of saturatable contractions of $\underline{K}$ removing $\underline{A}$ and considering all contractions obtainable by taking the meet of any subset of $S(\underline{K},\underline{A})$. We may suppose, as we did in Section 4.3, that relative to the basic partition, each saturatable contraction in $S(\underline{K},\underline{A})$ is assigned an M value and an informational value that decreases with an increase in M value. This informational value is what I have called *probability-based* informational value.

The initial corpus $\underline{K}$ also has an M value that, by hypothesis, we have assumed to be strictly less than the M value of any element of $S(\underline{K},\underline{A})$, so that every saturatable contraction of $\underline{K}$ by removing $\underline{A}$ incurs a positive loss in (probability-based) informational value.

Consider, then, any meet of saturatable contractions in a subset S^* of $S(\underline{K},\underline{A})$. Sometimes there will be saturatable contractions $\underline{K}'$ and $\underline{K}''$ in S^* such that $\underline{K}'$ is a subset of $\underline{K}''$. In that case, the meet of $\underline{K}'$ and $\underline{K}''$ will be identical to $\underline{K}'$. A saturatable contraction in S^* is *minimal* in S^* if and only if there is no element of S^* that is a proper subset of it. The meet of the elements of S^* is identical to the meet of the minimal elements of S^*. The M value of this meet will be the sum of the M values assigned the minimal saturatable contractions.

Since removing $\underline{A}$ from $\underline{K}$ incurs a positive loss of probability-based informational value, every saturatable contraction in $S(\underline{K},\underline{A})$ must do so. Hence, every such contraction must carry positive M value. If any carried o M value, its informational value would be at least as great as that of $\underline{K}$.

But the sum of positive M values must be greater than any of the summands. Hence, the probability-based informational value of any contraction in $S(\underline{K},\underline{A})$ that is the meet of two or more minimal saturatable contractions must be less than the probability-based informational value of any of the constituent minimal saturatable contractions.

It is this additive feature of probability-based assessments of informational value that yields the result that admissible contractions must be saturatable and the untoward result that adding $\sim\underline{A}$ to the contracted corpus expands to a maximally consistent set. To avoid this result, we need some way of taking the meet of two minimal saturatable contractions carrying equal informational value and saying that it takes the same informational value as the two components. Such an assessment of informational value will not be probability based. As is already apparent, I do not propose that it be used for assessing informational value in all contexts, but only for evaluating losses incurred in deciding how to contract.

Clearly, such an evaluation cannot be probability based in the sense that informational value increases with a decrease in the value of a probability measure M. Nonetheless, it can be generated by such a measure. Given a measure M defined relative to the basic partition, we obtain an index of *damped informational value* meeting the following conditions:

1. The damped informational value of $\underline{K}$ is its probability-based informational value.

2. The damped informational value of any saturatable contraction in $S(\underline{K},\underline{A})$ is its probability-based informational value.

3. The damped informational value of the meet of a set of saturatable contractions where each minimal saturatable contraction in the set has the same M value, and, hence, the same informational and damped informational value, is equal to that common (damped) informational value.

These three conditions do not fully characterize the structural properties of damped informational value.

Damped informational value, like probability-based informational value, should be subject to the weak monotonicity condition. From this it follows that a contraction that is the meet of a set of saturatable contractions cannot carry more damped informational value than the minimally saturatable contraction in the set carrying least damped informational value if there are only finitely many minimally saturatable contractions in the set or the greatest lower bound of the probability based informational values of the minimally saturatable contractions in the set.

The weak monotonicity condition applies only to comparisons of informational value where one corpus is a subset of another. However, we are supposing that the partial ordering with respect to set inclusion can be extended to a weak ordering over the elements of $C(\underline{K},\underline{A})$ by means of the M function and the probability-based measure of informational value derived thereby. This weak ordering, however, is unsatisfactory for reasons I have already explained. Nonetheless, it is plausible to require that the assessments of damped informational value cohere with assessments of probability-based informational value to the extent that if one contraction carries less probability-based informational value than another, it should not carry more damped informational value. Call this the *weak probabilistic monotonicity condition.*

This condition strengthens the weak monotonicity condition but does not require that assessments of damped informational value coincide with assessments of probability-based informational value.

Let $\underline{K}^*$ and $\underline{K}^{**}$ be saturatable contractions of $\underline{K}$ carrying equal informational value. Let $\underline{K}^{***}$ be a third saturatable contraction carrying more informational value than $\underline{K}^{**}$. All three saturatable contractions are minimal in the set of three and, hence, in any pair.

By condition 3, $\underline{K}_1$, which is the meet of $\underline{K}^*$ and $\underline{K}^{**}$, carries the same damped informational value as $\underline{K}^*$. By the weak monotonicity condition, $\underline{K}_2$, which is the meet of $\underline{K}^*$ and $\underline{K}^{***}$, carries no more damped informational value than $\underline{K}^*$. $\underline{K}_2$ carries lower M value and, hence, higher (undamped) informational value than $\underline{K}_1$. By the weak probabilistic monotonicity condition, it carries no less damped informational value than $\underline{K}_1$ – which is equal to the damped informational value of $\underline{K}^*$. Hence, the damped informational value of $\underline{K}_2$ must also equal that of $\underline{K}^*$.

Thus, given conditions 1–3, the weak monotonicity condition, and the weak probabilistic monotonicity condition, we can argue that the damped informational value of a potential contraction in $S(\underline{K},\underline{A})$ is the least damped informational value assigned a minimal saturatable contraction in the set of saturatable contractions whose meet is that contraction or the greatest lower bound of the damped informational values assigned such minimal saturatable contractions in case there is no minimum.[5] Hence, the loss of (damped) informational value incurred is equal to the maximum loss incurred by a minimal saturatable contraction in the set generating the meet or the least upper bound of such losses. Since the weak monotonicity condition is implied by the weak probabilistic monotonicity condition, this result is obtained from conditions 1–3 and the weak probabilistic monotonicity condition.

Given an information-determining probability function M defined relative to a basic partition and the probability-based assessment of informational value obtained thereby, an assessment of damped informational value of potential contractions in $C(\underline{K},\underline{A})$ is obtained by taking the damped informational value of $\underline{K}$ and all satiatable contractions to be equal to their probability-based values and taking the damped informational value of the meet of a set of satiatable contractions to be equal to the minimum (greatest lower bound) of the damped informational values assigned satiatable contractions in the set.

Assuming that the decision maker concerned to remove $\underline{A}$ from $\underline{K}$ aims to minimize loss of damped informational value, any contraction strategy in $C(\underline{K}, \underline{A})$ that minimizes loss of informational value is optimal. In general, there will be many optimal contraction strategies. These will include all satiatable contractions that carry maximum damped and, hence, probability-based informational value among the satiatable contractions, as well as meets of all subsets of the set of optimal satiatable contractions.

In Levi (1980), I suggested that ties in optimality in such cases should be broken by choosing the weakest contraction that is optimal. This has been the approach of Gärdenfors and his colleagues as well. But unlike them, I insist that in breaking ties, the recommended option should be optimal. If the assessment of damped informational value is the one that determines the "epistemic utilities" of the agent in this case, the rule for ties does recommend an optimal option as a tie breaker. If probability-based informational value is used, it does not.

Assuming that damped informational value is to be minimized, the contraction strategy that is uniquely admissible may be defined as follows:

$\underline{K}_{\underline{A}}^{-}$(the admissible contraction of $\underline{K}$ by removing $\underline{A}$) is the meet of all saturatable contractions of $\underline{K}$ removing $\underline{A}$ that minimize loss of informational value among saturatable contractions as determined by the given M function.

In contrast to the approach favored by Gärdenfors, Makinson, and others, an admissible contraction will not necessarily be the meet of maxichoice contractions. The reason may be explained as follows: Every saturatable contraction is a subset of exactly one maxichoice contraction. Consider, then, a saturatable contraction $\underline{K}^*$ that is not maxichoice and let $\underline{K}^{**}$ be the maxichoice contraction that contains it. Nothing in what we have said precludes $M(\underline{K}^{**})$ from being equal to rather than less than $M(\underline{K}^*)$. Neither the requirements of the probability calculus, the weak probabilistic monotonicity condition, nor the monotonicity condition do so.

One might wish to require that equality be precluded. But if one did this, that would be tantamount to specifying a strong monotonicity condition for evaluations of saturatable contractions with respect to both probability-based and damped informational value. Such a strong monotonicity condition would imply that if one saturatable contraction is contained in another, the second should carry more probability-based and more damped informational value than the first.

Observe, however, that if the strong monotonicity condition is in place for saturatable contractions and we use a probability-based assessment of informational value or losses of informational value for all elements of $C(\underline{K},\underline{A})$, the strong monotonicity condition must be satisfied for all such assessments. From this it follows that all admissible contractions must be maxichoice. This is a consequence that Gärdenfors and others do not want to endorse. We can avoid this implication by appealing to assessments of damped informational value. In that case, strong monotonicity can be restricted to elements of $S(\underline{K},\underline{A})$.

Gärdenfors (1988, p. 71) and Makinson (1987, pp. 383–94) both defend their restriction of admissible options to subsets of maxichoice contractions on the grounds that these are the strongest saturatable contractions. They are assuming that informational value increases with an increase of strength or information as the strong monotonicity condition requires. If this argument were cogent, then it would argue for using maxichoice contractions that they consider (and rightly so) to be objectionable. To be consistent, they must qualify this appeal to strong monotonicity by restricting its scope of applicability to saturatable contractions. But this means that they must explain why an increase in strength justifies assigning greater informational value when comparing saturatable contractions but not when comparing contractions that are not necessarily saturatable. Appeals to comparisons of strength without invoking other considerations will not do.

This point does not establish that the views of Alchourròn, Gärdenfors, and Makinson are untenable or inconsistent, but only that the arguments advanced by these authors and others for restricting admissible contractions to meets of maxichoice contractions are unconvincing.

What they need to defend is the strong monotonicity condition restricted to saturatable contractions as constraints on assessments of damped informational value. I contend, on the other hand, that this condition is untenable. It is tempting to complain about the ad hoc character of this suggestion. But a more profitable way to proceed is to explore the ramifications of the restrictions favored by Gärdenfors, Makinson, and others as compared to the more permissive view I favor. Gärdenfors and Makinson have indeed investigated some of the important ramifications. In my judgment, their results ought to have led them to abandon the restriction of admissible contractions to meets of maxichoice contractions. In Section 4.5, I explain why.

4.5 How to contract: The Recovery Postulate

The damped informational value of a contraction in $C(\underline{K},\underline{A})$ is the minimum probability-based informational value assigned a saturatable contraction belonging to the meet of a saturatable contraction identical to the given contraction. Assessments of damped informational value are characterized by the following conditions:

1. The damped informational value of $\underline{K}$ is its probability-based informational value $Cont(\underline{K})$.

2. The damped informational value of any element in $S(\underline{K},\underline{A})$ is its probability-based informational value.

3. If two or more saturatable contractions in $S(\underline{K},\underline{A})$ carry equal M value and, hence, equal probability-based informational value, their meet carries that common value as its damped informational value.

4. If one element of $C(\underline{K},\underline{A})$ carries less probability-based informational value than another, it should not carry more damped informational value (weak probabilistic monotonicity).

Weak probabilistic monotonicity implies, of course, weak monotonicity.

As we noted in Section 4.4, when we seek to minimize damped informational value using the rule for ties, the recommended contraction will be the meet of the set of saturatable contractions carrying minimum M value and, hence, maximum probability-based informational value. Suppose that we supplement conditions 1–4 by the strong monotonicity condition restricted to satiatable contractions. Optimal contraction strategies in $C(\underline{K},\underline{A})$ will be meets of subsets of optimal maxichoice contractions. The rule for ties implies that the uniquely admissible contraction $\underline{K}_{\underline{A}}^{-}$ is the meet of all optimal maxichoice contraction strategies removing $\underline{A}$ from $\underline{K}$.

Although I assume that the damped informational values of satiatable contractions are probability based, I do not impose the restricted version of strong monotonicity on them but only the weak probabilistic monotonicity condition. As a consequence, on my view $\underline{K}_{\underline{A}}^-$ is the meet of all optimal satiatable contractions where a satiatable contraction can be optimal even if it is not maxichoice and the meet of all optimal satiatable contractions can be contained as a proper subset of the meet of all optimal maxichoice contractions.

Thus, whether admissible contractions must be meets of maxichoice contractions or not pivots on whether the strong monotonicity condition restricted to satiatable contractions is acceptable.

Gärdenfors has proposed a set of conditions on what he calls *contraction functions*. These conditions imply that an admissible contraction should be the meet of a subset of the maxichoice contractions. Hence, informational value should be damped informational value satisfying the strong monotonicity condition. By reviewing these conditions, we may obtain another perspective from which to appreciate my disagreement with the approaches of Alchourròn, Gärdenfors, Makinson, and others.

For given $\underline{K}$ and $\underline{A}$, the value of a contraction function is what I take to be an admissible contraction. The conditions on contraction functions represent for Gärdenfors (1988, p. 61) "rationality postulates" that are motivated by what he takes to be considerations of "informational economy." The idea is that in contraction, the result should change the information carried in the contracted corpus as little as possible from what it was.

In a sense, this way of looking at the matter could be viewed as suggesting that the informational value lost by contraction should be as little as possible. We have seen, however, that there are many ways to construe loss in informational value: (1) as loss in information (so that the strong monotonicity condition is satisfied), (2) as loss in probability-based informational value, and (3) as loss in damped informational value. I have sought to identify what some of these construals are. Gärdenfors's appeal to informational economy does not explicitly appeal to questions of losses of informational value. Instead, one is supposed to intuit somehow that considerations of informational economy support these conditions. Let us see what the conditions are:

(K_1^-)   For any $\underline{A}$ and any $\underline{K}$, $\underline{K}_{\underline{A}}^-$ is a corpus – that is, a deductively closed set of sentences in $\underline{L}$.

($\underline{K}_2^-$) $\underline{K}_{\underline{A}}^-$ is a subset of $\underline{K}$.

Gärdenfors does not appeal to informational economy to sustain these two postulates but takes them to be definitional of contraction as giving up some assumption and moving to another state of full belief representable by a corpus.

He does appeal to informational economy to support the next postulate:

(K_3^-)   If $\underline{A}$ is not a member of $\underline{K}$, then $\underline{K}_{\underline{A}}^- = \underline{K}$.

Considerations of informational economy are not germane to the defense of this postulate. A contraction of $\underline{K}$ by giving up $\underline{A}$ is intended to be the result of giving up $\underline{A}$. If $\underline{A}$ is not in $\underline{K}$, then $\underline{A}$ is not given up. So there can be no contraction removing $\underline{A}$.

For purposes of systematic discussion, however, it may be useful to extend the definition of contraction to cover cases where $\underline{A}$ is not in $\underline{K}$. The contraction function then becomes a complete and not just a partial function. One could have picked out any arbitrary value for contraction in such a case. However, if we are instructed to give up $\underline{A}$ from $\underline{K}$ when $\underline{A}$ is not in $\underline{K}$, there is nothing we are instructed to give up. In effect, we are not instructed to make any change at all. So if we seek to convert the contraction function into a complete function, we should take the value of the contraction to be $\underline{K}$ itself. No appeal to considerations of informational economy is involved.

In contraction, $\underline{A}$ is removed from $\underline{K}$. This can happen consistent with (K_1^-) if and only if $\underline{A}$ is not a logical truth.

(K_4^-) If $\underline{A}$ is not a logical truth, then $\underline{A}$ is not in $\underline{K}_A^-$.

These postulates ought to be noncontroversial. So should the following:

(K_6^-) If $\underline{A}$ and $\underline{B}$ are logically equivalent, then $\underline{K}_A^- = \underline{K}_B^-$.

With the exception of (K_3^-), none of these postulates are motivated by considerations of informational economy, even according to Gärdenfors. In my judgment, (K_3^-) is not motivated in this way either. These conditions are motivated either by the presystematic understanding of contraction as the removal of an assumption from a corpus or by the condition that such a removal ought to be represented by a deductively closed set or corpus or by the idea that two logically equivalent sentences represent the same doxastic proposition.

The first four of these postulates imply that if one contracts from $\underline{K}$ by removing $\underline{A}$ and then reinstates $\underline{A}$ by expansion, the resulting corpus should be a subset of $\underline{K}$. If $\underline{A}$ is in $\underline{K}$, then $(\underline{K}_A^-)_A^+ \subseteq \underline{K}$. If $\underline{A}$ is a logical truth, the first postulate guarantees that $\underline{A}$ is not removed and no contraction is initiated. If $\underline{A}$ is not in $\underline{K}$, the third postulate guarantees that the contraction is degenerate. The serious case is where $\underline{A}$ is extralogical and in $\underline{K}$. The second and third postulates guarantee that $\underline{K}_A^-$ is a subset of $\underline{K}$ not containing $\underline{A}$. By the first postulate, it is deductively closed. Expansion by adding $\underline{A}$ and forming the deductive closure cannot, therefore, add sentences that are not already in $\underline{K}$.

As Gärdenfors points out, this result guarantees, quite sensibly, that one cannot acquire new information by first contracting by removing $\underline{A}$ and then just reinstating it.

There is one more postulate that Gärdenfors includes in his core postulates. It is the converse of the theorem just reported and is called the *Recovery Postulate*:

(K_5^-) If $\underline{A}$ is in $\underline{K}$, then $\underline{K} \subseteq (\underline{K}_A^-)_A^+$.

The Recovery Postulate implies that through contracting by removing $\underline{A}$ and then adding $\underline{A}$, one returns to the initial corpus $\underline{K}$.

Alchourròn, Gärdenfors, and Makinson (1985, observation 2.3, p. 513) have shown that every contraction satisfying the six conditions just cited is representable as the meet of a subset of the maxichoice contractions. However, postulates (K_1^-) to (K_4^-) and (K_6^-) are satisfied by meets of any subset of saturatable contractions. The pivotal assumption is the Recovery Postulate (K_5^-). Without it, the restriction of admissible contractions to meets of sets of maxichoice contractions does not obtain.

What case can be made for imposing the Recovery Postulate? Gärdenfors and Makinson have both argued that maxichoice contractions are strongest saturatable contractions, whereas no saturatable contraction that are not maxichoice contractions are strongest saturatable contractions. This is true, but it can be considered a relevant argument only by someone who concludes that maxichoice contractions are the only saturatable contractions that incur minimum loss of informational value. This conclusion cannot be endorsed by Gärdenfors and Makinson unless they presuppose a strong monotonicity condition. But an unrestricted strong monotonicity condition implies that an optimal contraction is a maxichoice contraction that they find objectionable, and rightly so.

To avoid this predicament, they must appeal to a strong monotonicity condition restricted to saturatable contractions. But then the issue becomes why one should impose such a restriction. The presystematic judgment or "intuition" they invoke appeals to the idea that stronger belief states carry more informational value in general. They need to explain why this intuition is to be taken seriously only for a very restricted class of contractions.

In my view, presystematic judgment sustains neither a restricted nor an unrestricted strong monotonicity condition.

Suppose that we know that Jones suffers from hepatitis and that he contracted it by eating tainted humus. Call "Jones ate tainted humus" $\underline{A}$ and "Jones suffers from hepatitis" $\underline{B}$.

Consider the contraction of our corpus $\underline{K}$ by giving up $\underline{B}$. We would be faced with giving up either $\sim\underline{A} \supset \underline{B}$ or $\underline{A} \supset \underline{B}$. We might quite plausibly regard giving up the claim $\underline{A} \supset \underline{B}$ as incurring greater loss of informational value than giving up $\sim\underline{A} \supset \underline{B}$ on the grounds that in doing so, we would be giving up the assumption that eating tainted humus tends to result in becoming infected with hepatitis, which has some explanatory value.[6] But then if we retain $\underline{A} \supset \underline{B}$, we shall be required to give up $\underline{A}$. The only question that remains is whether, in giving up $\underline{A}$, we should also give up $\sim\underline{A} \supset \sim\underline{B}$ or retain it. Advocates of the Recovery Postulate will say that we should retain it on the grounds that in not doing so we are losing informational value, which we do not need to do in order to give up $\underline{B}$. But if we put ourselves in the position of someone who does not know that Jones has hepatitis and does not know that he has eaten tainted humus, would we take ourselves as knowing that if the person has hepatitis, he has eaten tainted humus?

There are contexts in which we would respond affirmatively. We would do so if we had information that ruled out that Jones had sexual contact with an infected person, used tainted needles, undergone blood transfusions, and the like. Suppose, however, that we lacked such information. If the initial corpus that contained the information that Jones had eaten tainted humus did not rule out that he had sexual contact with someone infected with hepatitis or some other such source, then when $\underline{B}$ was removed and subsequently reinstated, we would not be in a position to conclude that Jones had eaten tainted humus. But this means that $\sim\underline{A} \supset \sim\underline{B}$ is not retained in the contraction. Yet, advocates of the Recovery Postulate seem committed to retaining it.

It seems to me that in situations such as the one envisaged, we do not think that the loss of $\sim\underline{A} \supset \sim\underline{B}$ adds to the loss of informational value incurred in giving up $\underline{B}$ additional to what is lost by giving up $\sim\underline{A} \supset \underline{B}$ even though it adds to the loss of information. The extra information lost is considered irrelevant. We might say that we initially believed $\sim\underline{A} \supset \sim\underline{B}$ only because of our initial conviction in the truth of $\underline{A}$. No loss of any explanatory information is incurred by giving up $\sim\underline{A} \supset \sim\underline{B}$ except that incurred in giving up $\underline{A}$.

To be sure, if the initial corpus did, indeed, contain information that ruled out explanations of the presence of hepatitis other than eating humus, the Recovery Postulate would be applicable. I am not arguing that it is never applicable. But we should not require it as a condition on admissible contractions in all contexts.

If this is right, the case for abandoning even a restricted version of the strong monotonicity condition is supported by presystematic precedent. Given the fact that the intuitive appeal of the strong monotonicity condition is to be resisted, there is no case for the restricted version at all.[7]

Abandoning the recovery postulate has some important ramifications, to which we now turn.

4.6 How to contract: Contraction and replacement

According to the commensuration requirement of Section 2.6, legitimate or admissible replacements and residual shifts are decomposable into sequences of legitimate or admissible contractions and expansions. No change of corpus or state of full belief from the status quo ought to count as legitimate unless it can be decomposed into a sequence of justified expansions and contractions. This commensuration requirement was distinguished from a commensurability thesis that states that every replacement (and every residual shift) can be formally constructed from expansions and contractions. The commensuration requirement is a prescriptive requirement for legitimate belief changes. The commensurability thesis is a condition of feasibility presupposed by the commensuration requirement.

Suppose that the state of full belief $\mathbf{K}_2$ is obtained from $\mathbf{K}_1$ by replacement. This means that $\mathbf{K}_2$ and $\mathbf{K}_1$ are inconsistent – that is, the complement of $\mathbf{K}_2$ is in the filter generated by $\mathbf{K}_1$. When states of full belief are represented by corpora in $\underline{L}$, $\underline{K}_2$ is a replacement of $\underline{K}_1$ if and only if, for some sentence $\underline{A}$, $\underline{K}_1$ entails $\sim\underline{A}$ and $\underline{K}_2$ entails $\underline{A}$.

Formally, such replacements can always be construed as expansions of contractions of $\underline{K}_1$. Consider the intersection $\underline{K}''$ of $\underline{K}_1$ and $\underline{K}_2$. It is a corpus and is a contraction of $\underline{K}_1$ and $\underline{K}_2$. Hence, $\underline{K}_2$ is an expansion of it.

As a general rule, there are several distinct expansions of contractions of $\underline{K}_1$ that will yield $\underline{K}_2$. Consider any contraction of $\underline{K}$ and form the intersection of it and $\underline{K}''$. It too is a contraction of $\underline{K}_1$, and $\underline{K}_2$ is an expansion of it.

Since the time that Stalnaker (1968) sought to motivate his possible worlds account of conditionals by generalizing the Ramsey Test with the aid of minimal revisions, attention has been focused on replacements described in the following way: Given a corpus $\underline{K}_1$ containing $\sim\underline{A}$, add $\underline{A}$ and make the minimal adjustments to $\underline{K}_1$ to retain a consistent corpus. As noted in section 2.9, Gärdenfors understands a minimal revision to be any change in belief state where a doxastic proposition is added to a belief state. Since he prohibits expanding into inconsistency, such changes are expansions if and only if the proposition added as input is consistent with the initial state. Otherwise, they are a replacements that call for minimal disturbance of the initial doctrine. Minimal revisions can be construed as the result of contracting the initial doctrine by removing $\sim\underline{A}$ if it is present in the corpus (otherwise, the contraction is degenerate) and then expanding by adding $\underline{A}$. The contraction is a transformation of $\underline{K}_1$ removing $\sim\underline{A}$, and the expansion is adding $\underline{A}$.

Of course, the appropriate contraction to make will depend upon what sort of replacement of $\sim\underline{A}$ by $\underline{A}$ is to count as minimal according to those who speak of minimal revisions. Whatever the answer might be, the formal point is that, given any specification of the minimal revision $\underline{K}_2$ from among those replacing $\sim\underline{A}$ by $\underline{A}$, there is at least one contraction of $\underline{K}_1$ by removing $\sim\underline{A}$ whose expansion by adding $\underline{A}$ yields $\underline{K}_2$. One need simply form the intersection $\underline{K}_3$ of $\underline{K}_1$ and $\underline{K}_2$.[8]

There are, however, other ways to achieve the same result. Consider any sentence $\underline{H} = \sim\underline{B} \supset \underline{A}$ that is not in the urcorpus $\underline{1}$. This sentence is in the corpus $\underline{K}_2$ because $\underline{A}$ is. Hence, it is a member of $\underline{K}_3$ (the corpus of "shared agreements" between $\underline{K}_1$ and $\underline{K}_2$) if and only if it is in $\underline{K}_1$. As long as $\underline{K}_1$ is not identical to the closure under consequence of $\sim\underline{A}$, there will be at least one such sentence $\underline{H}$ in $\underline{K}_1$. Contract $\underline{K}_3$ by removing $\underline{H}$. The result is a contraction of $\underline{K}_1$ removing $\sim\underline{A}$. Moreover, adding $\underline{A}$ yields $\underline{K}_2$.

The decomposability of replacements (or *minimal revisions*) into sequences of expansions and contractions is the commensurability thesis of section 2.9, and the formal representability of replacements as expansions of contractions (the *Levi Identity*) is a special application of this requirement. It is embedded in the demand that the space of potential states of full belief should have the structure of a boolean algebra, and is bound to be opposed by anyone sympathetic to the incommensurability doctrines of Kuhn and Feyerabend. It will also be opposed by advocates of that brand of modal realism that reifies judgments of serious possibility discussed in Section 3.7. But authors like Gärdenfors are not, so it seems, committed to rejecting the commensurability thesis. They reject the stronger commensuration requirement that I advocate, but not on the grounds of conceptual nonfeasibility. In disagreement with Gärdenfors, I hold that if an agent starting with corpus $\underline{K}_1$ is to be justified in shifting to $\underline{K}_2$, there must be some sequence of legitimate contractions and legitimate expansions, beginning with the former and terminating with the latter, that furnish the warrant. One possibility is that the inquirer is justified in removing $\sim\underline{A}$ from $\underline{K}_1$ in some specific way in an uncoerced contraction and then, relative to the contracted corpus, justified in adding $\underline{A}$. Another possibility is that the inquirer has expanded legitimately into contradiction from $\underline{K}_1$ by adding $\underline{A}$ in a routine expansion, contracted to $\underline{K}''$, and then expanded to $\underline{K}_2$. Both sequences satisfy the commensuration requirement as a condition of legitimate replacements. The first sequence can model belief changes where the testimony of the senses or of witnesses generates new information to be added to the initial doctrine. The second cannot. As we saw in Section 2.9, Gärdenfors contends that when the inquirer is entitled to add $\underline{A}$ to $\underline{K}_1$, as he thinks he sometimes is, through consulting witnesses or the testimony of the senses, the basic change should not be expansion. Inconsistency is hell! It should be revision that reduces to replacement in this type of case.

Notice that the contraction $\underline{K}_3$ is the strongest of the contractions removing $\sim\underline{A}$ from $\underline{K}_1$ whose expansion by adding $\underline{A}$ yields $\underline{K}_2$. Furthermore, adding $\sim\underline{A}$ to $\underline{K}_3$ reinstates $\underline{K}_1$, as the Recovery Postulate requires, whereas none of the other contractions removing $\sim\underline{A}$ whose exansions yield $\underline{K}_2$ obey Recovery.[9]

In Section 4.5, the point was made that contractions from $\underline{K}_1$ removing $\sim\underline{A}$ and only such contractions that satisfy the Recovery Postulate are meets of subsets of maxichoice contractions removing $\sim\underline{A}$. Thus, those who endorse the Recovery Postulate will conclude that the only way to contract by removing $\sim\underline{A}$ from $\underline{K}_1$ and then to expand by adding $\underline{A}$ to yield $\underline{K}_2$ is to contract to $\underline{K}_3$ that is the intersection (or meet if *meet* is construed as an intersection of sets and not as the greater lower bound of a pair of states of full belief in the partial ordering of potential states of belief) of a set of maxichoice contractions.

Recall, however, that $\underline{K}_3$ is the meet or intersection of $\underline{K}_1$ (the initial corpus containing $\sim\underline{A}$) and $\underline{K}_2$ (the replacement of $\sim\underline{A}$ by $\underline{A}$ that we are decomposing). What we have shown, in effect, is that not only are replacements formally decomposable via the so-called Levi Identity as expansions of contractions but that contractions are formally decomposable via the *Harper Identity* (Gärdenfors, 1988, p. 70) as the meets or intersections of the initial and final belief states or corpora in replacements.

The Levi Identity is a consequence of the thesis of commensurability and the assumption that there is exactly one admissible contraction (replacement) in a given context. Given that there is no issue between Gärdenfors and myself on these matters, we may leave them alone.

But the Harper Identity is controversial, for it implies that an admissible contraction must be the meet or intersection of a set of maxichoice contractions and, hence, that the Recovery Postulate should be obeyed.

Recall that Gärdenfors seems committed to the view that the only kinds of basically legitimate changes in belief state are minimal revisions and contractions – in violation of the commensuration requirement. What the Harper Identity allows one to do is to argue that when facing the question of how to contract, which is the only question about contraction Gärdenfors addresses systematically, the problem can be solved by determining how to make a minimal revision by adding $\underline{A}$.

This does not quite remove contraction from the status of a basic mode of change of belief. For the questions of whether and what to contract remain. But the question of how to contract by removing $\sim\underline{A}$ given that one is going to do so can be seen to be derivative from criteria for legitimate minimal revision if the Harper Identity is adopted. The price for achieving this bit of unification, however, is the imposition of the Recovery Postulate.

It may be thought that one need not take such a strong stand one way or the other on the matter of Recovery. If one is seeking to give an account of replacement of $\sim\underline{A}$ by $\underline{A}$, no matter which of the replacements available is considered admissible, there will be a unique way to represent it as an expansion of a contraction satisfying Recovery. There will be many alternative such representations violating Recovery. But if one violates Recovery in one of these ways, it will not make any difference to the replacement resulting once $\underline{A}$ is added.

This may suggest that it does not matter whether one endorses the Harper Identity and Recovery or not as far as an account of admissible replacement is concerned. If it does not matter, it may still be a question of convenience to favor representing the replacement as the product of an expansion adding $\underline{A}$ to the strongest contraction removing $\sim\underline{A}$ from $\underline{K}_1$ whose expansion by adding $\underline{A}$ yields $\underline{K}_2$. This contraction, as Makinson observed, is unique and is the meet of the initial corpus and its replacement.

For authors who want to see minimal revision and contraction as the basic types of legitimate belief change, the fact that Recovery allows for still further systematic unification by deriving an account of how to contract from an account of how to make minimal revisions will seem very attractive.

However, as Makinson (1987) clearly understands, beginning with the notion of minimal revision and defining admissible contractions in terms of this idea is more than a formal maneuver. It imposes the Recovery Postulate as a constraint on admissible contractions. And this is a constraint on how to contract in the sense that it is a restriction on what is to count as a justifiable contraction.

In Section 4.5, I argued that the Recovery Postulate is unwarranted if such justification is to be construed as showing that an admissible contraction minimizes loss of damped informational value. Even so, it makes no difference whether or not the Recovery Postulate is in place in deciding what is to count as an admissible replacement or a minimal revision. If, in the final analysis, what we are concerned to do in offering an account of belief revision is to rationalize replacements, the reservations expressed about the Recovery Postulate are mere pedantry.

The requirement of commensuration rejects this contention. It insists that to justify a replacement of $\sim\underline{A}$ by $\underline{A}$, one must move by some sequence of legitimate contractions and expansions to a position of suspense between $\sim\underline{A}$ and $\underline{A}$ – that is, either basically or derivatively justify contracting from $\underline{K}_1$ by removing $\sim\underline{A}$ and then justify the expansion of the contracted corpus by adding $\underline{A}$. But the process of inquiry is full of pitfalls. It can happen that an inquiring agent may open up his mind to some conjecture $\underline{A}$ inconsistent with his initial doctrine by contraction and have good reason to do so, and then engage in inquiry aimed at determining whether to add the conjecture to the contracted corpus, to expand by reinstating $\sim\underline{A}$ or, perhaps, some other alternative or, perhaps, to remain in a state of doubt. If it were automatic that the agent would be justified in expanding by adding the new conjecture $\underline{A}$, perhaps, a case could be made for ignoring the differences between contractions that satisfy the Recovery Postulate and those that do not.

But such justification is not automatic. For one thing, it may turn out that the inquirer is justified in reinstating $\sim\underline{A}$. In this case, if the justified contraction removing $\sim\underline{A}$ initially fails to satisfy Recovery, the net result will differ from the initial corpus.

Suppose, for example, that a coin assumed to be fair is tossed 1,000 times and the report is made that the coin landed heads every time. In some situations, the inquirer might question whether the coin is fair. But sometimes the inquirer might have good reason to question the report of the outcome of the thousand tosses, perhaps because she questions whether the experiment was actually run. Suppose that the inquirer does the latter and gives up the claim that the coin was tossed 1,000 times. If the inquirer takes for granted that the coin lands heads 1,000 times only if it is tossed 1,000 times and that giving up this assumption incurs an excessive loss of informational value, an admissible contraction would require her also giving up that the coin landed heads 1,000 times. If the inquirer subsequently became convinced that the coin was, indeed, tossed 1,000 times, she would not necessarily be warranted in also becoming convinced that it landed heads every time. Recovery would be violated.

There is yet another way in which breakdown of Recovery can be relevant. It is conceivable, as far as we have gone, that an inquiring agent may be justified in expanding a contraction removing $\sim\underline{A}$ by adding $\underline{A}$ if the contraction violates Recovery but not if the contraction obeys Recovery.

Consider the example of the coin once more. If the assumption that the coin was tossed 1,000 times is removed, but not the claim that if it is tossed 1,000 times, it lands heads every time, then there will be greater resistance to expanding by reinstating the claim that it was tossed 1,000 times given the conviction that the coin is fair than there would be if the material conditional is not retained at the contraction step.

These considerations indicate that the commensuration condition renders the rejection of the Recovery Postulate as a constraint on admissible contractions more than mere pedantry in the context of an account of justified belief revision.

It may, nonetheless, be maintained that the Recovery Postulate should be retained when developing a belief–change account of conditionals. In that case, the justification of the contraction and of the expansion steps is waived. It is stipulated that $\sim \underline{A}$ is to be removed and that $\underline{A}$ is to be added.

Two points may be made in response to this suggestion.

The first is that there is still a question of justifying how to contract by removing $\sim \underline{A}$. Unless the conditions on admissible contraction in hypothetical belief revision of the sort used in understanding conditionals differ from those that apply in nonhypothetical belief revision, our previous arguments suggest that the Recovery Postulate ought not to be imposed as a constraint.

The second point is that not all conditionals are counterfactual. There are conditionals in which the initial corpus does not contain $\sim \underline{A}$. In open conditionals, neither $\underline{A}$ nor $\sim \underline{A}$ is in the initial corpus. The Ramsey Test requires only that the initial corpus be expanded by adding $\underline{A}$. There are also conditionals in which $\underline{A}$ is in the initial corpus. Reverting to our coin example, suppose that the agent is certain that the coin was tossed 1,000 times and landed heads each time. She should not be prepared to assert that had the coin been tossed 1,000 times, it would have landed heads each time. To the contrary, she should be prepared to assert that had the coin been tossed 1,000 times, it could have landed tails at least one time.[10] This suggests that even in giving a belief revision account of conditionals, the Recovery Postulate should not be assumed.[11]

This situation is not restricted to cases where statistical examples are involved. Consider the example of the person who ate tainted humus and contracted hepatitis, discussed in Section 4.5. We should not assert that if the person had contracted hepatitis, he would have eaten tainted humus unless we had initially ruled out other possible sources of infection.[12]

The arguments just offered seek to undermine the Harper Identity as a constraint on legitimate contractions or at least legitimate basic contractions if there be such. If they succeed, they also undermine efforts to reduce criteria for how to contract by removing $\sim \underline{A}$ from $\underline{K}_1$ to criteria for how to revise $\underline{K}_1$ by replacing $\sim \underline{A}$ by $\underline{A}$.

Those who insist that inconsistency is hell might want to continue to reject the commensuration requirement and admit that contraction as well as revision is a basic mode of legitimate belief change. I am developing an argument to suggest that the very presystematic predicaments to which Gärdenfors and others appeal do not support this view. When an inquirer makes observations or receives testimony in conflict with his current doctrine, he does not replace his old convictions with the new data. Insofar as the inquirer first adds information to his initial doctrine, he expands inadvertently into inconsistency along lines I sought to render palatable in Chapter 3. In Section 4.7, I address the question of what is to be removed from the inconsistent doctrine to escape from hell. I suggest that often one not only gives up the background information in conflict with the new data but also questions the data. The net effect is not a minimal revision of the initial doctrine at all but a contraction. To obtain a replacement, further inquiry would be needed to settle the question of the truth value of $\underline{A}$, and this could turn out in favor of $\underline{A}$, or in favor of its negation, or could leave the inquirer in suspense. Derived replacement is just one of several possibilities. Nothing in this account provides for basic revision.

4.7 How to contract: Corrigibility and entrenchment

A corpus or the state of full belief it represents serves as a standard for serious possibility. It distinguishes between conjectures that are possibly true and claims whose falsity is settled.

One can be uncertain about a conjecture, and such uncertainty can come in degrees. Judgments of credal probability constitute one useful way of discriminating between serious possibilities with respect to such degrees of certainty. Observe, however, that such judgments do not distinguish between items in the corpus (or doxastic propositions that are in the filter generated by the current state of full belief). All of them are assigned the same maximum degree of certainty.

Yet items in $\underline{K}$ do not share the same epistemic status in all respects. Those sentences that are also in $\underline{1}$ or the urcorpus are not subject to removal from $\underline{K}$ by contraction (except in some kind of change of conceptual framework). They are, in this sense, maximally *incorrigible*. And other sentences in $\underline{K}$, though more corrigibile, may differ from one another with respect to their degrees of vulnerability to being given up.

The temptation to confuse grades of certainty with grades of incorrigibility should be resisted (Levi, 1980a, sects. 3.1 and 3.3.) Discriminations between doxastic propositions with respect to grades of certainty apply to serious possibilities – that is, to doxastic propositions consistent with the current state of belief. All doxastic propositions that lie in the ultrafilter generated by the current state are maximally certain according to that state, and there is no differentiation in this respect. Discriminations among such certainties concern degrees of corrigibility.[13]

Such evaluations do not apply to conjectures whose truth or falsity is not settled. They are not vulnerable to being removed from the corpus because they are not in the corpus. Because the question of their truth value is unsettled, they may be evaluated as more or less probable. We are not concerned in this discussion with degrees of probability or degrees of certainty, but with degrees of corrigibility.

We could have introduced another sort of discrimination. When the acceptance of $\underline{A}$ is considered more corrigible than the acceptance of $\underline{B}$, rejection of $\sim\underline{A}$ is considered more corrigible than rejection of $\sim\underline{B}$. In this way, we focus attention on an evaluation of sentences in $\underline{L}$ that are ruled out as impossible by $\underline{K}$. Items consistent with $\underline{K}$ are all minimally vulnerable to revision with respect to rejection, since they are not rejected at all.

We could have focused on degrees of *incorrigibility* or, as Gärdenfors (1988, p. 87) has called them, *degrees of entrenchment.* Degrees of entrenchment increase with a decrease in degrees of corrigibility. Moreover, we could speak both of degrees of corrigibility of acceptance and rejection and of how entrenched an acceptance is, and also how well entrenched a rejection is.

The four ways of making discriminations just identified (degrees of corrigibility of acceptance and of rejection, and degrees of entrenchment of acceptance and of rejection) all aim at conveying the same system of evaluations. Given a specification of one system, the other three are determined.

To obtain an account of how such assessments are to be made, we should return to our account of damped informational value. Recall that evaluations of damped informational value are evaluations of potential contractions of $\underline{K}$ by removing $\underline{A}$ – that is, of elements of $C(\underline{K},\underline{A})$. And any such contraction strategy is the intersection of a subset of the set $S(\underline{K},\underline{A})$ of satiatable contractions by removing $\underline{A}$ from $\underline{K}$. The account of damped informational value proposed began by assigning undamped informational values to the satu-ratable contractions and then assigning to the intersection of a set of saturatable contractions the minimum informational value assigned an element of the set.

The admissible contraction strategy was then the one that is the intersection of all saturatable contractions carrying maximum informational value, and the informational value thereby obtained was the informational value they all shared in common.

Suppose that $\underline{B}$ is in the admissible contraction strategy but $\underline{C}$ is not. Then $\underline{C}$ is more corrigible and less entrenched than $\underline{B}$ relative to $\underline{K}$ and $\underline{A}$.

Suppose that $\underline{B}$ and $\underline{C}$ are both in the admissible contraction strategy. Even though neither is given up in the admissible contraction strategy, we might ponder what would happen if we considered the intersection of all saturatable contractions carrying informational value at least as great as some specific satiatable contraction but less than the maximum informational value carried by a most informationally valuable saturatable contraction strategy. If $\underline{B}$ is in that corpus but $\underline{C}$ is not, then $\underline{C}$ is again more corrigible and less well entrenched than $\underline{B}$. In general, therefore, we may use the following definition:

$\underline{C}$ is at least as corrigible and no better entrenched than $\underline{B}$ relative to $\underline{K}$ and $\underline{A}$ if and only if no contraction $\underline{L}^*$ that is the intersection of all elements of $S(\underline{K},\underline{A})$ carrying at least as much informational value as some saturatable contraction $\underline{S}$ contains $\underline{C}$ but not $\underline{B}$.

In his book (1988, pp. 89–91), Gärdenfors introduces certain conditions on assessments of epistemic entrenchment. Gärdenfors assumes that entrenchment is defined for all sentences in $\underline{L}$. However, if $\underline{B}$ is not in $\underline{K}$, Gärdenfors assumes that it has minimum entrenchment rather than maximum entrenchment. He reasons (p. 90), that if it is not in $\underline{K}$, it is not entrenched at all and, hence, has minimum entrenchment. This corresponds to saying that because it is already removed, it is maximally vulnerable to removal. Gärdenfors also claims that the converse is true. If a sentence is maximally vulnerable to removal, it is not in $\underline{K}$. [See postulate (EE4).] This is not quite true. $\underline{A}$, which is the sentence to be removed from $\underline{K}$ no matter what else is removed, must be maximally vulnerable to removal relative to $\underline{K}$ and $\underline{A}$. Gardenfors also introduces postulate (EE1) ensuring transitivity of ordering with respect to entrenchment and postulate (EE2) guaranteeing that the logically stronger sentences are not more entrenched than logically weaker ones. Postulate (EE5) guarantees that all sentences in the urcorpus $\underline{1}$ are maximally entrenched. All of these postulates are satisfied when entrenchment or corrigibility is characterized along the lines I have suggested. The most interesting postulate, however, is (EE3), which, in effect, asserts that the degree of entrenchment of a conjunction is equal to the minimum degree of entrenchment assigned a conjunct. This too is satisfied by the interpretation I am suggesting.

According to the definition of corrigibility, the degree of corrigibility of $\underline{B}\&\underline{C}$ is equal to the maximum degree of corrigibility assigned to $\underline{B}$ and $\underline{C}$. Hence, the degree of entrenchment assigned to the conjunction is the minimum of the degrees of entrenchment assigned to the conjuncts as Gärdenfors's postulate (EE3) requires.

Observe, however, that if we consider the entrenchment of the rejections of sentences inconsistent with $\underline{K}$, the entrenchment of rejection for a disjunction is the minimum of the entrenchments of rejection assigned to disjuncts. The degree of vulnerability to rejection of such a disjunction is the maximum of the degrees assigned disjuncts.

It is interesting to notice that the evaluation of sentences with respect to corrigibility or entrenchment and the evaluation with respect to corrigibility or entrenchment of rejection have the formal properties of measures of degrees of belief (for entrenchment)) and degrees of potential surprise (for entrenchment of rejection) proposed by G. L. S. Shackle as early as 1949 (Shackle, 1949). Shackle's intentions in applying his formal scheme were not to capture degrees of entrenchment. The suitability of Shackle's idea for characterizing degrees of entrenchment indirectly adds to the case to be made for serious study of his relatively neglected idea.[14]

Gärdenfors and Makinson (1988) have suggested defining admissible contractions in terms of the assessment of epistemic entrenchment. Consider the set of sentences $\subseteq$ in $\underline{L}$ such that $\underline{A}$ is less well entrenched than $\sim\underline{A} \supset \underline{C}$ and form the intersection of the set of such $\subseteq$s with $\underline{K}$. This intersection is the admissible contraction of $\underline{K}$ removing $\underline{A}$.

If $\underline{B}$ is in $\underline{K}$, then so are $\underline{A} \supset \underline{B}$ and $\sim\underline{A} \supset \underline{B}$. If $\underline{A}$ is as well entrenched as $\sim\underline{A} \supset \underline{B}$, then $\sim\underline{A} \supset \underline{B}$ is not going to be retained in the admissible contraction. What about $\underline{A} \supset \underline{B}$? The proposed definition ensures that this will be retained; for it is in $\underline{K}$, and $\sim\underline{A} \supset (\underline{A} \supset \underline{B})$ is better entrenched than $\underline{A}$, since it is a logical truth.

In Section 4.5, however, it has been argued that retention of $\underline{A} \supset \underline{B}$ ought not to be mandatory. To make its retention mandatory is to insist on the Recovery Postulate. The Gärdenfors–Makinson definition of contraction by means of epistemic entrenchment is unacceptable because it presupposes a doubtful substantive assumption.

Once insistence on the Recovery Postulate is abandoned, a much simpler definition of the admissible contraction removing $\underline{A}$ can be given according to which it is the intersection of $\underline{K}$ with the set of sentences in $\underline{L}$ whose epistemic entrenchment relative to $\underline{K}$ and $\underline{A}$ is greater than that of $\underline{A}$ or whose corrigibility relative to $\underline{K}$ and $\underline{A}$ is less than that of $\underline{A}$.

The controversial status of Recovery does not, however, alter the basic structure of assessments of corrigibility or entrenchment.[15]

It should be emphasized that assessments of corrigibility and entrenchment are relative to the information-determining M function defined over the basic partition (see Section 4.3), the corpus $\underline{K}$, and the sentence $\underline{A}$ whose removal is required. The M values assigned corpora that are satiatable relative to $\underline{K}$ for some $\underline{A}$ in $\underline{K}$ can remain constant over variations of $\underline{K}$ and $\underline{A}$ (although this is not mandatory). Assuming that these values are fixed, comparisons of sentences $\underline{X}$ and $\underline{Y}$ with respect to corrigibility and entrenchment of acceptance and of rejection depend very much on both $\underline{K}$ and the sentence $\underline{A}$ that is required to be removed by stipulation. Clearly, if $\underline{X}$ is in $\underline{K}$ but not in $\underline{K}^*$, $\underline{Y}$ is in $\underline{K}^*$ but not in $\underline{K}$ while $\underline{A}$ belongs in both corpora, removing $\underline{A}$ from $\underline{K}$ can support the greater entrenchment of $\underline{X}$, whereas removing $\underline{A}$ from $\underline{K}^*$ can support the greater entrenchment of $\underline{Y}$. There is no inconsistency – only a relativity of degrees of entrenchment to the initial corpus. Similarly, when $\underline{A}$ is removed from $\underline{K}^{**}$ containing both $\underline{A}$ and $\underline{B}$, $\underline{B}$ might be retained, so that $\underline{B}$ has greater entrenchment than $\underline{A}$. But if $\underline{B}$ is removed from $\underline{K}^{**}$, $\underline{A}$ may have the greater entrenchment.

These variations in assessments of entrenchment or corrigibility do not depend on variation in the demands for informational value that are reflected in the information-determining M function. This does not mean that inquirers should never alter their demands for information. Research programs are subject to modification in the course of inquiry. An account of when they should and should not be altered ought to be incorporated into a fully satisfactory account of inquiry. Such an account is itself part of an account of the modification of cognitive value commitments and should, therefore, be seen as a special case of a more general account of the modification of value commitments (including economic, moral, political, and other value commitments). I do not claim to have a fully satisfactory account of this cluster of questions and, in any case, do not propose to examine it in this book. My point is that even though modifying the demands for information by changing the M function can lead to modification of comparisons with respect to entrenchment, changes in such comparisons can take place without alterations in the M function as well.

Gärdenfors (1988, p. 88) points out that the entrenchment of a sentence depends on the belief state or corpus in which it occurs. He also claims that a change in the Kuhnian paradigm involves a radical change of the ordering with respect to entrenchment. The tenor of his remarks suggests that he thinks that profound changes in orderings with respect to entrenchment attributable to deep-running changes in corpus or belief state are the stuff of which paradigm switches are made.

I am reluctant to venture a reconstruction of Kuhn's ideas. However, it is worth pointing out that Kuhn himself makes two claims about paradigm switches that do not fit too well into this analysis.

First, Kuhn seems to think that a paradigm switch or conversion arises in a situation where it is not feasible to suspend judgment between the rival theories and still be able to maintain a suitable non-question-begging account of truth conditions.[16] This aspect of the Kuhnian view implies rejection of the commensurability thesis. Gärdenfors does not seem to reject this claim, nor does it appear to be implicit in his account of large changes in the assessments of entrenchment.

Kuhn (1970a, pp. 199–200) does allow that even incommensurable theories can be compared with respect to several kinds of values such as accuracy, simplicity, fruitfulness, and the like. As I understand him, these values constitute different dimensions that contribute to the assessment of what I call *informational value*. Assessments with respect to these values do not correlate well with truth or probability of truth with respect to which incommensurable theories cannot be compared in a non-question-begging way. Kuhn thinks that individual inquirers advocating rival theories will disagree with one another in how they evaluate theories with respect to the several desiderata and, moreover, may weigh them differently in coming up with an aggregate assessment. The disputes are disputes over values and not disagreements about what is judged to be true. I paraphrase Kuhn's remarks about these matters as claiming that incommensurable theories can be compared with respect to informational value but that such comparisons depend on the demands for information to which the inquirer subscribes, which may differ from inquirer to inquirer. But such variations in demands for information are reflected, according to the scheme I am proposing, in differences in the information-determining M function. If this somewhat fanciful reconstruction is to the point, incommensurability for Kuhn may involve a change in the M function. Such incommensurability will surface in differences in assessments of entrenchment; but the changes will not necessarily reflect changes in states of full belief, as Gärdenfors suggests.

4.8 Coerced contraction: What to remove

In coerced contraction, the initial corpus $\underline{K}$ contains a sentence $\sim\underline{A}$. The inquiring agent carries out an investigation involving some sort of routine expansion either via observation and experimentation or through consulting witnesses or experts. Insofar as the agent is concerned to avoid error in routine expansion (as I am suggesting ought to be the case), we may suppose that the inquirer takes for granted that the program for routine expansion is sufficiently reliable. That is to say, prior to running the program, the inquirer assumes that the objective, statistical probability or chance of avoiding error on running the program, no matter what expansion will be adopted as a result, is sufficiently high to justify running the program for the sake of the benefits of the information to be obtained. This reliability assumption $\underline{R}$ itself may be a logical consequence of other assumptions in $\underline{K}$ concerning the physics, biology, psychology, or sociology of the matter. Once the routine has been run, an expansion is implemented. The agent is now certain (1) that he has run the program ($\underline{P}$) and (2) that $\underline{H}$ is true for some strongest sentence $\underline{H}$ added in response to the running of the program. Thus, the expanded corpus $\underline{K}_1$ contains, in addition to $\sim\underline{A}$ and $\underline{R}$ that are in $\underline{K}$, the further information $\underline{R}\&\underline{P}$ and $\underline{H}$. Suppose that $\underline{H} = \underline{A}$, so that $\underline{K}_1 = \underline{o}$ and is inconsistent. Expansion into inconsistency is inadvertent. Presumably, prior to running the program, the agent judged the chance of expanding into error sufficiently low to justify running the program. That is assumption $\underline{R}$. The chance of expanding by adding $\underline{A}$ is a fortiori no higher, according to the agent's initial point of view. The circumstance that the agent nonetheless expanded into inconsistency is therefore an inadvertency. Because the inquirer initially took for granted that $\underline{A}$ is false, he was not concerned to test for the truth or falsity of that statement. Such testing (pace Popper) would be pointless. Jones may be convinced at the outset that someone in the office owned a Ford with a given license number and wishes to find out who it is. She gains access to official registration files that she assumes at the outset give highly reliable information concerning ownership, and they state that the owner is not someone working in the office. At the outset, Jones is not concerned to test the claim that someone in the office owned the Ford. She wants to find out who in the office owned the Ford. She would not undertake the search through the files in order to find out whether the owner worked in the office. She takes for granted that the owner did work in the office, so that there is no point in looking into the matter. Given her conviction that the registration files are highly reliable, she may, nonetheless, recognize a small chance of error. But she may be prepared to risk the small chance of error for the sake of the new information to be gained. Hence, although Jones recognizes a small chance of her following the routine leading her to expand by adding the information that no one in the office owned the Ford that, she is convinced is false, she is prepared to incur the risk. However, as a result of her effort to find out who owned the Ford, she inadvertently stumbles into inconsistency.

Once the inconsistency has been injected, contraction from $\underline{K}_1 = \underline{o}$ is coerced. The question as to whether to contract or not is not a matter for debate. But the choice of contraction strategies remains to be decided.

The set of potential contraction strategies $C(\underline{o},\underline{H})$, for any extralogical $\underline{H}$, is well defined. It includes all intersections (meets) of maximally consistent sets in $\underline{L}$ at least one of which contains $\sim\underline{H}$. Given an information-determining M function, a uniquely admissible contraction from $\underline{o}$ removing $\underline{H}$ can be determined. The difficulty is that when the inquirer has stumbled into inconsistent $\underline{o}$ inadvertently and seeks to contract, it is unclear what sentence should be the input $\underline{H}$ for the contraction operation.

One way to approach the matter might be to pick the weakest consistent corpus carrying maximum damped informational value. Once this contraction is identified, one will be able to determine the class of sentences that qualify as inputs yielding this contraction.

There is a serious objection˙to this view. As long as the information-determining M function remains fixed, no matter how the inquirer happened to stumble into inconsistency, the contraction recommended will be the same. This result conflicts strongly with presystematic precedent.

The difficulty can be avoided by modifying the way damped informational value is determined so as to make its assessment sensitive to the provenance of the inconsistency.

We may obtain an idea of how evaluation of losses of damped informational value incurred in contracting from $\underline{o}$ depends on the initial corpus $\underline{K}$ that is expanded into inconsistency and the input sentence $\underline{A}$ that contradicts $\underline{K}$ by looking at the kinds of strategies that seem relevant to inquirers when they stumble into inconsistency. I suggest three main types of strategy need to be considered:

1. One may question $\sim\underline{A}$. The idea behind this strategy is to determine the admissible contraction $\underline{K}^-_A$ of $\underline{K}$ (the initial corpus) by removing $\sim\underline{A}$ and to expand the result by adding $\underline{P}\&\underline{A}$. Let this be $\underline{K}^*$. Notice that the contraction strategy just identified is also a contraction from $\underline{K}_1 = \underline{o}$ by removing $\sim\underline{A}$. In the case of Jones, she has given up the initial assumption that someone in the office owned the Ford. $\underline{K}^*$ is one of a set K^* of potential corpora derivable by taking an element of $C(\underline{K},\sim\underline{A})$ and expanding by adding $\underline{P}\&\underline{A}$. It is distinguished from the rest in being the weakest such corpus that maximizes damped informational value in the set. It represents the most

informative result the inquirer could have obtained had he been in a position to remove $\sim\underline{A}$ before routine expansion adding $\underline{A\&P}$.

2. One may question $\underline{A}$. That is to say, one may question the information obtained as a result of routine expansion. To do this, determine the admissible contraction of $\underline{K}^*$ by removing $\underline{A}$ and then expand the result by adding $\sim\underline{A}$. The result, $\underline{K}^{**}$, is a contraction of $\underline{K}_1 = \underline{o}$ by removing $\underline{A}$. $\underline{K}^{**}$ is the weakest corpus-carrying maximum damped informational value in the set K^{**} obtainable by removing $\underline{A}$ from an element of K^* and adding $\sim\underline{A}$. This strategy is tantamount to what would happen were the inquirer to implement the program up to the point where he faced contradiction and then abort the implementation.

Sometimes this may require removing either $\underline{R}$ (the reliability assumption) or $\underline{P}$ (the assumption that the program for routine expansion was implemented). This will be so if the assumption of reliability claims that the routine is perfectly reliable, so that the chance of error in implementing it is 0. In most cases, however, perfect reliability ought not to be assumed. Even so, as explained in Section 3.4, the pressure to remove either $\underline{R}$ or $\underline{P}$ or both is there.

For example, if Jones had followed the second strategy, she would have questioned the conclusion she obtained via routine expansion that no one in the office owned the Ford. The registration lists are not perfectly reliable indicators of ownership. But if they are sufficiently reliable, Jones may be justified via *deliberate* expansion in ruling out the possibility that she will expand into inconsistency. Having expanded into inconsistency, she could remove $\underline{A}$ from $\underline{K}^*$ and add $\sim\underline{A}$ to form $\underline{K}^{**}$ without jettisoning either the high-reliability assumption $\underline{R}$ or the implementation assumption $\underline{P}$.

Although the resulting $\underline{K}^{**}$ is consistent, it will, nonetheless, countenance anomaly. A highly improbable event will have occurred, and this itself may justify implementing an *uncoerced* contraction leading to the questioning of $\underline{R}$ or $\underline{P}$. Jones may very well want to question the reliability of the lists and seek additional sources of information such as, for example, an examination of the actual registration and ownership documents and a check of their authenticity.

We shall postpone detailed consideration of uncoerced contraction. However, it is important to appreciate that coerced contraction may (and, I dare say, typically will) lead to a second uncoerced contraction that raises doubts about the reliability or implementation of the routine. Let the resulting corpus be $\underline{K}^{***}$.

$\underline{K}^{**}$ is determined by $\underline{K}^*$ and $\underline{A}$, and $\underline{K}^*$ is determined by $\underline{K}$ and $\sim\underline{A}$. Hence, when we look upon $\underline{K}^{**}$ as a contraction from $\underline{o}$ removing $\underline{A}$, we are tacitly assuming the same approach to evaluating informational value as we did in connection with strategy 1.

3. One may question the initial assumption $\sim\underline{A}$, as strategy 1 requires, and question $\underline{A}$, as strategy 2 requires. That is to say, the contraction will be to the intersection of the first two contractions. The result will be the weakest

maximizing damped informational value in the set K' of all intersections of pairs of corpora, one from K^* and one from K^{**}

In the example of Jones that we have been tracking, it is quite likely that she would favor the first strategy of questioning the background assumption that someone in the office owns a Ford. But in special circumstances this need not be so, and there are other types of predicament where it is not likely to be so.

Michelson, Lorentz, and others responded to the results of experiments with the interferometer (which I take to have involved expansion into inconsistency) by questioning both the experiments and the background theory. Nor is this approach restricted to such sophisticated situations. If I were to stroll along 72nd Street near Columbus Avenue and spy a friend, Vic, who I am convinced before the event is in Sydney, Australia, I would look again and check the matter out. In doing so, I would be questioning both my initial response to sensory stimulation and the expansion into the conviction that Vic is on Columbus Avenue, as well as my background assumption that Vic is in Australia. Both convictions would be removed from the settled assumptions, and a subsequent investigation would ensue. I would not follow one of the first two contraction strategies to the exclusion of the other. These examples illustrate cases of following strategy 3. And the recent furor over experiments yielding cold tabletop nuclear fusion indicates that skepticism may be directed at experimental design and the reliability of a routine rather than at the initial background assumptions, as suggested by strategy 2.

Our primary concern here is to give a systematic decision theoretic rationalization of the choice among the several contraction strategies outlined earlier. We have not, however, given an explicit characterization of how losses in damped informational value are to be assessed in contracting from $\underline{o}$. The evaluations of such losses we have invoked in discussing strategies 1 and 2 have concerned contractions from $\underline{K}$ by removing $\sim\underline{A}$ and contractions from K^* by removing $\underline{A}$ respectively. We need to consider evaluations of losses when contracting from $\underline{o}$ by removing $\sim\underline{A}$ and by removing $\underline{A}$.

Consider now the set $MC(\underline{K},\underline{A})$ of all maximally consistent corpora that are expansions of elements of K^* or K^{**}. There will, in general, be maximally consistent corpora that are not elements of $MC(\underline{K},\underline{A})$.

My suggestion is this: When the inquirer has stumbled into inconsistency by inadvertently expanding $\underline{K}$ by adding $\underline{A}$ inconsistent with $\underline{K}$ to it, he should not contract from $\underline{o}$ to a corpus unless it is obtainable by one of the three strategies 1, 2, or 3. That is to say, he should not end up with more information than he would have gotten had he followed the program for routine expansion without stumbling into inconsistency or had he aborted the program before expanding into inconsistency. To do so would entail acquiring information that cannot be derived according to one of these three strategies. For example, relative to $\underline{K}$, Jones might be in doubt as to who will be elected president of the United States in 1992. She should not be entitled to become convinced of the result merely by contracting from $\underline{o}$ after having stumbled into inconsistency in virtue of routine expansion furnishing information quite irrelevant to this matter.

Thus, I suggest that contraction from $\underline{o}$ due to expansion of $\underline{K}$ by adding $\underline{A}$ should minimize loss of damped informational value subject to the constraint that all contraction strategies be intersections of elements of $MC(\underline{K},\underline{A})$ and subject to the proviso that the M values of the elements of these sets be the normalizations of the values initially assigned when all maximally consistent corpora not in the set are assigned the value o.

Under these conditions, the recommended contraction from $\underline{o}$ will be $\underline{K}^*$ if its (constrained) damped informational value is greater than that of $\underline{K}^{**}$, will be $\underline{K}^{**}$ if it carries the greater (constrained) damped informational value, and will be the intersection of the two if they are equal in (constrained) damped informational value.

The picture that emerges is that predicaments like my seeing someone who resembles Vic on Columbus Avenue exemplifies a case where not much difference in the loss of informational value is incurred by concluding that my visual observations were unreliable and that I was mistaken about Vic's whereabouts. However, when the background theory that is contradicted by the results of experiment is explanatorily powerful and well entrenched, one may well proceed by questioning the experimental design and other aspects of the conduct of the experiment while retaining the theory. Indeed, this is often the case when experiments are in the process of being designed and apparatus is calibrated and adjusted by relying on background theory. Conflict between background theory and the reliability of the routine is adjudicated in favor of the background theory. However, once the reliability of the experimental procedure and the program for routine expansion is settled and conflict between background theory and implementation of the routine ensues, the losses of informational value may be considerable regardless of whether one questions the background theory or the reliability of the routine, and both will be questioned. In the case of Jones, on the other hand, the loss of information incurred by giving up the information that someone in the office owned the Ford in question may be less than questioning the reliability of the registration lists.

The moral of the story is this: One cannot give a principled account of how to extricate oneself from inconsistency that arises inadvertently from coerced contraction without taking into account the informational values of the several available contraction strategies. In the absence of a standardized way of assessing informational value applicable to all situations, such assessments will have to be relativized to the demands for informational value that animate the inquirer's deliberations. These demands may reflect commitments to research programs and ideals of explanatory adequacy, simplicity, systematicity, precision, and the like, including commitments to certain types of theoretical frameworks (e.g., commitments to field theories, particle theories and the like) that may become sources of controversy between investigators.

In this respect, the situation is no different from the one that obtains in the context of expansion. There too, demands for information control the evaluation of potential answers or expansion strategies. The salient difference is that in expansion, risk of error also ought to be taken into account. Risk of error cannot play a role in contraction because nothing is being added to the corpus and, hence, there is no error to be incurred by adding a false claim. Moreover, there is no discrimination to be made within the corpus to be contracted with respect to truth value. If the corpus is consistent (as will be the case in uncoerced contraction), it is taken for granted that all elements of the corpus are true. If the corpus is inconsistent (as in coerced contraction), assessments of truth value collapse into incoherence and no discrimination with respect to truth value can sensibly be made.

Gärdenfors maintains that when one adds $\underline{A}$&$\underline{P}$ to $\underline{K}$ inconsistent with it, one does not expand into inconsistency but moves to a consistent minimal revision of the initial corpus $\underline{K}$. I have redescribed this kind of transformation as an expansion into inconsistency followed by a contraction to $\underline{K}^*$ corresponding to strategy 1. According to Gärdenfors, minimal revision is the only kind of transformation of a corpus that can occur in such cases. Because it is the only kind of transformation that can occur, it seems gratuitously complicated to describe the process as first expanding into inconsistency and then contracting.

Gärdenfors cannot complain, therefore, that I impose constraints on contraction from $\underline{o}$; for his conception of the process as minimal revision is equivalent to imposing a stronger constraint on potential contractions from $\underline{o}$ than the constraint I favor. And the constraint he favors makes reference to $\underline{K}$ and $\underline{A}$.[17]

The substantive difference between us concerns the constraints on the contraction strategies that are to be evaluated with respect to damped informational value in contracting from $\underline{o}$. Gärdenfors allows only those obtained via strategy 1, whereas I countenance the use of strategies 2 and 3 as well. My contention is that his view is far too restrictive. It does not provide for strategies that in some cases do seem to be endorsed, and with good sense. The account I am giving can accommodate them.

If the only strategy to be allowed were 1 when $\underline{A}$ inconsistent with $\underline{K}$ is added to $\underline{K}$, there would be no need to speak of expansion into inconsistency. One could follow Gärdenfors in speaking of minimal revisions. Characterizing the process as expansion into inconsistency followed by contraction would seem needlessly complicated. However, if I am right in maintaining that often either strategy 2 or strategy 3 is followed, the reference to expansion into inconsistency is not so easily bypassed. When $\underline{A}$&$\underline{P}$ is added to $\underline{K}$, the net result need not be a minimal revision. Transition to $\underline{K}^*$ is a minimal revision. But transition to $\underline{K}^{**}$ could be an expansion of $\underline{K}$ or a residual shift (if $\underline{P}$ remains), and transition subsequently by deliberate expansion to $\underline{K}^{***}$ could yield either a contraction or a residual shift. If $\underline{P}$ is removed in shifting to $\underline{K}^{**}$, the result could be either a contraction of $\underline{K}$ or $\underline{K}$ itself. Transition to the intersection of $\underline{K}^*$ and $\underline{K}^{**}$ will be a contraction if $\underline{P}$ is removed or a residual shift if it is not. In none of these cases will a minimal revision occur. And in none of these cases is $\underline{A}$ in the resulting corpus. But the problem to be faced was what to do when $\underline{A}$ inconsistent with $\underline{K}$ was *added* to $\underline{K}$.

In identifying the various available contraction strategies, it is important to furnish an account of how to contract given that one is going to give up some specific claim. That is the question of identifying admissible contractions that was discussed previously and that is the focus of the discussions of Alchourròn, Gärdenfors and Makinson, and other participants in their enterprise. What I have been emphasizing here is that, important as this question is, it constitutes only a fragment of an account of contraction. It addresses only the question of how to contract given that one is going to give up some specific claim. It does not consider whether one should contract at all and, given that one is going to contract, what claim ought initially to be given up. In coerced contraction, I have suggested that the question of whether one ought to contract is not an issue. The standard for serious possibility has lapsed into incoherence, and this suffices to make the case for contraction. But what to give up remains to be addressed. I have tried to indicate, in a general way, how this issue ought to be approached. In so doing, I have also sketched an account of how advocates of the commensuration requirement rejected by Gärdenfors and others can meet the worry that contradiction is hell. It is now time, therefore, to turn our attention to the question of uncoerced contraction.

4.9 Uncoerced contraction

When the inquirer expands inadvertently into inconsistency via routine expansion (normally because observation, experimental data, or reliable testimony contradicts background knowledge), the inquirer should contract to extricate himself from inconsistency. Contraction is coerced by the inadvertent stumbling into contradiction.

Sometimes, however, contraction is justified even though the initial belief state is consistent. In such uncoerced contraction, there is no need to escape from inconsistency. To be sure, the initial doctrine is in some sense in trouble. The inquiring agent should recognize some advantage in contracting from it. This advantage may accrue from the desirability of excising some defect from the initial corpus. Thus, the initial corpus $\underline{K}$ may contain some sort of anomaly. Anomaly, as I am construing it, is not to be confused with inconsistency. Rather, anomaly is present when $\underline{K}$ contains information that certain events occurred or certain conditions or laws obtain for which $\underline{K}$ fails to provide an explanation, and where the inquirer judges that the theories in K ought to furnish explanations of the occurrences of those events or of those laws or conditions. There is, in other words, a failure on the part of currently accepted theory to fulfill the demands for explanation being made on it. Newtonian gravitational theory failed to furnish an accurate account of the orbit of Mercury. From the point of view of the inquirer, there was no inconsistency in remaining committed to the truth of Newtonian mechanics. Such an inquirer will conclude that he lacks information on those factors in the solar system that would, together with Newtonian gravitational theory, explain the known behavior of Mercury. There is a defect in the initial doctrine. It lacks sufficient information to provide the desired explanation. There is an anomaly.

The existence of such an anomaly alone will not suffice to justify contracting so as to remove the theory whose performance as an explanatory scheme is so disappointing. To the contrary, the inquirer committed to Newtonian mechanics and concerned to remove the anomaly should seek to identify the unknown conditions that will, together with Newtonian mechanics, explain what is currently unexplained. One should not question a theory concerning whose truth one is currently certain merely because it has not yet proved capable of explaining, together with collateral information, some phenomenon. To contract deprives one of the information contained in the theory that normally has some value in explaining other phenomena. And the contracted corpus will not provide explanatory resources for removing the anomaly.

There is, of course, another way to remove anomaly besides identifying the unknown conditions. One might give up on Newtonian mechanics and replace it by an alternative theory that can explain the orbit of Mercury. But if avoidance of error is a desideratum in inquiry, as I claim it is, one cannot justify replacing a theory one is convinced is true with a theory one is convinced is false. One should first contract to give the alternative theory a hearing, and then investigate the merits of the old theory and the new, without begging any question concerning the truth or falsity of the rivals. If one can justify a subsequent expansion that endorses the new theory, the net effect of the contraction, inquiry, and expansion will be a replacement. But at no stage should an assumption concerning whose truth the agent is certain at the time be deliberately replaced by a doxastic proposition concerning whose falsity the agent is also convinced. That is to say, no such replacement should be undertaken if the agent is concerned to avoid error. On the other hand, contraction does not import error from the inquirer's point of view. It incurs a loss of information. But if this loss is accompanied by the opportunity to undertake an inquiry to settle the question as to the truth of the rival theories without begging the question, there may be a benefit in doing so to compensate for the initial loss of information. If this is right, a good reason for implementing an uncoerced contraction would be that it allows a promising theory incompatible with current doctrine to be examined without prejudice.

To justify questioning the initial theory (and, hence, contracting the initial corpus), one should have identified an alternative theory inconsistent with the one currently in the corpus that has some promise as a means for removing anomaly. Perhaps Brownian motion was an anomaly for advocates of classical thermodynamics, but they could tolerate the anomaly, saying that classical thermodynamics did not have the ambition to explain such phenomena. When Einstein showed how statistical mechanics could furnish a systematic account of important features of such motion of particles in colloidal suspension, he furnished an alternative theory and, hence, provided a good reason for moving to a position of suspense between classical thermodynamics and statistical mechanics.

Thus, the presence of an anomaly is not sufficient reason for coming to question a background theory or assumption. One needs an alternative candidate explanation.

Einstein's work on statistical mechanics actually allows one to illustrate a still stronger observation. Sometimes the construction of an alternative candidate explanation occurs antecedent to the recognition of the need for an explanation of some phenomenon and the failure of a currently accepted theory to supply the need. There was no urgent ongoing investigation within the scientific community of the Brownian motion or recognition of the failure of classical thermodynamics to account for it. It was part of Einstein's contribution to have created the demand and, hence, the existence of a sense of anomaly by introducing an alternative.

There is a tendency to think of anomaly as a type of generalized inconsistency or incoherence, and this may lead one to assimilate uncoerced contraction to the case of coerced contraction.

Consider, for example, two couples playing a game of bridge. One of the party deals, and the cards are all so distributed that each of the four players is dealt thirteen cards all of the same suit. That this happened is consistent with the background assumption that the cards were thoroughly shuffled and fairly dealt. But the chance of each player's receiving cards all of the same suit on a fair deal is extremely small, and it may seem that it is so small as to be stochastically inconsistent (whatever that may mean) with the assumption of a fair deal. Hence, so it may be argued, the players ought to become suspicious of the assumption of fairness via coerced contraction.[18]

This reasoning is unconvincing. If the deck is dealt out fairly, each possible deal is as probable or as improbable as any other. The reasoning just described ought to lead to the conclusion that no matter what happens, it is stochastically inconsistent with the assumption of a fair deal. Hence, the assumption of a fair deal is always stochastically inconsistent, and we should always be suspicious of its truth.

One may seek to finesse this difficulty by noting that there are many more ways in which the bridge players can obtain well-balanced hands than hands each of which contains exactly one suit. Deals that can be described as evenly balanced are more likely to be made on a fair deal than the other kind. Indeed, hands that are evenly balanced may be said to be statistically explicable by arguing that the deal was fair, whereas hands that are unevenly balanced cannot be explained on this assumption.

But this only shows that uneven hands are anomalous relative to the background assumption that the deal was fair. It does not show that uneven hands are inconsistent in some special sense of stochastic inconsistency with such a background assumption.

Does the existence of anomaly in such cases warrant contraction? I suggested that it should do so only if there is an alternative theory that can explain the anomalous event. In cases such as the bridge deal, one might indeed entertain the idea that the deal was foul. Of course, harboring such a suspicion is not the same as establishing that it is true. The idea is to contract to a position of suspense between the assumption that the deal was fair and was foul, so that both can be checked without begging questions one way or the other. Subsequent to contraction, investigation may be undertaken that could lead to expansion that settles the issue.

The same point applies to situations where the outcome of a stochastic experiment is somehow surprising. A coin known to be fair is tossed and yields a long, alternating series of heads and tails. One might well become suspicious about the fairness of the coin or the way it is tossed on the grounds that the alternating series of heads and tails could be explained as the product of a mechanism that realizes the instructions of a simple algorithm. The suspicion is expressed as a doubt about whether the sequence of heads and tails is random. There is some confusion here. Any sequence of heads and tails produced by a stochastic process of tossing is a random sequence – even if it yields alternating heads and tails ad infinitum. The idea that sequences computable by algorithms of low complexity are nonrandom derives from the fact that when such sequences are produced, alternative relatively simple hypotheses will be available to explain the sequences to the hypothesis that they are produced by a stochastic process. Then there will be a basis for questioning the assumption of production by a stochastic process. But we should not conclude that because a sequence generatable by a simple algorithm provides some basis for questioning the assumption of production by a stochastic process (i.e., production by a random process), such sequences are not random (i.e., produced by a stochastic or random process). I believe that the currently fashionable tendency to characterize random sequences in terms of the simplicity of algorithms generating them tends to perpetuate this confusion.

This does not mean that the investigation of simplicity of algorithms has no merit. I object only to the view that random sequences so construed characterize sequences generated by stochastic processes. In my judgment, random sequences in a sense determined by the complexity of the algorithms that generate the sequences have relevance to the topic of uncoerced contraction where the aim is to open up one's mind so as to give a hearing to a potential explanation that offers some hope of removing anomaly. If there is a simple way to account for the sequence alternative to the appeal to the occurrence of a stochastic process, there is a prima facie case for questioning the assumption that the sequence is generated by a stochastic process, should that assumption have been made initially.

These desultory remarks about stochastic processes and anomaly are intended to suggest that the issue of anomaly and uncoerced contraction is not restricted to cases where some grand theory is being challenged but is much more pervasive. The critical question to be faced for the program of giving a decision theoretic account of belief revision is how to rationalize uncoerced contraction.

Abstractly conceived, the predicament faced in uncoerced contraction may be characterized as follows: The inquiring agent begins with a corpus $\underline{K}$. The inquirer is confronted with a hypothesis $\underline{A}$ inconsistent with $\underline{K}$ and is concerned to decide whether he is justified in opening up his mind to the truth of $\underline{A}$ by removing $\sim\underline{A}$ from $\underline{K}$.

To assess the merits of such a move, the inquirer should first identify the admissible contraction $\underline{K}^* = \underline{K}^-_{\sim A}$ obtained by removing $\sim\underline{A}$ from $\underline{K}$. He should then construct the expansion $\underline{K}^{**} = (\underline{K}^-_{\sim A})^+_A$ of $\underline{K}^*$ by adding $\underline{A}$. There are three types of possible outcomes of shifting from $\underline{K}$ to $\underline{K}^*$ and engaging in inquiry:

1. After investigation, the inquirer might conclude that he should reinstate $\sim\underline{A}$ and, hence, return to $\underline{K}$ (if Recovery obtains) or to a subset of $\underline{K}$ (if Recovery fails). If Recovery fails, the inquirer will end up with a loss of information. However, there will be no loss of informational value.[19] Hence, in this case, there can be no loss of informational value eventuating from contracting and then inquiring. Indeed, there may be a gain in informational value since, in the course of the intermediate inquiry, new information carrying informational value will be obtained. But if we ignore this complication for the moment, there will be neither gain nor loss.

2. Suppose that inquiry is undertaken and, as a result, $\underline{A}$ is added to $\underline{K}^*$. The informational value of $\underline{K}^{**}$ could be greater than, less than, or equal to that of $\underline{K}$.

3. Finally, if inquiry is undertaken but neither $\underline{A}$ nor $\sim\underline{A}$ is added and the situation remains unsettled, the inquiring agent has suffered a positive loss in informational value.

Clearly, refusing to contract to $\underline{K}^*$ is the best response unless $\underline{K}^{**}$ carries more informational value than $\underline{K}$. Otherwise, the inquirer cannot benefit from contracting and may lose from doing so. There is no sense in incurring the risk of ending up with $\underline{K}^*$ unless there is a chance of benefiting by ending up with $\underline{K}^{**}$.

This fairly abstruse decision theoretic characterization of the situation fits well with the informal observations made previously. To justify opening up one's mind to the hypothesis $\underline{A}$ initially taken not to be seriously possible, the result of ending up with $\underline{A}$ in the corpus must be more valuable informationally than the status quo. This can happen when $\underline{A}$ contributes to systematizing or explaining some phenomenon that cannot be explained by the resources of the initial corpus $\underline{K}$ and where it is desirable to provide such explanation. In short, something like anomaly must be recognized relative to the initial corpus.

To say this, however, is not quite enough. Even if there is such a benefit from contraction, the inquiring agent may judge prior to contraction that the probability of his acquiring evidence justifying the addition of $\underline{A}$ in subsequent investigation is too low compared to the probability of remaining in suspense between $\underline{A}$ and $\sim\underline{A}$. In such a case, the expected informational value of contracting will be less than the informational value of the status quo, and the agent should not contract. To justify contraction, this expected value should be greater than the informational value of the status quo.

The comparisons of informational value made between $\underline{K}$, $\underline{K}^*$, and $\underline{K}^{**}$ are comparisons with respect to probability-based informational value as determined by the measure M. Assessments of damped informational value were introduced to evaluate contractions from a given corpus. In assessing potential expansions from a given corpus, probability-based informational value was used. In the present case, both $\underline{K}$ and $\underline{K}^{**}$ are expansions of $\underline{K}^*$ and, hence, we may look at them in the same way.

This procedure is introduced to indicate how in uncoerced contraction the question of whether to contract is to be answered. Unlike the case of coerced contraction, the issue is far from moot and demands some sort of justification.

It should also be emphasized that whether expansion by adding $\underline{A}$ to $\underline{K}^*$ or by adding $\sim\underline{A}$ to $\underline{K}^*$ is justified depends on the trade-off between risk of error (as assessed relative to $\underline{K}^*$) and the informational value obtained (as assessed relative to the same corpus). One cannot directly justify following the sequence (1), (2), or (3) so as to maximize informational value. The point of contracting to $\underline{K}^*$ is to move to a neutral basis relative to which the truth values of $\underline{A}$ and $\sim\underline{A}$ can be evaluated without begging the question. And relative to that neutral basis, which of the expansion strategies is justified depends not only on the informational value that will be added but also on the risk of error to be incurred *as assessed relative to* $\underline{K}^*$. Prior to contracting from $\underline{K}$ to $\underline{K}^*$, the inquirer might seek to predict or to make a probability judgment (relative to $\underline{K}$) as to what the result of inquiry relative to $\underline{K}^*$ will be. But such an estimate will include a judgment as to what his judgments of risk of error will be relative to $\underline{K}^*$.

For the sake of simplicity, consideration of an important factor has been omitted and should now be brought into play. As a general rule, when the inquirer shifts to $\underline{K}^*$, he will carry out investigations, make observations, conduct experiments, interrogate witnesses, and the like, which will lead to the addition of new information to $\underline{K}^*$ prior to deciding between $\underline{A}$ and $\sim\underline{A}$. This new information will yield a corpus $\underline{K}_1^*$ that carries more informational value than $\underline{K}^*$ and could, in principle, carry more informational value than $\underline{K}$. If the inquirer were to judge prior to contraction that it is likely to be the case that $\underline{K}_1^*$ will carry more informational value than $\underline{K}$, that would be sufficient for him to be justified in contracting. In that case, he would have little to lose by contracting and then inquiring even if he never settled the question of the truth of $\underline{A}$.

4.10 Messianic vs. secular realism

The requirement of commensuration is a central theme of this book. It insists that all legitimate changes of belief state should be rationalized as sequences of expansions and contractions. An important corollary is that all justifiable replacements should be rationalized as sequences of expansions and contractions. In the case of coerced contraction, such replacement can be the result of a routine expansion into inconsistency followed by a contraction or expansion into inconsistency followed by contraction followed by expansion. In uncoerced contraction, the replacement may result from the uncoerced contraction and inquiry followed by expansion.

My advocating the commensuration requirement is predicated on the thesis that avoidance of error is a desideratum of inquiry and that this desideratum demands that no inquirer should deliberately import error into his doctrine. To replace $\sim\underline{A}$ when one is certain that it is true by $\underline{A}$ is to deliberately replace truth with error as one judges it. It egregiously violates the demand that error be avoided.

My contention is that replacement is never basically justified. This contention allows one to respect the demand that error be avoided.

The claim that avoidance of error is a common feature of the goals relative to which changes of belief ought to be legitimated in science and in daily life represents a kind of realism that does more than insist that theories carry truth values but also insists that what these truth values are is a matter of concern to the inquirer in theory choice.

This view stands in opposition to the positions of Kuhn and Feyerabend, who insist that in certain kinds of changes (paradigm shifts), there is no neutral basis relative to which the truth values of rival hypotheses can be assessed without presupposing the truth or falsity of one or the other of the rivals in advance. Consequently, anyone who changes from one view to the other cannot do so in a way that manifests a concern to avoid error. The inquirer is compelled in such cases to shift from a doctrine he is certain is true to one he is certain is false. Pace Feyerabend, realists in the sense I am talking about cannot concede incommensurability with complacency.

The attack on the existence of a neutral basis often seems to be grounded on the view that even observation is "theory laden." I do not deny that the reports added to the corpus via routine expansion depend upon assumptions of reliability that often presuppose a rich theoretical background. Nor do I deny that, when deciding whether to add new information via deliberate expansion, such decisions are typically grounded in a rich background of information. But from this it does not follow that the background information needed must include the claims that are open to investigation. There may be no background assumptions that can be neutral with respect to every potential controversy. But for every potential controversy, it is entertainable that such a neutral background can be found.

One may find exceptions to this contention in the case of controversies as to whether logic should be two- or three-valued where three-valued logic is not to be construed in terms of modality or epistemic notions. Although one may use what Quine calls *semantic ascent* to compare rival logics without begging questions, one cannot do so if one is concerned to choose between them in a way that takes into account risk of error. Hence, avoidance of error cannot be accommodated in such accounts of changes in logic.

I suspect that the Kuhn–Feyerabend vision of paradigm switches or scientific revolutions claims that changes in scientific theories such as the shift from classical physics to quantum mechanics or from classical physics to special relativity involves a change of this nature. If it does, I do not know of any reason to think it correct.

Of course, those who think that, in revising scientific doctrine, avoidance of error is of no concern may not see much point in insisting that replacements be rationalized as sequences of contractions and expansions. And, in some moods, Kuhn seems to endorse just such a view. Kuhn has sought to defend himself against the charge that major revolutions are immune to reasoned criticism by taking note of several values that may be invoked to adjudicate between rival theories. The catalogue he offers appears to take into account various cognitive values relevant, as I understand it, to the assessment of informational value. Risk of error plays no role (Kuhn, 1970a).

As I understand the matter, controversies concerning the realism of claims either within science or without concern whether such claims bear truth values *in a sense that requires us to be concerned to avoid error with respect to these claims.* If someone (like B. van Fraassen, 1980) claims that a theory carries a truth value but that we need not take into account the risk of importing falsehood into the evolving doctrine when we contemplate adding it to the doctrine, I am not clear why it matters whether it carries a truth value at all. If, instead of embracing van Fraassen's *critical empiricism,* one denies the truth–bearing character of the theory, as authors like J. Dewey do, avoidance of error remains irrelevant to the revision of doctrine. From the perspective of the approach I am advocating, there is little difference.

Gärdenfors's argument for the basic nature of replacement seems, as I reconstruct it, to be predicated on the point that to expand into inconsistency is to expand into hell and, hence, should be forbidden. This view does display a respect for avoidance of error to the extent that it displays respect for the demand to avoid inconsistency.

As I explained in Section 2.6, this respect drives Gärdenfors to regard minimal revision as a basic type of legitimate belief change and, hence, to regard replacements in response to observations conflicting with the initial doctrine as sometimes legitimate. But this attitude displays a disregard for avoidance of error as a desideratum in inquiry in tension with the respect manifested by Gärdenfors's concern to avoid inconsistency.

I have sought to respond to the tensions that are displayed in Gärdenfors's account of belief change by suggesting that even though inquirers should be concerned to avoid error, they also should be concerned to obtain new information of value, and such curiosity can justify risking error to obtain new information. What should be prohibited is being prepared to add new information to one's evolving doctrine when one is certain that it is false. No amount of new information can be worth the importation of certain error. However, this prohibition argues against expanding into contradiction by a deliberate (= inferential = inductive) expansion; but it allows one to risk expanding into inconsistency via routine expansion, provided that the chances of importing contradiction are sufficiently low.

In this chapter, I have sought to show how contraction from inconsistency may be analyzed and evaluated. One of the advantages of the account given is that, unlike the views of Gärdenfors (and, for that matter, Stalnaker before him), the net effect of changes initiated by adding new information obtained from witnesses or observation that conflicts with initial doctrine need not be a minimal revision – that is, a replacement. I have argued that, in general, it neither is nor ought to be. On the other hand, in those examples, of the sort cited by Gärdenfors, where replacement does seem plausible, the account of coerced contraction remains applicable.

In addition, the account of uncoerced contraction I have offered can handle those types of replacement (not considered by Gärdenfors but much discussed by Feyerabend) where theory choice depends on the availability of rivals to the currently favored theory.

There remains, however, an important objection to the approach I have been advocating that needs to be addressed.

Avoidance of error is a desideratum of inquiry. Commitment to it implies that one should never deliberately import items into one's doctrine that one is currently certain are false. What about inadvertently importing such items into one's doctrine? I have defended inadvertent importation of error as legitimate, provided that the risk of error incurred is sufficiently low. As long as one is entitled to incur some positive risk of error, this seems reasonable – at least in the case of routine expansion.

Consider, however, uncoerced contraction. I have said that the inquirer incurs no risk of error in that case because no information whatsoever is being imported and, hence, no false information is being added.

However, it might be objected that this view is shortsighted. The inquiring agent can very well anticipate that upon contracting, he will engage in inquiries that may warrant subsequent expansions and that there is a positive probability of the agent's expanding by importing into his doctrine something he currently is certain is false. And in some cases, the probability of this happening is very high. Yet, the high probability need not deter him and, if the account of coerced contraction given previously is along the right lines, it might actually encourage him.

Thus, someone might not have been presented with Einstein's account of Brownian motion until after the experiments of Svedberg and Perrin, so that he would be virtually certain that upon contraction removing the classical thermodynamics, he would expand to endorse statistical mechanics. Surely such contraction entails deliberately importing items that one is currently certain are false into one's doctrine.

But even if matters are not so extreme, there is merely a good chance of this happening, and if one takes avoidance of error seriously, the risks of error would be too high to justify taking them for the informational benefits.

I suggest we distinguish between being concerned to avoid error *at the next change in belief state* and being concerned to avoid error *not only at the next stage but at n* (>2) *or all stages down the line* or being concerned to avoid error *at some ultimate stage* – perhaps in the limit – without regard to what happens in between.

I shall call those who advocate avoidance of error as a desideratum of inquiry in the first sense *secular realists* and those who favor one of the other two senses *messianic realists*.

The realism I favor is a secular realism. From the point of view of secular realism, the difficulty we are now considering presupposes that we are concerned with avoidance of error at subsequent states. This type of concern for progress toward the truth is a species of messianic realism that does, indeed, argue against uncoerced contraction from those assumptions one is certain are true. Messianic realists cannot give the account of uncoerced contraction I favor.

They must also stand opposed to routine expansion because of the risk of expansion into inconsistency. Because messianic realists care about converging on the truth at the End of Days, any time they are certain of the truth of some claim, giving it up will set back progress; but they incur the risk of doing so if they expand into inconsistency (because of coerced contraction) and, indeed, the risk will be considerable. Hence, making observations or acquiring testimony from reliable witnesses will not be conducive to progress.

I am a secular realist and, hence, do not feel the force of the difficulties just mentioned.

Charles Peirce, throughout his long career, advocated the idea that converging on the true, complete story of the world is the ultimate aim of inquiry. Like the view taken here, Peirce's "realism" is tied to his conception of truth as a value guiding the conduct of inquiry. However, Peirce's conception of the importance of truth differs in a fundamental way from the one advocated here. According to Peirce's conception, the inquiring agent is seeking a maximally specific answer to any given question that also avoids error and seeks to do so as the ultimate aim of the specific kind of inquiry under consideration. For secular realists, by contrast, avoidance of error is of concern as the proximate aim of efforts to revise doctrine at some specific step. Thus, in justifying expansion relative to $\underline{K}$, we should seek to avoid expanding into error on the assumption that all items in $\underline{K}$ are true. In contraction, we do not have to worry about importing error because no assumptions are being imported at all. To be sure, we might import new assumptions at the expansion step following contraction. But, for secular realists, the concern to avoid error is in the revision currently contemplated, and not at the step or steps after that. That is what I mean by suggesting that, for Peirce, avoidance of error tends to be an ultimate aim of inquiry rather than a proximate one.

The difference is an important one. If avoidance of error is an ultimate aim of inquiry, then when an inquirer begins with corpus $\underline{K}$ and contemplates removing $\sim\underline{A}$ in order to give $\underline{A}$ a hearing, he does run a risk of importing error at the expansion step from his current perspective. Relative to that perspective $\underline{A}$ is certainly false, and contracting to give it a hearing incurs a risk of importing error in a sense relevant to his ultimate goal. It makes no sense to incur such a risk given that the inquirer is certain that $\sim\underline{A}$ is true. Hence, everything in $\underline{K}$ is immune to revision.

Peirce, of course, denied that any claims other, perhaps, than logical truths are immune to revision. Hence, he was committed to denying that $\underline{K}$ should contain anything but logical truths. That is one reading of his celebrated fallibilism, a doctrine that seems to run together the idea that every claim is open to revision with the idea that every claim is uncertain.

This view seems to conflict with the important insight, expressed in Peirce's "Fixation of Belief," that in inquiry we start by counting only those items subject to a real and living doubt as uncertain and viewing what is certain as including a very substantial extralogical background.

I take it that this conflict reflects a genuine tension in Peirce's thought between the vision represented by his belief–doubt model of inquiry and his messianic realism according to which convergence on the true, complete story is the ultimate aim of inquiry. I do not believe that he ever eliminated the tension.

Perhaps Peirce and other messianic realists are best understood as endorsing the second version of messianic realism, according to which the ultimate aim of inquiry is to realize the true story of the world at the end of days, regardless of what happens in between. Even if the inquirer is certain that he runs the risk of importing error into his evolving doctrine at later stages of inquiry by removing assumptions he is currently certain are true, this brand of epistemic eschatology might wish to maintain that, at the End of Days, things will sort out and the ultimate goal will be attained. Such realists need to explain how the proximate goals of ongoing inquiries can be understood as promoting this end, except on the basis of an inexplicable albeit touching faith. In particular, they need to explain whether avoidance of error is a desideratum that directs our assessments and improvements of the methods of ongoing inquiry. As far as I can see, such messianic realists dispense with avoidance of error as a value in ongoing inquiry in practice by relegating it to the messianic future.

John Dewey, who followed Peirce in developing the belief–doubt model, avoided the tensions to which I have been pointing by denying that avoidance of error is a relevant value in inquiry altogether. Karl Popper, who independently of Peirce developed a version of messianic realism, had no use for the belief–doubt model.

In my judgment, the belief–doubt model represents the greatest insight in the pragmatist tradition, and I have sought to preserve it in my own thinking. On the other hand, Dewey's antirealism seems to me to represent too draconian a response to the difficulty facing Peirce. I have, therefore, suggested endorsing what I once called *myopic* but now prefer calling *secular* realism.

According to secular realism, the inquiring agent is committed to maximal certainty about the truth of the assumptions in his current corpus. He is concerned, moreover, to avoid error in the next alteration he makes in that corpus, where error is judged on the assumption that everything in the current corpus is true. Of course, the agent can recognize that in making changes in the current corpus, he might and probably will end up several stages down the chain of belief revision, becoming certain of claims he currently is certain are false. But as a secular realist, he is not concerned with the possibility that his beliefs several stages down the chain will be false as he currently judges truth and falsity. He is not concerned with progress toward the true, complete story, but only with avoiding error at the next step.

This view does, indeed, undermine the idea of scientific progress as progress toward the truth. It need not, however, undermine all conceptions of scientific progress. Inquiry does not get off the ground without demands for information, programs for research that aim, among other things, to obtain more comprehensive and informationally more valuable doctrines. Our goals in seeking more information are, on the view I have been advancing, far from myopic. We do look ahead many steps down the line. There is nothing in secular realism that mandates myopia with respect to demands for valuable information but only with respect to avoidance of error.

Secular realism seems to fall between two stools. It rejects the blanket claim of antirealists that truth doesn't matter except, perhaps, as regards the "phenomena" (whatever this may mean). And it also rejects the idea that

truth is a regulative ideal directing us toward the End of Days, when inquirers will have attained the true, complete story. This latter view renders the
importance of truth as a value relevant only to such eschatological aspira-
tions. Truth as a value has little bearing on the immediate concerns of special
inquiries.

Secular realism seeks to preserve the relevance of truth as a value in
carrying out the problem-solving inquiries that the Peircean belief–doubt
model was designed to illuminate. And it seeks to do so in a way that
preserves a coherent distinction between fallibilism (the claim that nothing
but the truths of logic are certain) and corrigibilism (the claim that all extralogical truths are open to revision).

Gärdenfors (1988, pp. 18–20) explicitly disavows any reliance on a conception of the relation between belief and the external world in his account of
belief change. I sympathize with the disavowal. However, secular realists like
myself insist that an account of belief change requires an account of how the
concern to avoid error controls legitimate changes in belief. To address this
question, one does not need to discuss the relation between belief and the
external world. Gärdenfors avoids this issue as well. If avoidance of error is
of no concern to the inquirer, worries about the legitimacy of replacement
because it requires the agent to deliberately import certain error cannot be
raised. But even if we students of belief change avoid speaking of the relations between belief states and the world, we can consider whether inquirers
ought to be concerned to avoid error in either a secular or a messianic sense.

But if avoidance of error is not a concern of the inquirer, why should
inconsistency be hell, as Gärdenfors proclaims it to be? As I have indicated, it
is possible to make sense out of contraction from inconsistency, provided that
one can appeal to the inputs that injected inconsistency in the first place.
One can, therefore, talk intelligently about extricating oneself from inconsistency. But why should one care about retreating from inconsistency or avoiding it altogether were it not that it is desirable to avoid error?

My point is that accounts of belief change that do not take into account
what the aims of the inquirer are or should be and what the conditions of
rational goal attainment are will yield at best partial accounts of rational belief
change. And failure to take account of the goals can lead to doubtful views of
what the basic kinds of legitimate change are. Much of the effort of this book
is designed to show that currently fashionable views according to which
minimal revision is the basic kind of legitimate change are misguided due to
debatable assumptions about belief revision derived from rejection of commensurability by students by Kuhn and Feyerabend, from mistaken under-
standings of the relations between belief states and modal judgments, and
from an excessive concern about expanding into inconsistency.

Notes

Chapter 2

1. From a so-called naturalistic point of view, such a reduction replaces two mysteries with one.

2. The set of potential belief states is, therefore, a set of predicates or properties or conditions. In discussing a structure imposed on this set, it is clear that there is a commitment to abstract entities of some kind. Whether such a commitment can be mitigated is not a matter of concern in this book. However, the distinction between X's current state of full belief and other potential states in the conceptual framework entails no further ontological commitment. To say that X is in the state of full belief **K** is to say that a certain predicate is true of him. To say that **K*** is a potential state of full belief for X that is not X's current state is deny that a certain predicate is of true of X and also to say that X is able (or permitted) to change, so that this predicate becomes true of him. Such an ability or entitlement is a condition that X currently satisfies. In general, to say that X is able to respond in manner $\underline{R}$ on a "trial" of kind $\underline{S}$ is to say that X lacks the sure-fire disposition to fail to $\underline{R}$ on a trial of kind $\underline{S}$. Such talk about abilities and dispositions can be analyzed without the benefit of a possible worlds semantics (see Levi, 1980a, ch. 11), I deny, therefore, that there is any covert commitment to modal realism of either the strong form advocated by D. Lewis (1986) or the "ersatzist" version favored by R. Stalnaker (1984). As to the question of whether we should be speaking of abilities or entitlements, further elaboration will be offered later in this chapter.

3. A relation $\underline{R}$ on a domain $\underline{D}$ is a partial ordering if and only if $\underline{R}$ is a quasi-ordering on $\underline{D}$ and $\underline{R}$ is antisymmetric. A relation $\underline{R}$ on $\underline{D}$ is a quasi-ordering if and only if it is reflexive (so that every element of $\underline{D}$ bears the relation to itself) and transitive (so that if $\underline{x}$ is $\underline{R}$ to $\underline{y}$ and $\underline{y}$ to $\underline{z}$, $\underline{x}$ is $\underline{R}$ to $\underline{z}$). $\underline{R}$ is antisymmetric if and only if for every $\underline{x}$ and $\underline{y}$, if both $\underline{xRy}$ and $\underline{yRx}$, $\underline{x} = \underline{y}$.

4. The partial ordering associated with a boolean algebra has the following properties: (a) if $\underline{x}$ and $\underline{y}$ are both elements of the boolean algebra, there is an element $\underline{z}$ such that $\underline{x} \leq \underline{z}$ and $\underline{y} \leq \underline{z}$ and there is no $\underline{z}'$ meeting this condition that precedes $\underline{z}$ in the partial ordering. In that case, $\underline{z} = \underline{x} \lor \underline{y}$. (b) If $\underline{x}$ and $\underline{y}$ are both elements of the boolean algebra, there is an element $\underline{w}$ such that $\underline{w} \leq \underline{x}$ and $\underline{w} \leq \underline{y}$ and there is no $\underline{w}'$ meeting this condition that succeeds $\underline{w}$ in the partial ordering. $\underline{w} = \underline{x} \land \underline{y}$. (c) The elements of the boolean algebra are such that $\lor$ distributes over $\land$ and vice versa. (d) There is a unique element **1** of the boolean algebra that is a "maximum" in the sense that it succeeds every other element and a unique element **0** that is a "minimum." For every element $\underline{x}$ of the boolean algebra, there is another element $\underline{x}^*$ (the complement of $\underline{x}$) such that $\underline{x} \land \underline{x}^* = \mathbf{0}$ and $\underline{x} \lor \underline{x}^* = \mathbf{1}$. A pseudo-boolean algebra satisfies all these conditions but (d), which is weakened to posit only the existence of a pseudocomplement for $\underline{x}$ whose meet with $\underline{x}$ is **0** but whose join need not be identical to **1**.

   For future reference, the following technical terminology is introduced. (See

Bell and Slomson, 1969, ch. 1, and Rasiowa and Sikorsky, 1963, ch. 1, for a discussion of boolean algebras and this terminology.)

A filter on the boolean algebra is a set $\underline{F}$ of elements of the algebra such that if $\underline{x}$ and $\underline{y}$ are in $\underline{F}$, so is $\underline{x} \wedge \underline{y}$, and if $\underline{x} \le \underline{y}$ and $\underline{x}$ is in $\underline{F}$, so is $\underline{y}$. An ultrafilter on the boolean algebra is a filter on the algebra such that for every element $\underline{x}$ of the algebra, either $\underline{x}$ or $\underline{x}^*$ is in the filter. The filter (ultrafilter) generated by element $\underline{x}$ of the boolean algebra is the set of elements of the algebra that $\underline{x}$ precedes in the partial ordering. A filter (ultrafilter) is principal if it is generated by some element of the algebra. It is proper if it is not identical to the set of all elements of the algebra.

An element $\underline{x}$ of the boolean algebra is an atom of the algebra if and only if the filter generated by it is a proper ultrafilter. A boolean algebra is atomic if and only if every element of the algebra other than 0 or an atom is preceded in the partial ordering by an atom of the algebra. It is atomless if and only if it contains no atoms.

5. Suppose, for example, that there were a countable set of atoms in the algebra. We may think of them as hypotheses about which of the integers is to be selected in a lottery. The ultrafilter according to which all of the atoms are judged false is a nonprincipal ultrafilter. Such a network of judgments of truth and error does not constitute a potential state of full belief if the conceptual framework is the boolean algebra generated by these atoms. If such a set of judgments is, indeed, available to the inquirer, there should be an element of the algebra whose complement has as consequences the complements of these atoms. But then the conceptual framework is a different algebra than the one that was initially contemplated. It is possible to construct formally a boolean algebra whose atoms are the proper ultrafilters of the original algebra, whether they are principal or not; but if the original algebra represents only potential states of full belief, this constructed algebra does not. I do not mean to impose a strong restriction on conceptual frameworks. There is no injunction against enriching the conceptual framework. However, according to the approach being proposed, potential states are elements of the algebra. If there is no element of the conceptual framework generating a system of judgments of truth and error, in that framework such a system of judgments is conceptually inaccessible and needs to be modified in order to render the system of judgments conceptually available.

6. I think that when Davidson (1984, ch. 13) argues against there being more than one conceptual scheme, he must be thinking of conceptual schemes in this second sense.

7. This taxonomy appears in this form in Levi (1980a, ch. 1.8). Earlier versions were published in Levi (1974) and (1976). I first used this terminology to make these distinctions in a paper, "Truth, Fallibility and the Growth of Knowledge," that I read at various universities, including Rockefeller, Pittsburgh, Michigan, and Boston universities from 1971 on. However, it was not submitted for publication until 1975 and was not published until 1983 (as Levi, 1983). P. Gärdenfors uses the notions of expansion and contraction in a sense similar to mine. He sometimes uses the term *revision* for changes that are expansions when the information added is consistent with the initial state and that are replacements otherwise. He has no term for what I call *residual shifts*. In the past, I used *revision* to cover all changes in states of belief. I shall, for the most part, use *change* in this book. The relation between replacement and Gärdenfors's revision will be explained in Section 2.9. See Gärdenfors (1988, ch. 3).

8. The structure induced by X's state of credal probability judgment on the **K** propositions is best represented by a set of conditional probability functions

satisfying a certain convexity condition as proposed in Levi (1980a). This representation generates a quasi-ordering of the K propositions of the sort mentioned in the text. However, several such sets may generate the same quasi-ordering. I contend that the differences between convex set representations are significant for deliberation and inquiry and, hence, for many purposes ought not to be neglected.

9. Thus, potential corpora need not be finitely axiomatizable. When they are not, the potential states they represent may not be representable by single sentences in L.

10. In virtue of introducing a Tarskilike conception of truth, we are in a position to deploy the model theoretic notion of logical consequence. (For a discussion of the notion of logical consequence and the contrast with the notion of deductive consequence in formalized theories, see Tarski, 1956, ch. 16.) The question arises as to whether potential corpora should be closed under the model theoretic notion of logical consequence, as well as under deductive consequence characterized syntactically. If the urcorpus of sentences mapped onto 1 includes set theory and the truths of arithmetic, the set of elements of the urcorpus and, hence, of any potential corpus will not be recursively enumerable. Potential corpora will be closed under deduction; but no axiomatization will yield all the sentences that are judged true according to the belief state being represented. However, the total set of sentences true in L if the potential state of full belief is error-free will be closed under logical consequence.

11. The details sketched here concerned the use of a regimented formal language L to represent potential states of full belief in a conceptual framework. In practice, the linguistic means deployed by inquirers and observers of their conduct to characterize their states of full belief are more wide-ranging. One can characterize a corpus of sentences K without listing the sentences. (Indeed, giving a list would be an impossibility.) One might offer a characterization by means of a set of axioms or axiom schemas. Or one might use other, even more indirect means. X may declare that he fully believes that quantum mechanics is true. Yet X might not (in an extreme case) be in a position to identify a single axiom or theorem of quantum theory. Even so, given the sincerity of his declaration (which is to be firmly distinguished from its foolhardiness), X may be taken to be committed to the truth in L of a system of sentences in L representing quantum mechanics. Suppose that X utters the sentence token "What I am now saying is not true." This linguistic performance is, of course, not in the regimented language L. Nor is it in a regimentable fragment of English (or any other natural language) because the designator "What I am now saying" is not a standardized designator (as, for example, the numerals are taken to be and legally recognized names for cities sometimes are). Still, the linguistic performance is an attempt at full recognition. Unlike the utterance "What I am now saying is true," however, it is abortive. We should refrain from considering the linguistic performance as being true or false and should instead assign it the truth value Gap. Indeed, X himself is committed to fully recognizing that his effort at full recognition is abortive. When sentence tokens are uttered or written in an effort to fulfill a doxastic commitment and the performances are recognized (either by X or by an observer) to fail, then X or the observer, as the case may be, may assign them the value Gap. Notice that on this view there is nothing to prevent either X or an outside observer from saying "What X said is not true" and, through that utterance, to succeed in manifesting full recognition that X's original utterance is not true (because it is a Gap). My concern here is not with either the weak or strong liar paradox. On these matters, I am following the suggestions of Parsons (1983, ch. 9) and Gaifman (1988).

What I am claiming is that the challenge of addressing the liar paradoxes is related to accounts of how linguistic performances succeed and fail to manifest doxastic performances. When discussing revisions of doxastic commitments in abstraction from doxastic performance, these questions may be set to one side. Indeed, when the error-free potential states are characterized as the elements of a privileged ultrafilter of the conceptual framework, there is no room for liar paradoxes to arise. Yet, we do need to represent states of full belief linguistically. In the systematic investigation of belief revision, we may take the representation to be in a standardized (and, hence, regimented) language where care is taken that sentences in $\underline{L}$ represent doxastic propositions and, hence, potential corpora in $\underline{L}$ do so as well. To represent all that we wish to say about the inquirer's doxastic commitment, the introduction of a hierarchy of metalanguages with Tarskilike truth predicates for languages in the hierarchy, and so on, proves useful. Observe, however, that given the hierarchy of languages, the hierarchy of metacorpora expressible in languages in the hierarchy is determined by the lowest-level corpus. Hence, it is not, strictly speaking, necessary to appeal to anything more than the lowest-level corpus in representing the agent's state of full belief except insofar as we seek to render explicit the agent's commitments to judgments of truth value, serious possibility, credal probability, utility, and so on.

12.   Gärdenfors (1988, p. 23). See sects. 3.6 and 3.7 for a more accurate comparison of potential corpora and belief sets.

13.   It may be suggested that the behavior is explained in a covering law sense by appealing to the information that the agent is, on this occasion, rational. Here the term *rational* is construed as a disposition term – to wit, characterizing the disposition to fulfill commitments. According to the position taken in Levi and Morgenbesser (1964, pp. 221–32), disposition predicates are placeholders for theoretically and explanatorily more satisfactory terms in covering law explanation. Because I am inclined to think that "is rational" is not likely to be integrated into a satisfactory explanatory theory (although I cannot prove this) and, more crucially, because I do not think that it makes any difference to the status of models of rationality whether they can be so integrated, I deny that principles of rationality are primarily intended for purposes of explanation.

Nonetheless, if an agent's behavior can be described as living up to his or her commitments and, hence, as being rational, it can be seen as conforming to a certain pattern and to this extent can be explained or understood. But the understanding is best construed as conforming to regularities that the agent undertook to satisfy. I think it may be preferable to call this *rationalization* rather than *explanation*.

14.   The question arises as to the standards for assessing costs here. A lazy inquirer may regard the effort to fulfill his commitments as too costly where a more energetic inquirer suffering from the same disabilities does not. Is the lazy inquirer failing to do what he ought to do to fulfill his commitments, in contrast to the more energetic inquirer? I have no firm answer to this question. It seems to me that the issues involved here resemble disputes over when a person has fulfilled his contract to buy his house. We can recognize the question as a prescriptive one without pretending that we are always in a position to answer it in advance.

15.   Gärdenfors (1988, p. 10). Gärdenfors is not alone in this view. Carnap's "inductive logic" (1962) sought to identify rather strong commitments inquirers should have concerning the credal states they adopt where these commitments are generated by the inquirer's state of full belief (total available evidence). H.

E. Kyburg (1983, pp. 221–31) also regards inductive logic as characterizing the commitments an inquirer has "in an atemporal sense" (p. 226). Kyburg, like Carnap, thinks that the state of credal probability judgment to which the inquirer is committed is uniquely determined by his state of full belief. However, for Kyburg, inductive inference is accepting some hypotheses "with practical certainty" on the basis of what is accepted "with moral certainty" in the corpus corresponding to the state full belief (pp. 226–7). Indeed, it is astonishing to see how few authors writing about induction in the twentieth century have thought of induction as involving a genuinely ampliative change in the inquirer's state of full belief. However, very few have been as explicit as Gärdenfors and Kyburg have been about the matter.

16. For a development of this view of Peirce, see Levi, (1980b).

17. I am not denying the importance of giving an account of justification of changes in belief state. Nor am I denying that, even from the point of view of the inquirer X, there is a distinction to be made between coming to fully believe that h through belief change, coming to do so without error, and coming to do so with justification. Prior to instituting the change, these are clearly distinct conditions. Moreover, from X's view prior to changing his belief state, he would not consider himself entitled to say that he will come to know that h by coming to full belief that h. For at that stage, he is not certain that h is true and, according to the view I favor, knowledge is true full belief. To be entitled, he would need a good reason for adding the doxastic proposition that h to the consequences of his state of full belief. But if such justification were available, then X's coming to full belief would be a justified coming to full belief that h and a justified coming to full belief that error is thereby avoided. (Notice that what is justified is that the future state is one where X has full belief that error is avoided and not the current state where X is in doubt on this score.) See Levi (1980a, ch. 1).

18. Thus, the "deductive closure" condition on the set of "accepted" sentences is abandoned. Care should be taken to distinguish this rejection of deductive closure, which is due to applying the requirement to doxastic performances to rejections of deductive closure, as a constraint on commitments. Kyburg (in, e.g., 1983, pp. 221–63) denies that one ought to be committed to accepting all the deductive consequences of what one accepts. However, acceptance involves levels. At the highest level are what I would call the *full beliefs*. Kyburg does require deductive closure for these "moral certainties." On the other hand, there are those sentences accepted because they are sufficiently probable – that is, carry probability at least as great as some threshold level. These are the *practical certainties*. The set of these need not be deductively closed. Kyburg is not motivated by the problem of bounded rationality – that is, the limitations on our computational capacity and our emotional stability that preclude our satisfying the conditions of ideal rationality. He thinks that there is an important sense of "acceptance" corresponding to his notion of practical certainty for which it is implausible to require deductive closure. I have no doubt that one can define *acceptance* in a way that allows for such failures of deductive closure, but I have not been convinced of the value of the idea of acceptance constructed in this way. I am not concerned to settle this issue here, but only to point out that Kyburg's rejection of deductive closure is not motivated by worries about bounded rationality, and his views ought not to be confused with those we are now examining.

19. This point is discussed in Levi (1984, ch. 6). See especially pp. 80–1.

20. The insistence on a "regulative" rather than an "ontological" conception of

logic implied by the position taken here is, of course, reminiscent of the views of
E. Nagel (1949, pp. 191–210). Nagel does not, however, discuss Frege's views
about the regulative view.

21. See especially P. Gärdenfors (1988), C. E. Alchourrón, P. Gärdenfors, and D.
Makinson (1985), and papers by Alchourrón, Gärdenfors, Makinson, H. Rott,
and K. Segerberg listed in the bibliography of Gärdenfors's book.

22. Matters are not quite so convenient when we focus on potential corpora as
representations of belief states. Let $\underline{A}$ be a sentence in regimented language $\underline{L}$
that represents the doxastic proposition **A**. Let $\underline{K}$ be the set of sentences in $\underline{L}$
that represents the state of full belief **L**. Then $\mathbf{K} \wedge \mathbf{A}$ is representable in $\underline{L}$ by the
corpus $\underline{K}_A^+$, which is the closure under deductive consequence of $\underline{K} \cup \underline{A}$. We
shall call this corpus the expansion of the corpus $\underline{K}$ obtained by adding $\underline{A}$ and
adding all consequences of the consequences of $\underline{K}$ and $\underline{A}$.

Since some doxastic propositions representable by potential corpora express-
ible in $\underline{L}$ are not representable by single sentences in $\underline{L}$, some expansions of
corpora cannot be characterized as adding an input sentence to a corpus $\underline{K}$ and
forming the deductive closure. To this extent, Gärdenfors's approach is excessively restrictive. It remains true, however, that for, the most part, expansions of
corpora of interest will tend to be representable along lines in keeping with
Gärdenfors's approach. In any case, it is in keeping with Gärdenfors's approach
to think of adding doxastic propositions to belief state.

23. Gärdenfors (1988, p. 68) correctly represents my commensuration requirement
as a condition on legitimate changes in belief. Yet because of his well-
intentioned attempt to describe my view within his framework, he misleadingly
claims that I advance the thesis that "revisions can be analyzed as a sequence of
contractions and expansions." The claim is misleading because, in my previous
work and in this one, the term *revision* is used to describe any kind of change in
belief state, and not the special sort of change considered by Gärdenfors.
Moreover, and more crucially, the relevant passages on pp. 64–5 of Levi
(1988a) concern legitimate changes in belief state and distinguish in effect, if
not in so many words, between basically legitimate changes and changes whose
legitimacy is derived. As I have pointed out in the text, however, the only kinds
of revisions in Gärdenfors's sense that are legitimate on my view are expansions. The *Levi Identity* according to which the minimal revision $\mathbf{K}_A^*$ adding **A** to
K is identical to $(\mathbf{K}_{\sim A}^-)_A^+$ where $\mathbf{K}_{\sim A}^-$ is the admissible (in Gärdenfors's language,
the minimal) contraction removing $\sim$A from **K** and $\mathbf{K}_A^+$ is the expansion of **K** by
adding **A** may, in the light of this, be understood in one of two ways: It can be
understood as claiming that a minimal revision can be decomposed, for purposes of analysis, into an expansion by adding **A** to the result of contracting **K**
by removing $\sim$A. This is, indeed, a claim I would endorse. So would Gärdenfors. It is a corollary of the uniqueness condition on legitimate contractions
and minimal revisions together with the requirement that the space of potential
states of belief constitute a boolean algebra – the claim that supports the commensurability thesis. So construed, the Levi Identity is innocuous and ought to
be noncontroversial. The Levi Identity can also be understood as claiming that
every legitimate revision should be shown to be a legitimate expansion by
adding **A** of a legitimate contraction of **K** by deleting $\sim$A if $\sim$A is a consequence of **K**. So construed, it is too strong and too restrictive for me to endorse
it. The commensuration requirement that I do accept implies that all replacements are derivative. None are basic. But it does not imply that all are derived
by first justifying the contraction from **K** by removing $\sim$A and then justifying
the expansion of that result by adding **A**. In the subsequent discussion, I

understand the Levi Identity in the first, more trivial way. The more substantive proposal I have made is the commensuration requirement.

Chapter 3

1. More elaborate accounts of deliberate expansion are found in Levi (1967; 1980a, chs. 2 and 6; 1984, chs. 5, 6, and 7; and 1986, ch. 3).
2. In Section 2.5, I proposed to use *full belief* to characterize doxastic commitment and *full recognition* to characterize doxastic performance. A further distinction can be made between such performances. X fully recognizes that h̲ if he has a disposition to various kinds of behavior. When that disposition is activated, the resultant behavior manifests full recognition that h̲. Both the disposition and its manifestation satisfy the agent's doxastic commitment.

    Reporting that h̲ is in some respects indistinguishable from manifesting full recognition that h̲. Both types of events may be linguistic utterances, psychic episodes, or neurophysiological processes. Moreover, both are described intensionally (as reporting that h̲ and manifesting full recognition that h̲, respectively). The difference is that manifesting full recognition that h̲ is construed as a manifestation of a disposition of the agent conforming to his doxastic commitments, whereas reporting that h̲ is construed as a manifestation of some external condition of the environment when the agent interacts with it. There is no presumption that the agent's report is a manifestation of a disposition conforming to a doxastic commitment.

    For those who fail to recognize a distinction between commitment and performance, no sense can be made of the contrast between describing such episodes as reports and as occurent manifestations of full recognitions.
3. I suspect that C. Misak (1987) is correct in suggesting that Peirce was inclined to this view.
4. Notice that when the testimony of the senses conflicts with settled background information, we do not give priority to the deliverances of the senses and abandon the background assumptions in favor of the data. Michelson's experiments were not crucial experiments deciding against classical theory. On the other hand, when the product of routine expansion via observation conflicts with a *conjecture* given background information, there is no pressure to question background assumptions. Pace Duhem, there are crucial experiments. The case for a rival view refuses to take seriously the distinction between background assumptions that are a settled ingredient in a state of full belief and tentatively or conjecturally held collateral claims. When a theory is tested using collateral assumptions tentatively or conjecturally held, the reports of experiment do not deductively refute the theory relative to the state of full belief. But when the collateral assumptions are part of the state of full belief, they do. Once one insists on a distinction between conjecture and certainty, Duhem's thesis ought to lose its force.
5. There is, to be sure, a difference between the case of seeing Dudman in New York and Michelson's predicament. In the former case, one might question the result of routine expansion without questioning the general reliability of the program for routine expansion that was employed. For that reason, it might be enough to take a second look. In the Michelson case, the question of the design of the experiment and, hence, the reliability of the program itself was called into question. And even the case of seeing someone who looks like Dudman might involve taking a second look at closer quarters, which does bring into question the reliability of visual reports from across the street. So although, on some occasions, the reliability of the programs for routine expansion that inject inconsistency is not brought into question, it can be and frequently is.

6. In the 1870s and 1880s, Peirce took both induction and abduction to be ampliative, and this view of his is often cited. However, early in the twentieth century, Peirce shifted explicitly to a task-oriented distinction between abduction, induction and deduction. One of the by-products of this shift was a reclassification of those "inferences" he initially called abductive as cases of "qualitative induction." Hence, all ampliative changes in states of full belief became versions of induction. Abduction understood to be the task of constructing potential answers to questions cannot be ampliative in the required sense because the "conclusion" of an abduction is not a revision of the state of full belief but the formation of a conjecture. In his later years, Peirce was quite clear on this point.

7. Peirce devoted substantial effort to characterizing the differences between deduction, abduction, and induction as differences in the formal structure of arguments. At the beginning of the twentieth century he abandoned the project. It would be useful if contemporary writers would take the lessons Peirce learned nearly a century ago to heart.

8. This reading is supported by the passage from Peirce referenced in the text. Peirce explicitly associates carrying more information with carrying more truth and contrasts both with liability to error. Peirce predicates information of terms and truth of propositions or theories. My conjecture is that he tended to say that terms carry more or less information, whereas propositions carry more or less truth, meaning what I mean by saying that they carry more or less information. I am less convinced that James had this understanding in mind, but think it charitable to understand him as following Peirce's usage.

9. Recall that expansions can be represented as meets of the current state of full belief K with other doxastic propositions or potential states of full belief. For this reason, we can induce a partial ordering on all potential states or doxastic propositions with respect to new information rather than just on those representing potential expansions. Let A be any doxastic proposition. The expansion of K by adding A is $K \wedge A$. This meet is an expansion even if A is not and will find a place in the partial ordering of expansions with respect to new information. Clearly, if A is inconsistent with K, the meet is 0 and A will be ranked with expansion into inconsistency. If A carries less information than K unconditionally, the meet will be identical to K and will carry no new information. If A is a nondegenerate expansion of K, it will be located in the partial ordering as in the text. All other doxastic propositions will be equivalent given K with an element of the filter generated by K (i.e., will be the same K-proposition) and will be located in the partial ordering accordingly.

    Similar remarks apply *mutatis mutandis* to the new information carried by sentences in L that are the strongest sentences added to K according to the expansions they characterize.

10. Some authors seem to think that simplicity is in tension with strength. The thought seems to derive from the notion that Ockham's razor counsels partiality to simpler theories. Since partiality for ontological economy seems to be a partiality for weaker rather than stronger theories, simplicity is thought to vary inversely with strength or information. But an ontologically more economical theory is not, in general, a weaker one. A theory that is committed to the existence of horses and denies the existence of cows is neither stronger nor weaker than a theory that is committed to the existence of both horses and cows. To be sure, such a theory is stronger than a theory that is committed to horses but leaves open whether there are cows. But the latter theory is not committed to the existence of cows and, hence, is not ontologically more complex than the

former. Ockham's razor, in our example, offers comparisons between theories that are noncomparable with respect to strength.

Simplicity is well known for being both ambiguous and vague. Ontological simplicity is one thing. Simplicity of axiomatization is another. When it comes to simplicity of axiomatization, we make comparisons with respect to simplicity of equivalent formulations of a single theory. Such comparisons are of no concern here. We are focusing on theories that are rival relative to the initial state of full belief $\mathbf{K}$ and, hence, noncomparable with respect to strength. If considerations of simplicity are relevant at all here, they are relevant because they render what is noncomparable comparable. What about two theories $\underline{T}$ and $\underline{T}'$ where $\underline{T}$ is stronger than $\underline{T}'$ and where $\underline{T}$ is obtained from $\underline{T}'$ by adding an additional premise – say $\underline{A}$? Shall we say that $\underline{T}$ is more complex than $\underline{T}'$?

It would be futile to engage in word battles concerning this point. But insofar as inquiring agents invoke considerations of simplicity in theory choice, the function of such appeals would appear to be to complete the quasi-ordering with respect to strength and not to invoke a desideratum at odds with strength or informational value. I am not denying that there is a relevant evaluation of rival conjectures that is in tension with strength. But that desideratum is to minimize the risk of error.

John Earman (1986, pp. 87–90) takes it on the authority of David Lewis (1973) that simplicity as a desideratum in theory choice increases with decreasing strength. Earman is proccupied with the problem of justifying the refusal to accept gratuitous additions to otherwise attractive theories. He wants to say that simplicity and systematicity prevent this when they outweigh the desideratum of strength.

But such gratuitous additions are examples of increases in information that carry no increase in informational value. Even though informational value is not increased, the risk of error is, so that there is a built-in deterrent to endorsing such gratuitous additions without, in the slightest, invoking a notion of simplicity that decreases with an increase in information.

Earman himself suggests (p. 89) that we are not concerned with strength but "strength in intended applications" – which is a tacit acknowledgment that some strengthenings do not increase informational value. Once this is conceded, there is no need to invoke simplicity rather than risk of error as a countervailing desideratum.

Earman's concern is to characterize laws of nature. I would characterize a law as a true universal generalization (pace Earman, probability distributions are not generalizations and, hence, not laws) that gratify demands for information to a high degree. It may be the case that what he calls *deterministic* generalizations gratify demands for information to a maximal degree. In some inquiries, I suspect this is so, but I doubt whether it holds generally. In any case, Earman thinks deterministic generalizations gratify demands for information maximally. Although I am skeptical of the correctness of this claim in full generality, that is not my chief reservation about what Earman has to say. Earman seems to think that even though there is a strong incentive to endorse deterministic laws, there is a deterrent that sometimes wins out. That deterrent is simplicity in those cases where deterministic laws are excessively complex as compared to alternatives. In my judgment, the deterrent is risk of error.

In Levi (1967) I took the position that desiderata like explanatory power and simplicity were desiderata additional to and possibly competing with content or information. But in "Information and Inference" (also published in 1967 in *Synthese* and republished as chapter 5 of Levi, 1984), I amended my view by suggesting that explanatory power, simplicity, and the like are considerations invoked in completing the quasi-order induced according to the monotonicity condition.

11.   I do assume that an inquirer's evaluation should be representable by a convex set of such utility functions. This will include cases where the evaluation does not complete the quasi-ordering with respect to informational value according to the monotonicity requirement. The set of utility functions that conform to the quasi-ordering is a convex set of the required sort.

12.   This assumes that the aggregation of utility functions for informational value and for truth value are weighted averages of these functions. I have argued elsewhere (e.g., Levi, 1984, ch. 5, and 1986) that potential resolutions of conflicts between different values should be represented as weighted averages and shall not rehearse this issue here.

13.   In logic, it is possible for disagreement to be so severe between minimally coherent or rational agents that the only shared agreements between them are trivial or so near triviality as to render serious inquiry hopeless. But anxiety on this score should not preclude our acknowledging that, in most cases, consensus as shared agreement is feasible.

14.   For a discussion of the more general case where informational value is evaluated by a nonempty convex set of content measures, see Levi (1980, sect. 8.6; 1984, ch. 7).

15.   In Levi (1967, 1980a, 1984, ch. 5, 1986, 1990a, 1990b). In Levi (1986) I offered an argument based on results of Blackwell and Girshick and Harsanyi for using weighted averages. Seidenfeld, Kadane, and Shervish (1989) point out, in effect, that the argument I deploy applies only when there is no indeterminacy in the probability distributions over the states of nature and that arguments for the convexity of the set of probability functions in a credal state depend on there being no conflict in the utility function over consequences. They argue that when there is indeterminacy both in the probabilities and in the utilities of consequences, convexity fails for both utility of consequences and of states. Their argument depends on a strict endorsement of a form of pareto unanimity in the evaluations of options. I argue (1990b) that pareto unanimity should not be endorsed in all cases and that when the cases where it should be violated are identified correctly, convexity is restored. Whether my view is accepted or not, at least conditions sufficient for justifying the convexity requirement have been identified.

16.   Expanding to **A** and to **B** could both be optimal if and only if expanding to $A \lor B$ is also optimal (Levi, 1967, sect. 5.5).

17.   Serious possibility is possibility that a doxastic proposition is true or error-free according to an agent (i.e., relative to the agent's state of full belief). Logical possibility is serious relative to **1** – the minimal state of full belief – or, perhaps, relative to the truths of logic. The ability of an object or system or person to respond in a certain way on a trial of a certain type is not *de dicto* in one of these senses but is a property that an object or system may or may not have. If an agent is sure that object x has the ability on a trial of kind T to respond in manner R and also is sure that x has been subjected to a trial of kind T at time t and knows nothing else that is relevant, it is seriously possible that x responds in manner R at t. However, the agent may be sure that x failed to respond in manner R at time t and, hence, may not regard it as a serious possibility that it did. Yet, he may be sure that x had the ability to respond in manner R on that particular instance of a trial of kind T. The inquiring agent may be sure that x has the ability at t to respond in manner R on a trial of kind T and also that on a

trial of kind $\underline{T}$ that is also $\underline{T}'$, $\underline{x}$ lacks the ability at $\underline{t}$ to respond in manner $\underline{R}$. For further discussion, see Levi (1980a, ch. 11).

18. Either the inquirer was committed to the view that he would implement the program all along, or he has just deliberately chosen to be committed. In addition to expansion via routine and via inference, we need to make room for expansion via choice. If an agent is convinced that he has control over certain conditions through his choices, then when he chooses to realize such conditions, he becomes convinced that those conditions are or will be realized. This is a species of expansion distinct from routine and inferential expansion. See Section 3.8.

19. Statistical probabilities or chances are not to be confused with credal probabilities any more than objective possibility in the sense of ability on a trial is to be confused with serious possibility. See Levi (1980a, chs. 11 and 12).

20. See Levi (1980a, 1986) for a general approach to decision making when probabilities, utilities, and, hence, expected utilities become indeterminate and how considerations of security may then be invoked.

21. The informational values of the two remaining elements of Θ constituting the inquirer's ultimate partition are now both equal to ½.

22. The conception of surprise is discussed in Levi (1984, ch. 14), and the sense in which the occurrence of an event (under a description) may be regarded as inexplicable as unsurprising and, hence, anomalous is considered in Levi (1988).

23. This distinction is discussed in Section 2.6. I return to it here in order to elaborate on its significance in connection with expansion.

24. In commenting on an earlier draft of this essay, Gärdenfors contended that because his analysis of epistemic entrenchment "can be seen as an explanation of the 'forces' that govern belief changes," it is appropriate to claim that he is discussing the dynamics of belief change. In the theory of consumer demand, the indifference maps and budgetary constraints of consumers can be regarded as "forces" regulating consumer demand with as much justice as entrenchment can in Gärdenfors's account of belief change. However, when economists study how a change in the price of a commodity alters the equilibrium state without exploring the details of the "path" from one state to the other, that is an investigation of what P. A. Samuelson (1947, ch. 2) called *comparative statics* and not dynamics.

I do not want to quibble over terminology here but merely to emphasize the importance of distinguishing between what I have called *comparative statics* and dynamic explanations that are designed to explain the path of a system from one state to another. Neither Gärdenfors's account nor mine offers a dynamics in this sense, and that is all I mean to emphasize.

25. I first introduced a contrast between expansion, contraction, and replacement in early 1971 when I read Levi (1984, ch. 8) to several audiences. (This paper, was finally published as Levi, 1983. The idea was repeated in Levi, 1974 and 1976). I took the position that all changes in belief state (I called them *revisions* but avoid that usage now because Gärdenfors uses *revision* for a special kind of belief change and not as a generic term covering all kinds of belief changes, as I did) ought to be representable as sequences of expansions and contractions. This is the thesis of commensurability of Section 2.9. I defended the position in Levi (1980a). In that essay, I also defended the requirement of commensuration requiring that all legitimate changes be decomposable into sequences of legitimate expansions and contractions. In all these writings, I took expansion by adding sentence $\underline{A}$ to be adding $\underline{A}$ to the current corpus and forming the deductive closure.

Gärdenfors tends to use the term *revision* in two ways. Sometimes it means what I have in mind by *replacement*. Sometimes it means the result of the basic change involving the addition of information to a belief state as input. In that sense, revision is replacement only when the new information contradicts the contents of the initial state. Otherwise the revision is an expansion. I shall continue to use *replacement* for revision in the first sense and *revision* for revision in the second.

26. Suppose that one represents a belief state by a set of possible worlds as, for example, in J. Hintikka (1962) and R. Stalnaker (1984, pp. 68–9), so that a corpus in $\underline{L}^*$ consists of all sentences that are true at all possible worlds in that particular set. Let $\underline{A}$ be a nonmodal "contingent" sentence such that neither it nor its negation is in that corpus. Given a semantics for S5 propositional modal logic, it will be true at every possible world in the given set that $\underline{A}$ is possibly false and that it is possibly true. Suppose that we now add $\underline{A}$ to the corpus in $\underline{L}^*$ and thereby reduce the set of possible worlds in the belief set. It still remains the case that $\underline{A}$ is possibly false. But it will not be seriously possible that it is false according to the commitments of the inquirer in that belief state. So the semantics for modality we have provided is not for serious possibility.

To make the semantics relevant, we might consider excluding as alternative worlds to worlds in the given set associated with the state of full-belief worlds that are not in the set and otherwise use an S5 structure. Then, relative to the expanded corpus, it will be false that $\underline{A}$ is possibly false according to the resulting semantics. But, with this modification of the semantics, according to the initial corpus that did not contain $\underline{A}$, it was true that $\underline{A}$ is possibly false, whereas in the new corpus it is false. My contention is that when the inquirer is contemplating adding $\underline{A}$ to his state of full belief, he should be concerned with whether $\underline{A}$ is false but not with whether "It is possible that $\underline{A}$ is false" is true or is false.

27. Among those who include modal judgments and conditionals in an agent's state of full belief, the practice of focusing on replacements (or minimal revisions) as the basic kind of change in belief state is more or less standard for cases where new information is added to the evolving doctrine conflicting with the initial belief state but not for cases where new information fails to conflict. Thus, writers like R. Stalnaker (1984) contrast cases of belief change where new information is added that conflicts with what is already in the belief state from cases where there is no conflict. The latter type of case is one where possible worlds are eliminated from the set representing the state of full belief. Stalnaker nowhere, to my knowledge, considers the point raised earlier that such changes, when represented linguistically in a modal language $\underline{L}^*$, become replacements. So it would appear that, at least tacitly, the truth values of such modal claims are of no concern in the revision of states of full belief. But Stalnaker does appear to think that modal claims are true or false and that this is somehow an interesting philosophical thesis. In any case, when it comes to situations where the new information is false in all possible worlds allowed by the initial state of full belief, Stalnaker is quite explicit in thinking of the new information as calling for a decision between rival revisions (replacements in my sense) (p. 96). And in discussing conditionals, he appears to endorse some conception of minimal revision (p. 129). It does not occur to him to consider analyzing replacements as sequences of expansions and contractions. Indeed, Stalnaker fails to mention contraction in his essay.

28. This challenge ought to be taken seriously by advocates of "ersatzist" applications of possible worlds semantics who are more prone to appeal to examples of

judgments of possibility that may be readily construed as judgments of serious possibility either relative to the current belief state or to some transformation of the the current belief state in the case of conditional judgments. Modal realists of a more radical variety who insist that some modal judgments cannot be accommodated in this fashion, or that even judgments of epistemic modality presuppose a realist notion of objective modality, may regard themselves as exempt from the challenge. They deny what I am taking for granted − to wit, that the judgments of possibility indispensable for inquiry and deliberation are epistemic or "subjective." Their strongest case, perhaps, is that judgments of epistemic or serious possibility presuppose a conception of consistency that invokes an antecedent conception of objective possibility. There is a half-truth in this observation. The conception of consistency I have deployed relies on an antecedently given space of potential states of full belief possessing the structure of a boolean algebra. The notion of a *potential* state of full belief may be alleged to invoke the antecedent notion of possibility. But, as I argued in Chapter 2, a potential state of full belief is to be understood as a state to which the inquirer is able or, better yet, is entitled to be in. The underlying notion of modality is that of ability or permissibility. I deny that such modal notions are to be cashed out in terms of possible worlds semantics. If I am right about this, such modal realists need to explain why one should not stare incredulously by identifying more convincingly than I believe they have why their hyperrealism meets a demand for explanation that skeptics ought to take seriously.

Chapter 4

1. The notion of saturability has thus been defined relative to a language $\underline{L}$. It can also be applied to an atomic boolean algebra of potential states of full belief. A contraction from **K** by removing A is saturatable if and only if the expansion of that contraction by adding $\sim A$ is an atom of the algebra. In an atomless boolean algebra of potential states of full belief, we may characterize a saturatable contraction as one that is saturatable in all atomic subalgebras containing **K** and **A**. In the subsequent discussion, we focus on saturatability relative to a language $\underline{L}$.

A note on terminology is in order here. I use *contraction* by removing $\underline{A}$ from $\underline{K}$ as a generic term to characterize all shifts to corpora that are subsets of $\underline{K}$ not containing $\underline{A}$. Every such contraction in $C(\underline{K},\underline{A})$ is the meet (strictly speaking, intersection) of a subset of the saturatable contractions in $S(\underline{K},\underline{A})$. A *maxichoice* contraction refers to any saturatable contraction removing $\underline{A}$ from $\underline{K}$ that contains $\sim\underline{B}\vee\underline{A}$ for every $\underline{B}$ in $\underline{K}$ but not in the contraction. (See Section 4.3.) Alchourròn, Gärdenfors, and Makinson (1985) restrict the term *contraction* to meets of subsets of maxichoice contractions. Makinson (1987), Gärdenfors (1988, p. 71), and H. Rott (1989) are aware that there are what I call *contractions* that are not meets of maxichoice contractions. The term *withdrawal* is used by these authors to cover the generic case. Since I always used *contraction* to cover the generic case, I stubbornly persist in my terminological practice. There is also a small rhetorical purpose in doing so. The problem, as these authors and I agree, concerns what to give up when removing $\underline{A}$ from the evolving doctrine. And they themselves regarded this as the problem of contraction. Indeed, in Alchourròn, Gärdenfors, and Makinson (1985), the so-called Recovery Postulate is taken for granted, which, as they show, is tantamount to requiring that when removing $\underline{A}$, one is going to be restricted to meets of maxichoice contractions. They do not even consider why one should be so restrictive. The issue is addressed in Makinson (1987), and the term *withdrawal* is introduced. The rhetorical point is this: If we are going to agree that the problem of contraction is the problem of what else to give up when removing $\underline{A}$ from $\underline{K}$, as Makinson, others, and I do, we should avoid prejudicing the discussion by giving a specialized construal to the term *contraction*. It is immaterial to me whether *withdrawal* is substituted for *contraction*, provided that we now call the problem of what to give up the problem of *withdrawal*. But we should avoid rhetoric that carries a question-begging message by calling the problem of what to give up the problem of contraction and then construing *contraction* as a meet of maxichoice contractions.

2. Minimizing strategies can fail to exist if there are infinitely many contraction strategies or if the evaluation of contraction strategies with respect to losses of informational value does not yield a weak ordering. In this discussion, I assume that such evaluations do yield weak orderings and that minimizing strategies do exist relative to such weak orderings.

3. This claim may be established by the following line of reasoning:

$\underline{A}\&\underline{B}$ is logically equivalent to the conjunction of the following three sentences for every $\underline{B}$ in $\underline{L}$: (i) $\sim\underline{A} \supset \underline{B}(=\sim\underline{B} \supset \underline{A})$, (ii) $\sim\underline{A} \supset \sim\underline{B}$, and (iii) $\sim\underline{B} \supset \sim\underline{A}$. $\underline{A}$ alone is equivalent to the conjunction of (i) and (ii). It is a constraint of the contraction problem that $\underline{A}$ be removed from $\underline{K}$. This means that for each $\underline{B}$ in $\underline{L}$, either (i) or (ii) must be removed, and possibly both.

If for every sentence $\underline{B}$ that is in $\underline{L}$ either (i) or (ii) is removed but not both, then the contraction strategy is saturatable. If for some such $\underline{B}$ both are removed, the contraction strategy is nonsaturatable. [Recall that a saturatable contraction removing $\underline{A}$ from $\underline{A}$ is such that if it is expanded by adding $\sim\underline{A}$ to the contraction, the result is maximally consistent. Such a maximally consistent corpus will contain either $\underline{B}$ or $\sim\underline{B}$ for every sentence $\underline{B}$ in $\underline{L}$. Hence, for every such $\underline{B}$, either (i) or (ii) must be in the contraction.]

By hypothesis, contracting $\underline{K}$ by removing $\underline{A}$ incurs a positive loss of informational value no matter which contraction is used. This means that for every $\underline{B}$ in $\underline{L}$, whether (i) or (ii) is removed, a positive loss of informational value is incurred. Hence, the M function must assign positive M values to their negations $\sim\underline{A}\&\sim\underline{B}$ and $\sim\underline{A}\&\underline{B}$, respectively. Since these propositions are logical contraries, neither can carry M value equal to 1.

The probability-based informational value of the conjunction of (i) and (ii) is a decreasing function of the M value of the disjunction of their negations. Given that both disjuncts are positive and that the M value of the disjunction must be the sum of the separate M values of the disjuncts, the M value of the disjunction must be greater than the M value of either disjunct. Hence, the loss in informational value incurred by removing both (i) and (ii) must be greater than the loss incurred by removing one but not the other.

Hence, a nonsaturatable contraction will incur a greater loss of informational value than the result of adding either (i) or (ii) to that contraction for each $\underline{B}$ such that both (i) and (ii) are removed. This suffices to establish the thesis.

4. Gärdenfors (1988, pp. 76−7). Consider a saturatable contraction such that for every $\underline{B}$ in $\underline{K}$, $\underline{A} \supset \underline{B}$ is in the contraction. For every $\underline{B}$, let $\underline{X}$ be the sentence $\sim\underline{A} \supset \underline{B}$ and let $\underline{Y}$ be the sentence $\sim\underline{A} \supset \sim\underline{B}$. Since the contraction is saturatable, exactly one of these sentences must be removed for each $\underline{B}$ and the other retained. If $\underline{B}$ is removed from $\underline{K}$, then $\underline{Y}$ must be retained and $\underline{X}$ removed. But $\underline{Y}$ is equivalent to $\underline{B} \supset \underline{A}$. Hence, all saturatable contractions passing the test mentioned earlier are maxichoice.

Conversely, if a contraction is maxichoice, then for every $\underline{B}$ in $\underline{K}$ but not in the contraction, either $\underline{X}$ or $\underline{A} \supset \underline{B} = \underline{Z}$ is removed from $\underline{K}$. The maxichoice criterion requires that $\underline{Z} \supset \underline{A}$ be in the contraction if $\underline{Z}$ is not. But this logically implies $\underline{A}$, which must, therefore, be in the contraction. But $\underline{A}$ is to be removed from $\underline{K}$.

Hence, we cannot remove $\underline{Z}$ from $\underline{K}$ and satisfy the maxichoice definition. So the maxichoice contraction must pass the test.

5. Since the damped informational value of a saturatable contraction is its probability-based informational value relative to a given M function, if there is no minimum, we may suppose that there is a greatest lower bound to the values assigned. Because I begin with the assumption that probability-based informational value yields a weak ordering of elements of $C(\underline{K},\underline{A})$ representable by an index that increases with a decrease in M value relative to some M function, there is no need to postulate the existence of a minimum informational value in the minimal saturatable contractions whose meet yields a given contraction. Those who wish to begin with a relational structure on the domain of potential contractions in $C(\underline{K},\underline{A})$ and derive a representation of the weak ordering by means of a probability measure M will find this unsatisfactory. But they will have difficulty in obtaining a desired result without postulating the existence of a minimal saturatable contraction in the set whose meet yields a given contraction that carries minimum informational value, and this seems unnecessarily restrictive. Since Gärdenfors, Makinson, and others themselves appeal to intuitions appealing to ideas about probability-based indices of informational value, it seems to me preferable to begin explicitly with a probability-based measure and relax the restriction.

6. It may, perhaps, be argued that we are not required to give up the claim that eating tainted humus tends to infect the consumer with hepatitis on the grounds that the tendency is not strictly universal. The point is well taken. But if we are certain initially that Jones contracted hepatitis from eating tainted humus, we are sure that the humus contained a sufficiently virulent culture of a hepatitis virus to overcome Jones's immune system. If subsequently, we give up the conviction that Jones contracted hepatitis, we cannot at the same time retain (a) the claim that he ate the humus and (b) the claim that the viral culture of the humus was sufficiently virulent to overcome his immune system. Let $\underline{A}$ be the conjunction of (a) and (b) or whatever more fine-grained claim yields a lawlike sufficient condition for Jones's contracting hepatitis through eating humus. Giving up $\underline{A} \supset \underline{B}$ would require giving up the conviction that the condition was sufficient, whereas giving up $\sim\underline{A} \supset \underline{B}$ would not. By appropriately adjusting the remaining features of the example, the point I seek to make will still be sustained.

7. A. Fuhrmann (1991) has offered an argument against recovery based on a characterization of a contraction from $\underline{K}$ removing $\underline{A}$ as relative to any set of sentences whose closure is $\underline{K}$. A minimal base contraction removing $\underline{A}$ from $\underline{K}$ will depend on the base that is selected. Fuhrmann then shows (pp. 7–8) an abstract counterinstance to Recovery. The argument I have offered does not depend upon relativizing contractions to bases. The approach taken in this book is that contraction, in the first instance, applies to states of full belief and not to corpora or theories that are linguistic representations of them. Only corpora or theories can have bases. States of full belief cannot. See also Niederée (1991).

8. If $\underline{K}_2$ is a replacement of $\underline{K}_1$, $\underline{K}'' = \underline{K}_3$. With $\underline{K}''$ we are not given a specific sentence or doxastic proposition that is replaced. With $\underline{K}_3$, we are.

   Gärdenfors (1988, p. 69) calls the condition $(\underline{K}_A^-)^+_{\sim A} = \underline{K}^*_{\sim A}$ = the admissible replacement of $\sim\underline{A}$ by $\underline{A}$ (a *minimal revision* in the terminology of Stalnaker and Gärdenfors) when construed as a definition of admissible replacement the Levi Identity. It is a definition of an admissible or legitimate replacement if and only if we understand the contraction and the expansion to be legitimate. That, at any rate, is what the commensuration requirement demands. Gärdenfors clearly and explicitly states my commitment to the commensuration requirement and then offers the Levi Identity as a formal representation of it in the case of replacement.

This formal definition neither explicitly nor implicitly imposes any demand of legitimacy on the contraction and expansion steps. But without such restraints, the Levi Identity imposes no restrictions on legitimate replacements (revisions). Every replacement, whether legitimate or not, can be formally decomposed into an expansion of a contraction. (And every residual shift can be decomposed into a sequence of contractions and expansions.) I do, therefore, endorse the Levi Identity taken as a formal requirement because it is an implication of the commensurability thesis or, more generally, the requirement that potential states of full belief should constitute a boolean algebra, along with the normative assumption that there should not be more than one admissible change of belief state in a given context (the uniqueness condition of section 2.9).

However, in my earlier writing, I intended to advocate a claim substantially stronger than the formal Levi Identity – to wit, the commensuration requirement. The Levi Identity does not preclude regarding some replacements as basically legitimate. The commensuration requirement does. The only replacements that are legitimate, according to the commensuration requirement, are those that can be decomposed into sequences of legitimate contractions and expansions.

Gärdenfors does sometimes seem to recognize that I am advocating something stronger than the formal Levi Identity. However, he seems to understand me as imposing a requirement insisting that the legitimacy of a replacement must be derived by first justifying a contraction from $\underline{K}_1$ by removing $\sim\underline{A}$ and then justifying an expansion by adding $\underline{A}$ to the result. Such a requirement would be stronger than the commensuration requirement demands. Any sequence of legitimate expansions and replacements yielding the desired replacement will do. The scenario Gärdenfors envisages as representing my view captures cases where one first engages in uncoerced contraction to give $\underline{A}$ a hearing and subsequently expands by adding $\underline{A}$. But when one first inadvertently (but legitimately) expands into inconsistency through the use of a program for routine expansion, contracts under coercion, and then expands (either routinely or deliberately), the net result can also be replacement of $\sim\underline{A}$ by $\underline{A}$. Nothing in the commensuration requirement or my previous discussion precludes this.

9. These features of contraction and replacement are discussed in a note by D. Makinson (1987).

10. Instead of asserting that if the coin had been tossed 1,000 times it might have landed tails at least one time, it is more customary to assert that the coin might have landed heads 1,000 times without explicitly expressing the "if" clause.

11. This point indicates one of several respects in which an adequate belief revision account of conditionals differs from possible worlds accounts of conditionals of the sort advanced by Stalnaker or Lewis. Possible worlds accounts of conditionals appeal to comparisons of elements of a domain of possible worlds with the world for which the truth of a conditional is being assessed with respect to "overall similarity" or "nearness." Given the intuitive motivations (such as they are) for speaking of similarity between possible worlds or the nearness of a possible world to another, it should be axiomatic that there is a uniquely nearest (or most similar) world to any given possible world and that is the given world itself. That is the postulate Lewis (1973, pp. 14–15) calls *centering*. Although Lewis accepts the centering postulate in his own work, he has expressed misgivings about it and has toyed with the idea of requiring only a weak centering postulate that insists only that no world is more similar to a given world than itself. He reiterates his commitment to centering and also his openness to weak centering in Lewis (1981, pp. 233–4).

I would have thought that any other world similar to the actual world as weak centering countenances is to all intents and purposes identical to it. That is to say, any respect in which it differed would not be of any interest. Hence, if a given sentence $\underline{A}$ is true and $\underline{B}$ is false, the conditional "If $\underline{A}$ were true, $\underline{B}$ would be false" should be false except, perhaps, for sentences $\underline{B}$ whose truth value is of little interest to the inquirer. To all intents and purposes, the strict centering condition will be obeyed even in those cases where weak centering but not strict centering is officially endorsed. In any case, if we are to use possible worlds semantics to give an account of belief revisions and a belief revision explication of the assertability conditions for conditionals, it will do no good to invoke comparisons of possible worlds with respect to how similar or close they are to the actual world. But we might consider comparisons of possible worlds with respect to how similar or close they are to worlds not ruled out by the current corpus $\underline{K}$.

Thanks to the work of Adam Grove (1988, pp. 157–70), we have a good idea of why abandoning Recovery renders ordinary possible world modeling quite hopeless even when the comparisons of possible worlds are reconstructed along the lines just indicated. Grove represents potential corpora by the sets of their maximally consistent extensions (which are analogues of possible worlds) in which the sentences in a corpus are true and considers an ordering of all maximally consistent sets in $\underline{L}$ by means of *spheres* similar to those considered by Lewis. The most significant difference is that the system of spheres is not centered on a possible world or maximally consistent set but on a corpus or set of worlds normally containing more than one set. Grove shows that the conditions on contraction required by Gärdenfors (including Recovery) and on minimal revision or admissible replacement are satisfied, and points out how the representation of contractions of $\underline{K}$ by removing $\underline{A}$ satisfying Recovery as intersections of sets of maxichoice contractions correspond to representations of the associated replacements (i.e., revisions) by sets of possible worlds. Grove's system of spheres contains a centering postulate different from Lewis's. The central sphere is the set of possible worlds representing $\underline{K}$ that is the current corpus and not the single actual world. Possible worlds are not ordered with respect to how similar or how close they are to the actual world but to that set of worlds not ruled out by the current corpus $\underline{K}$. Formally, Grove's suggestion amounts to endorsing Lewis's requirement of weak centering except, of course, that the comparisons of possible worlds are not with respect to similarity to the actual world but with respect to some kind of affinity with worlds in $\underline{K}$.

As Grove appreciates, he can get away with this because, as long as Recovery obtains, there is a one-to-one mapping of the maxichoice contractions onto the maximally consistent corpora that contain $\underline{A}$ (where we start with a $\underline{K}$ that does not contain $\underline{A}$). Thus, the weak ordering Grove proposes corresponds to an evaluation of maxichoice contractions that remove $\sim\underline{A}$ from $\underline{K}$ with respect to informational value. The mapping becomes many-one, however, once we consider satiatable contractions that are not maxichoice. And if we break ties in informational value, when feasible, by favoring the weaker of two contractions, the lexicographical order that results does not determine a consistent partial ordering of the maximally consistent sets or possible worlds. The same possible world can receive distinct places in the ordering, which determines which contraction strategy is admissible. Thus, comparisons between possible worlds will be too coarse-grained to determine admissible contractions or replacements (minimal revisions). Observe, however, that in spite of this, weak centering is satisfied, just as it is by Grove's scheme. Lewis's idea of weak centering cannot, therefore, capture the impact of rejecting Recovery. The rejection of Recovery entails a far more radical abandonment of the Stalnaker–Lewis approach to possible worlds. Yet, such rejection seems clearly called for. The fact is that the Lewis–Stalnaker approach secures the truth of "If the coin would have been tossed a 1,000 times, it would have landed heads 1,000 times" in any world in which the coin is tossed 1,000 times and lands heads every time. This is obviously wrong. According to the belief revision view I favor, if an agent is convinced that the coin was tossed 1,000 times and that it landed heads every time, the conditional may still remain unassertable.

12. Gärdenfors (1988, p. 62) has admitted the dubiety of the Recovery Postulate in probabilistic contexts. However, he claims that in nonprobabilistic contexts, it "seems to be a valid principle." The case of the tainted humus calls this contention into question.

13. Agents working in a given conceptual framework are committed to fully recognizing the doxastic proposition 1 or all sentences in the urcorpus corpus $\underline{1}$, no matter which potential state of full belief they are in or the potential corpus representing that state. All sentences in the urcorpus (which include the logical truths in $\underline{L}$) are incorrigible to the maximum degree (or corrigible to the minimum degree). They are incorrigible. All such agents are also committed to fully recognizing that they are true and, in this sense, they are maximally certain. However, for agent X who is committed to corpus $\underline{K}$, the elements of $\underline{1}$ all of which are also in $\underline{K}$ are no more certain than the other sentences in $\underline{K}$. The difference is that the latter are open to removal from the set of certainties.

14. For further discussion of applications of Shackle's formalism, see Levi (1984, ch. 14). Among the many authors who have rediscovered Shackle's formalism for some purpose or other are L. J. Cohen (1977), G. Shafer (1976), and W. Spohn (1988).

15. For an excellent critical discussion of the various ideas considered here from the vantage point of those who take the Recovery Postulate for granted, see H. Rott (1991).

16. This is my reading of passages where Kuhn criticizes a neutral observation language and, with it, the intelligibility of anything but "intratheoretic" notions of truth. See T. Kuhn (1970b, p. 262). The point is not only that there is no neutral observation language but that, when there is a choice between competing incommensurable theories, there is no system of shared assumptions relative to which an assessment of the merits of the competing theory with respect to truth value or even probability of truth can be made without begging the question.

17. In correspondence related to an earlier version of these remarks, Gärdenfors does complain. He points out that he, Makinson, Alchourròn, and others have always taken contraction to be a function of the corpus on which contraction is performed and the input sentence which is to be removed. It follows that removing $\underline{A}$ from $\underline{o}$ must yield the same result no matter how inconsistency was obtained. I have never required contraction to be so context independent as that. Only if the information-determining M function is held fixed must this be so. But I contend that in contraction from $\underline{o}$, the information-determining M function is modified in order to meet the constraints on the problem. And I am pointing out that Gärdenfors's account of minimal revision is equivalent to expanding into inconsistency and contracting from $\underline{o}$ under constraints of a similar and more severe kind. I grant that were his constraints otherwise acceptable, the difference between us would be terminological and I would also grant that his terminology might plausibly be recommended as simpler. But I question the acceptability of his constraints. And this changes the picture.

18. R. A. Fisher (1936) did, indeed, argue in this way. He contended that the data Mendel obtained in his experiments were sometimes "too good to be true" and suggested that, perhaps, an overzealous assistant had tampered with the data.

19. Suppose that the initial corpus $\underline{K}$ contains $\underline{A}$ and $\underline{B}$. The set of consequences of these two sentences is the same as the set of consequences of $\sim\underline{A} \supset \underline{B}$, $\sim\underline{A} \supset \bar{\underline{B}}$, and $\underline{A} \supset \underline{B}$. Assume further that the inquirer gives up $\underline{B}$. If $\underline{A} \supset \underline{B}$ is a consequence of a law in $\underline{K}$, this will not be given up. $\sim\underline{A} \supset \underline{B}$ will be given up instead. The informational value to the inquirer of the corpus consisting of $\sim\underline{A} \supset \underline{B}$ without $\sim\underline{A} \supset \underline{B}$ could be the same as the informational value that also contains this latter conditional. Under these circumstances, the probability-based informational value of adding $\underline{B}$ to each of these corpora would also be the same.

Strictly speaking, the situation is more complicated than this. During the process of inquiry discussed in the text where $\sim\underline{A}$ is in the initial corpus $\underline{K}$, and where $\sim\underline{A}$ is initially removed and then reinstated, the inquirer will obtain new information via routine expansion (e.g., by running experiments and obtaining new data or via collateral deliberate expansions) that may carry positive informational value. Consequently, it is unlikely that a sequence of changes in states of full belief will involve giving up $\sim\underline{A}$ and then restoring it without any other modifications taking place. This qualification is neglected in this (over)simplified discussion of outcomes 1, 2, and 3. See, however, the final paragraph of this section, where the chief significance of taking it into account is pointed out.

References

Alchourròn, C. E., Gärdenfors, P., and Makinson, D. (1985), "On the Logic of Theory Change: Partial Meet Functions for Contraction and Revision," *Journal of Symbolic Logic*, 50; 510–30.

Alchourròn, C. E., and Makinson, D. (1982), "On the Logic of Theory Change: Contraction Functions and Their Associated Revision Functions," *Theoria*, 48: 14–37.

Bell, J. L., and Slomson, A. B. (1969), *Models and Ultraproducts*, Amsterdam: North Holland.

Carnap, R. (1962), *The Logical Foundations of Probability*, 2nd ed., Chicago: University of Chicago Press.

Cohen, L. J. (1977), *The Probable and the Provable*, Oxford: Oxford University Press.

Cohen, R. S., and Wartofsky, M. (1983), *Language, Logic and Method*, Dordrecht: Reidel.

Davidson, D. (1984), *Inquiries into Truth and Interpretation*, Oxford: Oxford University Press.

Dretske, F. (1981), *Knowledge and Flow of Information*, Cambridge, Mass.: MIT Press.

Earman, J. (1986), *A Primer on Determinism*, Dordrecht: Reidel.

Ellis, B. (1979), *Rational Belief Systems*, Oxford: Blackwell.

Fisher, R. A. (1936), "Has Mendel's Work Been Rediscovered?" *Annals of Science*, I: 115–37.

Frege, G. (1967), *The Basic Laws of Arithmetic*, trans. M. Furth, Los Angeles: University of California Press.

Fuhrman, A. (1991)), "Theory Contraction Through Base Contraction," *Journal of Philosophical Logic*, 20: 175–205.

Gaifman, H. (1988), "Operational Pointer Semantics: Solution to Self-Referential Puzzles I," *Proceedings of the Second Conference on Theoretical Aspects of Reasoning about Knowledge*, ed. M. Y. Vardi, Los Angeles: Morgan-Kaufman, pp. 43–60.

Gärdenfors, P. (1988), *Knowledge in Flux: Modeling the Dynamics of Epistemic States*, Cambridge, Mass: MIT Press.

Gärdenfors, P., and Makinson, D. (1988), "Revisions of Knowledge Systems Using Epistemic Entrenchment," *Proceedings of the Second Conference on Theoretical Aspects of Reasoning about Knowledge*, ed. M. Y. Vardi, Los Angeles: Morgan Kaufman, pp. 157–180.

Gärdenfors, P., and Sahlin, N.-E. (1988), *Decision, Probability and Utility*, Cambridge: Cambridge University Press.

Good, I. J. (1983), *Good Thinking*, Minneapolis: University of Minnesota Press.

Grove, A. (1988), "Two Modellings for Theory Change," *Journal of Philosophical Logic*, 17: 157–70.

Hacking, I. (1967), "A Slightly More Realistic Personalist Probability," *Philosophy of Science*, 34: 311–25.

Harman, G. (1986), *Change in View: Principles of Reasoning*, Cambridge, Mass.: MIT Press.

Hintikka, K.J.J. (1962), *Knowledge and Belief*, Ithica, N.Y.: Cornell University Press.

James, W. (1897), *The Will to Believe and Other Essays*, New York: Longman.

Koslow, A. (in press), *A Structuralist Theory of Logic*, Cambridge:, Cambridge University Press. Press.

Kuhn, T. (1970a), *The Structure of Scientific Revolutions*, 2nd ed., Chicago: University of Chicago Press.

(1970b), "Reflections on My Critics," in *Criticism and the Growth of Knowledge*, ed. I. Lakatos and A. Musgrave, Cambridge: Cambridge University. Press, pp. 231–78.

Kyburg, H. E. (1983), *Epistemology and Inference*, Minneapolis: University of Minnesota Press.

Levi, I. (1967), *Gambling with Truth*, New York: Knopf (reprinted in paperback by MIT Press, 1973).

(1970), "Probability and Evidence," in *Induction, Acceptance and Rational Belief*, ed. M. Swain, Dordrecht: Reidel, pp. 134–56.

(1974), "On Indeterminate Probabilities," *Journal of Philosophy*, 71: 391–418 (reprinted with modifications in Gärdenfors and Sahlin, 1988, pp. 287–312).

(1976), "Acceptance Revisited," in *Local Induction*, ed. R. Bogdan, Dordrecht: Reidel, pp. 1–71.

(1980a), *The Enterprise of Knowledge*, Cambridge, Mass.: MIT Press.

(1980b), "Induction as Self-Correcting According to Peirce," in *Science, Belief and Behaviour, Essays in Honour of R. B. Braithwaite*, ed. D. H. Mellor, Cambridge: Cambridge University Press, pp. 127–40.

(1983), "Truth, Fallibility and the Growth of Knowledge," in Cohen and Wartofsky (1983), pp. 153–74, with discussion by I. Scheffler and A. Margalit with replies, pp. 175–198.

(1984), *Decisions and Revisions*, Cambridge: Cambridge University Press.

(1986), *Hard Choices*, Cambridge: Cambridge University Press.

(1988), "Four Themes in Statistical Explanation," in *Causation in Decision, Belief Change and Statistics*, Vol. 2, ed. W. L. Harper and B. Skyrms, Dordrecht: Reidel, pp. 195–222.

(1990a), "Consensus and Pareto Unanimity," *The Journal of Philosophy*, 87: 481–92.

(1990b), "Compromising Bayesianism: A Plea for Indeterminacy," *Journal of Statistical Planning and Inference*, 25: 347–62.

(1991), "Consequentialism and Sequential Choice," in *Foundations of Decision Theory*, eds. M. Bacharach and S. Hurley, Oxford: Blackwell.

Levi, I., and Morgenbesser, S. (1964), "Belief and Disposition," *American Philosophical Quarterly*, 1: 221–32.

Lewis, D. (1973), *Counterfactuals*, Cambridge, Mass.: Harvard University Press.

(1981), "Ordering Semantics and Premise Semantics for Counterfactuals," *Journal of Philosophical Logic*, 10: 233–4.

(1986), *On the Plurality of Worlds*, Oxford: Blackwell.

Makinson, D. (1987), "On the Status of the Postulate of Recovery in the Logic of Theory Change," *Journal of Philosophical Logic*, 16: 383–94.

Misak, C. (1987), "Peirce, Levi and the Aims of Inquiry," *Philosophy of Science*, 4: 256–65.

Nagel, E. (1949), "Logic without Ontology," in *Readings in Philosophical Analysis*, ed. H. Feigl and W. Sellars, New York: Appleton-Century-Crofts, pp. 191–210.

Niederée, R. (1991), "Multiple Contraction: A Further Case Against Gärdenfors' Principle of Recovery," in *The Logic of Theory Change*, ed. A. Fuhrmann and Morreau, Berlin: Springer Verlag, pp. 322–34.

Neyman, J., and Pearson, E. S. (1933), "On the Problem of the Most Efficient Tests of Statistical Hypotheses," *Philosophical Transactions of the Royal Society*, Ser. A., 231: 289–337.

Parsons, C. (1983), *Mathematics in Philosophy*, Ithica, N.Y.: Cornell University Press.

Peirce, C. S. (1982), *Writings of Charles S. Peirce*, Vol. 1, ed. M. Fisch, Bloomington: University of Indiana Press.

Rasiowa, H., and Sikorski, R. (1963), *The Mathematics of Metamathematics*, Warsaw: Panstwowe Wydawnictwo Naukowe.

Rott, H. (1991), "Two Methods of Constructing Contractions and Revisions of Knowledge Systems," *Journal of Philosophical Logic*, 20: 149–173.

Shackle, G. L. S. (1949), *Expectation in Economics*, Cambridge: Cambridge University Press.

(1961), *Decision, Order and Time*, Cambridge: Cambridge University Press.

Shafer, G. (1976), *A Mathematical Theory of Evidence*, Princeton, N.J.: Princeton University Press.

Shapere, D. (1982), "The Concept of Observation in Science and Philosophy," *Philosophy of Science*, 49: 485–525.

Simon, H. A. (1972), "Theories of Bounded Rationality," in *Decision and Organization*, ed C. B. Radner and R. Radner, Amsterdam: North Holland, pp. 161–76.

Spohn, W. (1988), "Ordinal Conditional Functions: A Dynamic Theory of Epistemic States," in *Causation in Decision, Belief Change and Statistics*, ed. W. Harper and B Skyrms, Dordrecht: Reidel, pp. 105–34.

Stalnaker, R., (1968), "A Theory of Conditionals," in *Studies in Logical Theory*, ed. N. Rescher, Oxford: Blackwell, pp. 98–112.

(1984), *Inquiry*, Cambridge, Mass.: MIT Press.

Tarski, A. (1956), *Logic, Semantics, Metamathematics*, Oxford: Oxford University Press.

Van Fraassen, B. (1980), *The Scientific Image*, Oxford: Oxford University Press.

Name index

Subject index